Teaching Science as Investigations

Modeling Inquiry Through Learning Cycle Lessons

Richard H. Moyer
University of Michigan–Dearborn

Jay K. Hackett
Emeritus, University of Northern Colorado

Susan A. Everett
University of Michigan–Dearborn

Upper Saddle River, New Jersey
Columbus, Ohio

Library of Congress Cataloging-in-Publication Data

Moyer, Richard.
Teaching science as investigations: modeling inquiry through learning cycle lessons / Richard H. Moyer, Jay K. Hackett, Susan A. Everett.
p. cm.
Includes bibliographical references and index.
ISBN 0-13-218627-6
1. Science—Study and teaching (Elementary) 2. Science—Study and teaching (Middle school) 3. Inquiry-based learning. I. Hackett, Jay K. II. Everett, Susan A. III. Title.
LB1585.M69 2007
372.3'5—dc22

2006016483

Vice President and Executive Publisher: Jeffery W. Johnston
Editor: Meredith D. Sarver
Senior Editorial Assistant: Kathleen S. Burk
Production Editor: Alexandrina Benedicto Wolf
Production Coordination: Carlisle Publishers Services
Design Coordinator: Diane C. Lorenzo
Cover Designer: Candace Rowley
Cover Image: Corbis
Production Manager: Pamela D. Bennett
Director of Marketing: David Gesell
Senior Marketing Manager: Darcy Betts Prybella
Marketing Coordinator: Brian Mounts

This book was set in Times by Carlisle Publishing Services and was printed and bound by Command Web. The cover was printed by Phoenix Color Corp.

Pearson Education Ltd.
Pearson Education Singapore, Pte. Ltd.
Pearson Education Canada, Ltd.
Pearson Education—Japan
Pearson Education Australia Pty, Limited
Pearson Education North Asia Ltd.
Pearson Educación de Mexico, S.A. de C.V.
Pearson Education Malaysia, Pte. Ltd.

10 9 8 7 6 5 4 3 2 1
ISBN: 0-13-218627-6

Preface

Our experience in teaching elementary and middle school science has indicated the need for a different kind of science methods text. We wanted our students to experience inquiry-based science as described by the *National Science Education Standards* (NSES) through an approach that integrates science content and pedagogy in a manner consistent with inquiry. This is the approach we and many others have used to teach science methods in our own teacher education programs. Therefore, we decided to write a text on inquiry-based methodology that students could use in their future classrooms and that would encourage teachers to teach science as inquiry. The result is a very different type of methods book for use with pre-service and practicing elementary teachers about the teaching of science as they are learning science. We teach our course in precisely this manner.

A DIFFERENT APPROACH TO A METHODS TEXT

Many of today's science methods texts are intended for traditional courses, not for courses that teach inquiry by having students experience inquiry. *Teaching Science as Investigations: Modeling Inquiry Through Learning Cycle Lessons* is a nontraditional text. It offers science investigations for use as class activities to engage students in inquiry. It also suggests that the instructor model effective teaching strategies as the students *do* inquiry. Each investigation in the text is revisited with an emphasis on the inquiry teaching strategies—effective questioning strategies, for example—in the context of that lesson or investigation. The instructional pedagogy is embedded into learning cycle lessons in the form of *Teaching Focus* features. These illustrate various effective instructional methodologies while engaging students in lessons that use the Learning Cycle format, in the true spirit of *NSES*. Thus, the teaching pedagogy shared in this text is demonstrated in the context of each investigative lesson, allowing students to focus on the how-tos of different pedagogical concepts throughout the text.

We believe that this method serves several purposes. First, pre-service and practicing teachers use pedagogy through firsthand experiences. Second, they learn science content that supports their need to understand the science concepts that they will teach. And third, they experience inquiry-based science because, as the research shows, people tend to teach in the same way that they were taught. We hope that by using this text pre- and inservice teachers will become more confident and proficient in teaching science as inquiry.

ORGANIZATION OF THE BOOK

Teaching Science as Investigations: Modeling Inquiry Through Learning Cycle Lessons opens with an introduction on how children learn science. In fact, research on how children learn science has driven the development of this book and also drives its intended use. Instructors who want to model constructivist inquiry, however, may want to skip to an investigation rather than begin with the Introduction.

After the Introduction, the text follows a predictable format. It covers not only the three major content disciplines of science education, but also the pedagogy of teaching science as inquiry.

To navigate the text you will want to know how it is organized—as units, investigations within units, and lessons that make up individual investigations.

UNITS. All the investigations in the text fall within three units: Unit I, Physical Science; Unit II, Life Science; and Unit III, Earth/Space Science.

INVESTIGATIONS. Within each unit are four investigations. Each investigation contains three learning cycle lessons and begins with possible student misconceptions and a list of misconception resources. The first investigation in each unit is appropriate for grades K–4. Three additional investigations present conceptual lessons for grades 5–8.

INDIVIDUAL LESSONS. The science lessons have both a predictable format and predictable pedagogical features.

- Each lesson is a scientific inquiry driven by an explorable question in the 5-E Learning Cycle lesson format.
- Each lesson provides a coherent conceptual development of standards-based concepts.
- Each lesson has a student version that can be reproduced for classroom use, and an expanded teacher version that includes all the content and pedagogy needed to teach the lesson in a constructivist manner.
- Each lesson includes a complete explanation of its science content.
- Each lesson presents the *Teaching Focus* at their point of use. These elements cover various instructional methodologies or strategies including the Learning Cycle, guided versus open inquiry, assessment, integrating mathematics, materials management, integrating reading, questioning strategies, educational technology, inquiry abilities, misconceptions, integrating writing and communication, and integrating inquiry into textbook instruction.
- Each lesson contains *Teaching Tips,* a variety of practical suggestions to help teachers further implement the lesson.

The Conclusion of the text provides material to enable teachers to develop their own investigations with lessons that follow a 5-E Learning Cycle model. It furnishes directives to help them develop each phase of a 5-E lesson model, and presents guidelines to ensure that any science activity found on the Web or in a science book is set up as a valid scientific inquiry with an explorable question.

ACKNOWLEDGMENTS

This book is the result of our experiences and has been greatly influenced by our interactions with, and contributions from our many colleagues. We are grateful on their help in preparing this book and as colleagues on a daily basis:

Charlotte Otto, professor of chemistry and associate provost at the University of Michigan—Dearborn (UMD), answered all of our chemistry queries with concise and concrete aplomb.

Judy Nesmith, senior lecturer in biology at UMD, for her creative ideas for the lessons on heredity.

Harold Pratt, Jefferson County (Colorado) Schools and past president of NSTA, for his professional encouragement and mentoring.

Henry Heikkinen, professor emeritus of chemistry education at the University of Northern Colorado, for countless hours of stimulating discussion on science teaching and learning.

Rodger Bybee, executive director of the Biological Sciences Curriculum Study (BSCS), for his guidance and profound influence on science education.

We also are constantly renewed by our interaction with our faculty colleagues at the Inquiry Institute at the University of Michigan-Dearborn: Stein Brunvand, Christopher Burke, John Devlin, Patricia Hartshorn, Gail Luera, Judy Nesmith, Charlotte Otto, Robert Simpson II, Carrie Swift, and

Paul Zitzewitz. In addition, we would like to recognize the hundreds of students and teachers with whom we have worked—their questions, suggestions, and zeal for teaching science the "right way" have been a steady source of energy for us.

Our thanks also to the following reviewers of this text whose guidance helped shape its contents and usefulness: Margaret S. Carter, James Madison University; Cynthia H. Geer, Xavier University; Terrie Kielborn, State University of West Georgia; Michelle Scribner-MacLean, University of Massachusetts, Lowell; Leah Melber, California State University, Los Angeles; Michael Odell, Illinois State University; Bruce Patterson, Central Michigan University; and Kathleen Sillman, Pennsylvania State University.

And finally, we would also like to acknowledge our editor, Linda Ashe Bishop, who over the years has helped us become better authors.

Richard Moyer
Jay Hackett
Susan Everett

About the Authors

Richard H. Moyer, EdD, is Professor of science education and natural sciences at the University of Michigan–Dearborn. He and Jay K. Hackett are senior authors of the *McGraw-Hill Science* text series. He has conducted hundreds of workshops on inquiry science teaching.

Jay K. Hackett, EdD, is Professor Emeritus of earth science education at the University of Northern Colorado. He and Richard Moyer have collaborated on their elementary science textbook series for more than 25 years. He is also a contributing writer of *Inquiry in the National Science Education Standards* and *Teaching About Evolution and the Nature of Science* for the National Academy of Sciences.

Susan A. Everett, PhD, is Assistant Professor of science education at the University of Michigan–Dearborn. She has extensive experience with teaching science at the pre-primary level and is also a coauthor of *Pre-AP: Strategies in Science—Inquiry-Based Laboratories for Middle School.*

Teacher Preparation Classroom

See a demo at
www.prenhall.com/teacherprep/demo

Your Class. Their Careers. Our Future. Will your students be prepared?

We invite you to explore our new, innovative and engaging website and all that it has to offer you, your course, and tomorrow's educators! Organized around the major courses pre-service teachers take, the Teacher Preparation site provides media, student/teacher artifacts, strategies, research articles, and other resources to equip your students with the quality tools needed to excel in their courses and prepare them for their first classroom.

This ultimate on-line education resource is available at no cost, when packaged with a Merrill text, and will provide you and your students access to:

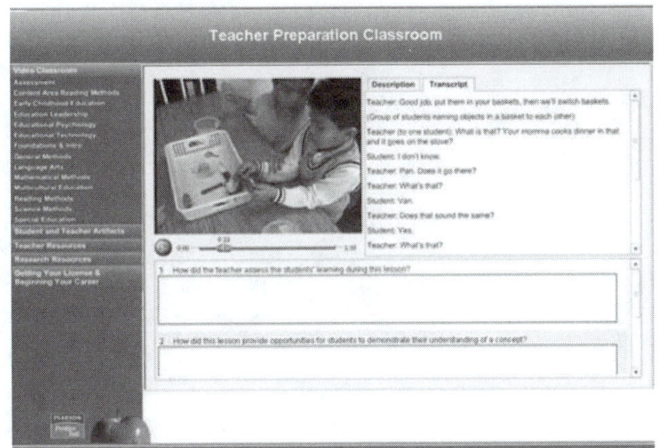

Online Video Library. More than 150 video clips—each tied to a course topic and framed by learning goals and Praxis-type questions—capture real teachers and students working in real classrooms, as well as in-depth interviews with both students and educators.

Student and Teacher Artifacts. More than 200 student and teacher classroom artifacts—each tied to a course topic and framed by learning goals and application questions—provide a wealth of materials and experiences to help make your study to become a professional teacher more concrete and hands-on.

Research Articles. Over 500 articles from ASCD's renowned journal *Educational Leadership*. The site also includes Research Navigator, a searchable database of additional educational journals.

Teaching Strategies. Over 500 strategies and lesson plans for you to use when you become a practicing professional.

Licensure and Career Tools. Resources devoted to helping you pass your licensure exam; learn standards, law, and public policies; plan a teaching portfolio; and succeed in your first year of teaching.

How to ORDER *Teacher Prep* for you and your students:
For students to receive a *Teacher Prep* Access Code with this text, instructors *must* provide a special value pack ISBN number on their textbook order form. To receive this special ISBN, please email *Merrill.marketing@pearsoned.com* and provide the following information:

- Name and Affiliation
- Author/Title/Edition of Merrill text

Upon ordering *Teacher Prep* for their students, instructors will be given a lifetime *Teacher Prep* Access Code.

Contents

An Introduction to Science Learning

How Children Learn Science

Science is constructed of facts, as a house is of stones. But a collection of facts is no more a science than a heap of stones is a house.

Henri Poincaré

LAURA'S SECOND GRADE CLASSROOM*

Laura was ready to begin teaching a second grade unit on light and shadows. She began by reading the first two verses of a poem to her class.

MY SHADOW

I have a little shadow that goes in and out with me,
And what can be the use of him is more than I can see.
He is very, very like me from the heels up to the head;
And I see him jump before me, when I jump into my bed.

The funniest thing about this is the way he likes to grow—
Not at all like proper children, which is always very slow;
For he sometimes shoots up taller like an india-rubber ball,
And he sometimes gets so little that there's none of him at all.

Robert Louis Stevenson (1906)

Afterward the children talked about the parts of the poem they liked best and why. Laura told the children that during science, for the next two weeks, they would learn all about light and shadows like those in the poem. Next, Laura gave the children a list of vocabulary terms they would use in learning about light and shadows.

---

*A significant portion of the following vignettes is based on an article by Pratt and Hackett (1998) that appeared in *The Principal*. Reprinted with permission. Copyright [1998] National Association of Elementary School Principals. All rights reserved.

The children used the glossary in the back of their texts to find the definitions for the words (e.g., *light*, *reflection*, *transparent*, *translucent*, *opaque*, and *shadow*) and wrote them in their learning logs.

When finished with the vocabulary lesson, the class read aloud and discussed the chapter on sources and behavior of light from their textbooks. Now it was time to do several hands-on activities. The first activity demonstrated how light travels in a straight line. In the second activity, the children used flashlights, clear plastic, wax paper, and a book to demonstrate the meanings of the terms *transparent*, *translucent*, and *opaque*. Next, the students completed a worksheet showing a flashlight in four different positions and the resultant shadows cast by a small post. Then they used a flashlight and a short straw to duplicate and verify each diagram. In the final lesson, the students wrote a story entitled "My Friend the Shadow."

CARLA'S SECOND GRADE CLASSROOM

Down the hall, in the same school, Carla and her second graders were ready to begin their unit, "Light and Shadows." With the children gathered around, Carla read aloud the poem "My Shadow." After finishing the poem, Carla asked the children a number of questions: "What do you think it means when it says that sometimes my shadow is very tall and sometimes it gets little until there is none at all? Where and when have you seen your shadow look like this? What makes your shadow get long? Why does it sometimes get very small? When don't you have a shadow? Why? What do you need to make a shadow?" After finding out what her students already knew about shadows, Carla said, "What other questions do you have about shadows? Let's make a list of all of your questions and put them in our learning logs." (See Figure I.1.)

Investigating Shadows

The following day, Carla asked the children: "How could we make shadows and make them change? Do you suppose we could find answers to your questions from

Figure I.1 Children's shadow questions

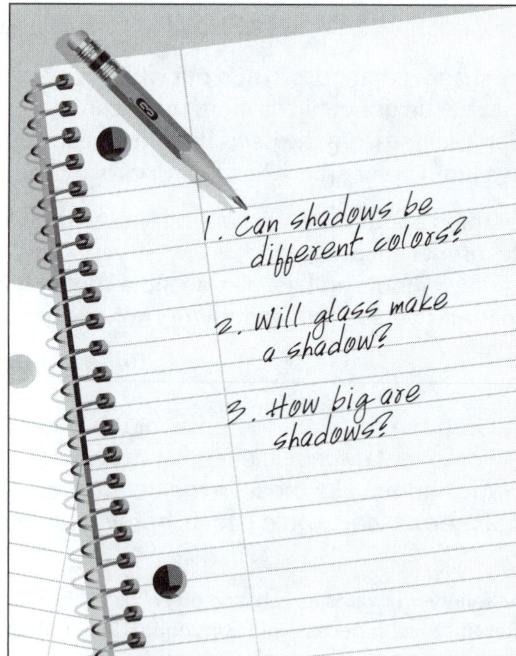
1. Can shadows be different colors?
2. Will glass make a shadow?
3. How big are shadows?

yesterday? Let's try it and see." Carla divided the class into groups and gave each group a flashlight, a small lump of clay, a short section of drinking straw, and a large sheet of paper. The students explored the following questions: "How can you make a long shadow? What can you do to make a short shadow? How can you shine the light so there is no shadow at all? How can you make a shadow that points left? Right? Have your partner turn out the light and point it at the straw. Predict where and how long the shadow will be when the light is turned on." Carla asked the children to keep a record of all investigations in their learning logs. The students measured shadows using a ruler. When the activities were completed, Carla and the students discussed each question and the results, and then worked together to develop explanations for what happened.

Developing Conceptual Understanding

After several days, Carla then asked, "What do you think would happen if we put clear plastic, wax paper, or a book in front of our flashlights and tried to make shadows?" After listening to the children's predictions and explanations, she said, "Would you like to try it?" The students then gathered their materials and explored the problem. After finishing these investigations, Carla and the students discussed the terms *light, shadow, transparent, translucent,* and *opaque,* referring to their questions and explorations. The children developed a definition for each term and compared their definitions to the glossary in their text.

> **Science Background**
>
> In this activity, students work with various objects to determine if they make a shadow. There are some objects through which light is unable to pass. These *opaque* objects form shadows. Objects, such as clear plastic, that you can see through (because light is able to pass) are referred to as *transparent*. Objects, such as wax paper, that block part of the light passing through them are known as *translucent*.

Next, Carla selected relevant pages in the "Light and Shadows" chapter in their text. After reading these passages, Carla and the students compared what they had read to what they had done with the flashlights and straws. They compared the flashlights and straws to the sun and opaque objects. The next day the students traced their own shadows with chalk on the outside play area, then predicted where and how large their shadows would be later in the afternoon (verifying their predictions later). To conclude the unit, each child wrote and illustrated a story entitled "What Makes My Shadow Shrink and Grow?"

COMPARING THE CLASSROOM SCENARIOS

Consider the descriptions of the science lessons conducted by Laura and Carla. Although both scenes are brief and incomplete, nonetheless they provide a window through which to view two different learning environments. Compare them for the type of physical and mental processes required in learning the science content: (1) In which class were hands-on investigations designed around scientific questions generated by both the teacher and the students? (2) In which class were explanations based upon evidence gathered through observations and measurement? (3) In which class did students acquire information organized and presented by the teacher? (4) In which class did students use their curiosity to generate ideas, and means to test those ideas?

HOW DID YOU LEARN SCIENCE?

Reflect for a moment on how you learned science in elementary, middle, and high school. Your view of science today is most likely a reflection of how you learned it. Was your experience like that in Laura's class, or that in Carla's class? Students in Laura's class, and in many other classrooms today, are learning science in a passive way: Information is organized and presented to them by their teacher. Often, the teachers pay little attention to what students already know about science. In this learning model, the information transmitted by the teacher and the curriculum materials is assumed to make sense and seem reasonable to the students. Each of us, however, has listened to many well-organized and articulated explanations that we did not understand. Even though we recognized and could probably spell each word, there was no way that we could explain what we had heard to someone else.

Two Views of Science

As a result, most of us view science from a very limited perspective. This perception of science has been influenced by the manner in which we studied it. Thus, we may see science as only an organized body of information about the natural world. Or, we may see science as a collection of terms and definitions—a body of knowledge to be memorized. Or, we may see science as the dynamic interaction of thought processes, skills, and attitudes that help us develop a richer understanding of the natural world and its impact on society. The latter view sees science as not just a body of knowledge but rather a "process for producing knowledge" (American Association for the Advancement of Science, 1990, p. 2). This view of science is the one that scientists, science educators, and many science teachers have today.

Impact of Science

The impact of science on our lives has never been greater. Each day, advances in science and technology affect the quality of our food, water, medicine, consumer products, and safety. To assume that science's impact will always be positive, however, is naïve and potentially foolish. As more people in the world demand newer products and access technology to produce them, it becomes increasingly important that we better understand how science, technology, and society are related. Thus, it is critical that our society be scientifically literate—have the day-to-day knowledge needed to make informed decisions about science and technology. The road to a more scientifically literate society begins with the opportunity for all students to develop a better understanding of fundamental science concepts, principles, and ways of thinking.

Like Scientists, Children Are Curious

Children seem to have an unending supply of questions about things around them: What makes my shadow grow longer? How do fish breathe under water? Why does the moon change its shape? What happened to the dinosaurs? Children are innately curious. This curiosity is a powerful stimulant for learning. Unfortunately, in many schools, curiosity is not valued. Students are not encouraged to ask questions like those listed above. They are more likely to be involved in lessons where they simply follow the directions of the teacher or text as if they were following a recipe in a cookbook.

A CLOSER LOOK AT INQUIRY AND THE NATIONAL SCIENCE EDUCATION STANDARDS

One major reform effort of the 1990s was the development of the National Science Education Standards (*NSES*), a broad effort that included hundreds of scientists, science educators, and teachers. The *National Science Education Standards* (National Research Council, 1996, p. 20) emphasize that learning science is an active process. "Learning science is something that students do, not something that is done to them." Doing science requires students to be involved in both the physical and mental processes collectively known as *scientific inquiry*. This implies that "hands-on" science activities alone are not enough. Students must have their "minds-on" as well. Clearly, the children in Laura's class were engaged in physical activities. Because they were merely confirming (verifying) what they had already read or been told, however, their minds-on quotient was significantly less than that of the children in Carla's class. Recall, Carla's students were performing physical activities designed to answer some question(s) and thus they were more mentally engaged.

Inquiry as a Process in Science

Student inquiry in science should mirror the active physical and mental processes conducted by scientists themselves. Employing inquiry in science classrooms requires a shift from teachers organizing and presenting content to active student involvement in investigations driven by scientific questions. Recorded observations and measurements provide students with evidence upon which to develop explanations, or answers to these questions. During science investigations, students make connections between their current knowledge and the recognized scientific explanations found in textbooks and other sources. The children can then apply this understanding to new questions, and communicate this knowledge to others.

Inquiry as Content in Science

The developers of the *National Science Education Standards* took a unique position with respect to school science inquiry. They viewed scientific inquiry as more than just a way to teach and learn science. In their judgment, scientific inquiry also involves an understanding of how scientific inquiry results in the continuing development of scientific knowledge. Therefore, they designated scientific inquiry as a content standard along with more familiar subject matter content areas: physical science, life science, and earth and space science. The *NSES* state, "As a result of activities in grades K–12, all students should develop . . . abilities necessary to do scientific inquiry [and] . . . understandings about scientific inquiry" (National Research Council, 1996, p. 105).

Inquiry abilities. This inquiry standard includes specific abilities necessary for students to do inquiry. Because inquiry abilities are actually mental processes, they become more complex as students mature cognitively. Compare the inquiry abilities (Figure I.2) for students in grades K–4 with those for students in grades 5–8 (National Research Council, 1996, pp. 122, 145, 148).[1]

Note that K–4 students "employ simple equipment and tools to gather data," while 5–8 students should also be able to "analyze" and "interpret" data. K–4 students should be able to "use data to construct reasonable explanations," while 5–8 students should be able to "recognize and analyze alternative explanations and predictions." These processes require students to use more sophisticated tools and critical thinking to engage with scientific inquiry. This increasing complexity of inquiry abilities mirrors the growth in cognitive development of students. As can be seen from Figure I.2, the developers of the inquiry content standard emphasize that employing these cognitive abilities requires the learner to go beyond typical science process skills such as observing, classifying, predicting, and experimenting.

Developing inquiry abilities requires active and thoughtful participation in science investigations. Although students are naturally curious and continually ask questions, they must learn the difference between broad, general questions and scientific questions. They need help in learning how to refine and focus questions about objects or phenomena that can be answered from evidence.

---

[1]What does scientific inquiry look like in the classroom? The addendum to the *National Science Education Standards* focusing on inquiry (National Research Council, 2000, p. 25) describes what they term the *Essential Features of Classroom Inquiry*.

Essential Features of Classroom Inquiry

- Learners are engaged by scientifically oriented questions.
- Learners give priority to evidence that allows them to develop and evaluate explanations that address scientifically oriented questions.
- Learners formulate explanations from evidence to address scientifically oriented questions.
- Learners evaluate their explanations in light of alternative explanations, particularly those reflecting scientific understanding.
- Learners communicate and justify their proposed explanations.

Figure I.2 Inquiry abilities

Grades K–4: Abilities necessary to do scientific inquiry	**Grades 5–8: Abilities necessary to do scientific inquiry**
Ask a question about objects, organisms, and events in the environment.	Identify questions that can be answered through scientific investigations.
Plan and conduct a simple investigation.	Design and conduct a scientific investigation.
Employ simple equipment and tools to gather data and extend the senses.	Use appropriate tools and techniques to gather, analyze, and interpret data.
Use data to construct a reasonable explanation.	Develop descriptions, explanations, predictions, and models using evidence.
	Think critically and logically to make the relationships between evidence and explanations.
	Recognize and analyze alternative explanations and predictions.
Communicate investigations and explanations.	Communicate scientific procedures and explanations.
	Use mathematics in all aspects of scientific inquiry.

Experience in designing and conducting scientific investigations followed by reflective discussions of the mental and physical processes involved enable students to develop the idea of a fair test. Inexperienced investigators do not always discriminate between observations or measurements to know which data they should use to answer their question. The goal is to help students develop the ability to think critically—to analyze data and form logical explanations based upon cause-and-effect relationships in their investigation. Central to developing these physical and mental processes is helping students understand the "evidence to explanation" nature of scientific inquiry that sets it apart from other ways of thinking. If this is a new idea for you as well, be assured that working through the learning cycle lessons in this text will enable you also to enhance your ability to use observations and data from experiments to develop explanations for natural phenomena.

Inquiry understandings. To this end, the *NSES* (National Research Council, 1996, p. 123) also include what are known as the "inquiry understandings." These understandings parallel the inquiry abilities but also extend them to include how scientists create new knowledge through inquiry. They also reveal how scientists modify their explanations of natural phenomena as they present and debate new evidence and reasoning through publication and peer review.

Inquiry in the Classroom

Return to the snapshots describing teaching and learning in the classrooms of Laura and Carla. Examine each for the presence of the inquiry abilities. Which classroom scene demonstrates classroom inquiry? Students conducted investigations in both classes. In Laura's class, the investigations followed explanations provided by the teacher and instructional materials. The investigations were designed to verify explanations provided by others. Carla's students were given the opportunity to raise questions about light and shadows based upon their prior understanding. They designed and conducted investigations to answer their questions. The answers or explanations were constructed from evidence gathered from observations and measurements. The students then compared their explanations to accepted scientific explanations presented in readings from their text. Carla's students then defended their knowledge by writing and illustrating a story explaining the cause and effect of light and shadows. Employing science as inquiry helped Carla's students understand the cause-and-effect relationship of light and shadows, in much the same way as scientists had done before them.

NSES FOR TEACHING STANDARDS

To this point we have treated the topic of inquiry from the perspective of what children should understand and be able to do. What implications do these learning outcomes have for how teachers teach science? Just as there are science content standards for inquiry, there are also science teaching standards (National Research Council, 1996, pp. 27–53). These teaching standards are comprehensive and include many different teaching strategies, among them inquiry. Teaching Standard A states: "Teachers of science plan an inquiry based science program for their students" (National Research Council, 1996, p. 30). The *NSES* emphasize that effective teachers use multiple strategies. They point out that hands-on science activities do not necessarily result in students developing inquiry abilities and understandings. Instead, a variety of teaching strategies, including inquiry, are found to be most effective in helping students learn with understanding. This text provides a series of student investigations that use inquiry pedagogy coupled with teaching tips and other strategies consistent with the above standards. As you work through the investigations in this text, you will experience several of these different teaching strategies, which are integrated into the science lessons.

EARLY ADVOCATES OF INQUIRY TEACHING

Inquiry teaching and learning is not a new idea. It has not always been called *inquiry*, but the idea has been around for about a century although its popularity has been cyclical. In the early 1900s, science was taught in a passive mode, generally focusing on nature studies. Learning was generally limited to the acquisition of information presented by the teacher and through readings. We now turn our attention to four prominent learning theorists and their contributions to inquiry.

John Dewey

Around 1910, John Dewey appeared on the scene as a prominent advocate of reasoning rather than of memorization (Dewey, 1910). Dewey believed that instruction, particularly in science, should emphasize inquiry through problem solving. He also believed that students, when engaged in solving interesting and relevant problems, learned more effectively. He proposed that when challenged by a meaningful problem, learners actively reflect on what they already know from earlier experiences deemed similar in nature. After actively comparing and contrasting ideas, the learner begins to form a reasonable hypothesis or explanation to be tested.

Dewey emphasized the importance of providing problems that are personally relevant and interesting for the learner. Consequently, concepts or problems deemed important by the teacher and the curriculum are not always sufficient, in Dewey's view. Dewey believed that, to effectively engage meaningful thought processes, learners had to perceive problems as *personally interesting and relevant to daily events and experiences* in their world. Dewey also felt that enabling students to interact with each other, comparing their thoughts and ideas, was extremely important.

Jean Piaget

From 1920 until late in the 1970s, the contributions of Jean Piaget heavily influenced the field of cognitive development. This Swiss biologist was intrigued with what he perceived as the progressional development of mental structures that influence thinking in children. Although Piaget did not address inquiry specifically, one could argue that his views on the mental processes involved in learning are directly related to the concept of inquiry. Piaget viewed learning as an active process in which the learner compares and contrasts modes of thinking about new experiences with those of prior experiences. Often the child realizes that the explanation used for an earlier experience just does not seem to fit with a new experience. This results in a kind of puzzlement Piaget referred to as *cognitive disequilibrium*. To resolve this type of problem, learners may need to modify their way of thinking to come to a conclusion that seems personally reasonable. Piaget called this process of thought adjustment *equilibration* (Inhelder & Piaget, 1958).

The process of equilibration has unique and important implications for the teaching of science (Bybee & Sund, 1982). Equilibration is the process through which children learn by altering or adapting a mental structure. This adaptation occurs through two active thought processes, assimilation and accommodation. *Assimilation* occurs when learners compare the new experience (and its explanation) with an earlier one and decide the two are very similar. The new experience is then incorporated or assimilated into the already-existing mental structure. When learners encounter an experience for which they have no preexisting mental structure available for assimilation, the mind adapts by changing its thought processes and adding a new mental structure. This process is known as *accommodation*. For example, suppose some of Carla's students believed that all solid objects cast shadows. During one of the investigations, they place a small card-shaped piece of clear plastic in front of a flashlight and one of them shouts, "Look, there's no shadow! Where did it go?" How might the students deal with this discrepant event? If the problem were truly perplexing to them, and they were encouraged with probing questions to explore and test it further, the students might accommodate the problem of the clear plastic by constructing a new understanding about how a transparent object creates essentially no shadow.

Assimilation and accommodation are dynamic processes and occur together rather than in isolation. Learning through equilibration requires that learning be an active process, like that described in the *National Science Education Standards*, in which students are involved in both hands-on and minds-on investigations.

Lev Vygotsky

Vygotsky was a Russian psychologist who died at the age of 38. At a very young age, he became interested in developmental psychology after a period in medical and law school. Vygotsky was especially interested in social interactions and their influence on cognitive development. He noted that "Culture creates special forms of behavior, modifies the activities of mental functions and adds new stories to the developing system of human behavior" (Vygotsky, 1966, p. 19). Vygotsky is probably best known for his concept of the *Zone of Proximal Development*, which he defined as "the distance between the actual developmental level as determined by independent problem solving and the level of potential development as determined through problem solving under adult guidance or in collaboration with more capable peers" (Vygotsky, 1978, p. 86). In other words, Vygotsky believed that a student's learning development is facilitated by social interaction with more sophisticated individuals that provide guidance during the learning process. From Vygotsky's work, we can see that the value of students working in small groups to conduct science investigations comes from the discourse that takes place. It also follows that the skillful intervention of a teacher can elevate the level of students' thinking and learning.

Jerome Bruner

An exceptionally bright young man, Bruner was educated at Duke University and Harvard. He became intrigued with psychology and focused on the study of how people learn. Bruner contended that learners should not spend their time *talking about* science, they should be *doing* science. Much of his learning research centered upon *active-discovery learning through inductive reasoning*. Inductive approaches involve the use of specific concrete experiences in which the learner organizes objects and events to discover patterns and relationships, then develops solutions or explanations (Bruner, 1960).

The work of Dewey, Piaget, Vygotsky, and Bruner has contributed significantly to both elementary and middle-level science curriculum development and approaches to teaching science. Their theories of intellectual development and how students learn provide the foundation for what the *NSES* refer to as *active-learning through inquiry-oriented investigations*.

Implications for Instructional Materials

The United States during the 1950s and 1960s saw large-scale efforts that deliberately moved away from passive learning approaches. Locked in a race with Russia to land people on the moon, the nation felt the need for citizens who better understood not only science concepts and principles, but also the nature of science and how it works. In response, governmental agencies, primarily the National Science Foundation, and private foundations provided funds for the development of new elementary and secondary science curricula that emphasized learning through inquiry. Three large-scale programs were developed for elementary school classrooms. The *Science Curriculum Improvement Study* (SCIS), the *Elementary Science Study* (ESS), and the *Science—A Process Approach* (SAPA) each involved children in *active* physical and mental processing of questions and problems through science investigations. SCIS and ESS, in particular, emphasized developing an understanding of concepts and their cause-and-effect relationships. Terminology and definitions were constructed from the active hands-on and minds-on experiences of the children. New, more inquiry-oriented programs were also developed for junior high and high school students. Funds were also made available for teacher in-service and professional development.

Implications today. While research showed that students in the new elementary science programs understood science concepts better than did their counterparts who were taught in more-passive environments, the acceptance of programs like ESS, SAPA, and SCIS was disappointing and short-lived for the most part (Bredderman, 1982; Harms & Kahl, 1980). Many classroom teachers who learned science by acquisition of information apparently found it difficult to teach using inquiry approaches and strategies. Others have argued that elementary school teachers did not have sufficient time and support to maintain instruction in these programs. The long-term impact of these programs, however, has been significant. Influenced by the philosophy and approach guiding the new programs, teachers and instructional materials developers began using more hands-on laboratory activities in their classrooms. A shift from using activities to verify concepts to that of investigating first became more common. Modifications of ESS, SAPA, and SCIS investigations made their way into laboratory manuals and textbooks. The focus on inquiry began to take shape and formed the backbone for the National Science Education Standards and the recommended science teaching and learning methodology.

HOW LEARNERS CONSTRUCT MEANING

Misconceptions

Earlier we asked you to reflect on how you learned science in classes you had taken from elementary school through college. Our premise was that most of us learned through instructional models patterned after time-honored practices in passive learning. These approaches have come under close scrutiny for a number of reasons. While it is true that the general public holds many misconceptions about science, a surprising number of college science majors as well as graduate students also demonstrate a lack of understanding of basic scientific concepts (Bodner, 1991; diSessa, 1982; Meltzer, 2004). Their explanations of certain fundamental concepts are inconsistent with accepted scientific explanations and, thus, are referred to as misconceptions. This finding is a bit disconcerting when you consider that these young men and women were highly interested in the study of science and deliberately chose to study it! It emphasizes, however, the need to provide students with lots of hands-on experiences and minds-on thinking to steer them toward more-accurate understandings of science concepts and principles.

Common misconceptions. The following is a list of common misconceptions held by high school students (Hapkiewicz, 1992). Read through the list and think about your own understanding of each statement.

- Earth's seasons are caused by the distance from Earth to the sun.
- The phases of the moon are caused by Earth's shadow covering up different parts of the moon.

- Heat rises.
- Electrical current in a flashlight flows from the battery to the bulb, not from the bulb to the battery as well.
- All metals are attracted to magnets.
- The bubbles in boiling water contain hydrogen and oxygen.
- Objects float in water because they are lighter than water.
- If you back away from a mirror, you can see more of yourself.
- The sun is directly overhead at noon each day.

Adults' misconceptions. In all probability you have, in various science courses in your schooling, studied most of the topics covered in this list of misconceptions. Many of you also will undoubtedly share some of the same misconceptions. If you are feeling a little uncomfortable with your thinking on several of these examples, you are in good company. In a video entitled *A Private Universe* (Pyramid Film and Video, 1988) 23 graduating Harvard seniors, alumni, and faculty were interviewed to find out their understanding of simple astronomy questions related to seasons and the phases of the moon. Twenty-one of the 23 gave explanations that exhibited misconceptions. For example, they stated that Earth's seasons were the result of its distance from the sun—winter occurring when the Earth was farther away and summer when closer. It is reasonable to assume that each of these educated persons had, at some point in their schooling, received formal instruction about this concept. The distance between the Earth and the sun has virtually nothing to do with why we have seasons. In fact, the Earth is slightly closer to the sun during the winter season in the northern hemisphere. The relationship between the tilt of the Earth on its axis as it revolves around the sun and the angle at which solar energy strikes Earth's surface, however, directly affects the amount of energy absorbed, producing the seasons (see Figure I.3).

Children's misconceptions. Elementary school children, naturally, exhibit similar misconceptions. Particularly interesting is the fact that, even after completing units of study in science, many children still do not change their explanations. These *naive* or *alternate explanations*, or *misconceptions,* seem to persist in spite of direct instruction in the concepts. For example, Beverly Bell, a New Zealand researcher, found that a surprising number of children ages 6 through 12 when queried about plants and animals did not classify grass, carrots, or oak trees as plants (Bell, 1981). Whereas most adults tend to classify living things into two general groups, plants and animals, children often use different reasoning and construct different systems for classifying these living things.

Science and misconceptions. Since the emergence of modern science, the understanding of basic concepts explaining the behavior of objects and events in the universe was obtained through inquiry. Scientists pursued intriguing questions and problems through active exploration. They

Figure I.3 The sun's energy is spread over a wider area of earth as its angle decreases

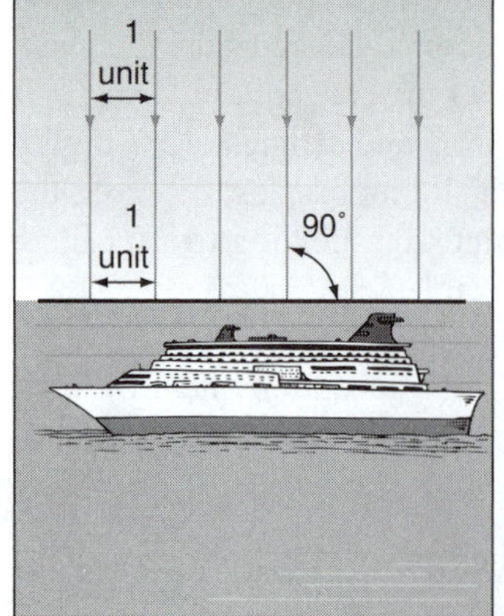

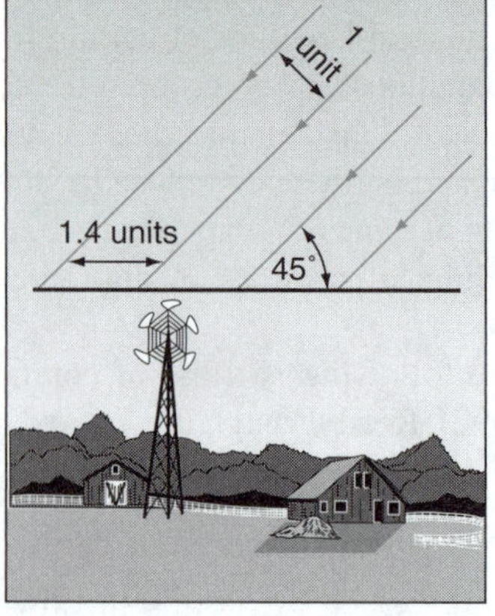

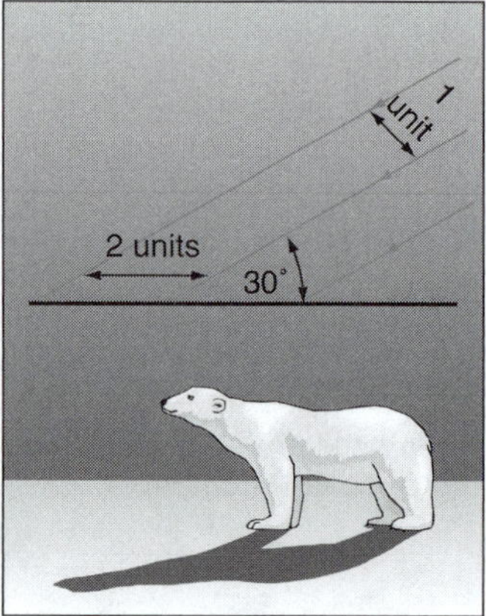

tested their hypotheses and compared results with what was known at the time. When data were not consistent with their hypotheses, they tried different ways of thinking about the phenomena until reconstructed explanations began to make sense and could be verified through further testing. This is what actually distinguishes modern science from previous ways of explaining phenomena. This may explain why geocentric (earth-centered) explanations of the solar system persisted for thousands of years—even in light of many observations to the contrary.

Constructivism

Cognitive psychologists and science educators, influenced by the work of misconception researchers, have added much to the work of early discovery learning advocates. What follows is a blend of ideas from Dewey, Piaget, Vygotsky, and Bruner together with more-recent findings. Underlying this research is the notion that all people normally try to make sense of their world. Although most of us operate with far less precision than does a scientist, we still seek to explain, predict, and control our experiences.

Revisiting Laura's and Carla's classrooms. Let's begin by reconsidering the scenarios presented earlier regarding the teaching of light and shadows. Recall that in Laura's classroom:

> Laura gave the children a list of vocabulary terms they would use in learning about light and shadows. The children used the glossary in the back of their text to find the definitions for the words (e.g., *light*, *reflection*, *transparent*, *translucent*, *opaque*, and *shadow*) and wrote them in their learning logs. When finished with the vocabulary lesson, the class read aloud and discussed the chapter on sources and behavior of light from their textbooks.

This teaching methodology assumes that knowledge can be transferred directly from the textbook to the student—in the manner one would download information from a computer. Indeed, this method works with some students—those whose prior experiences allow them to make sense of the new information. For many students, however, the new information will be difficult to understand, and to some it will be meaningless!

In contrast, let's look once again at Carla's classroom:

> After finishing these investigations, Carla and the students discussed the terms *light*, *shadow*, *transparent*, *translucent*, and *opaque*, referring to their questions and explorations. The children developed a definition for each term and compared their definitions to the glossary in their text. Next, Carla selected relevant pages in the "Light and Shadows" chapter in their text. After reading these passages, Carla and the students compared what they had read to what they had done with the flashlights and straws.

In this case the students began by exploring shadows through a series of inquiry activities using a variety of materials. From these experiences they developed their own understandings of the concepts. Not until after this did Carla provide the accepted scientific vocabulary and have students read their text. Note that in this method the teacher facilitated the students' construction of their own understandings. A broader range of students will more likely be able to make sense of information when it is presented in this manner (Shymansky, Kyle, & Allport, 1983).

Constructing meaning. Students are not always ready to receive or absorb incoming information as presented by their teacher or textbook. Nor do they "discover" concepts just by manipulating hands-on materials. Instead, when students are challenged by something they want to learn, they try (with varying degrees of success) to consider any incoming data in the light of related information already stored in their long-range memories from previous experiences. In other words, they *construct* new meanings by combining incoming information with what they already know. This view of learning is called *constructivism.* The basic premise of constructivism is that learners receive sensory input, compare it to existing memory networks of what appears to be a similar event, modify if necessary, and then construct explanations that seem to make sense. What learners actually construct from a given learning experience varies from student to student and often deviates from what the teacher intended. Constructivists contend that there is no "fiber optic cable" from one person's mind to another. This means that one person's understanding of a concept does not necessarily transmit as personal understanding to the person receiving the information. The learner *always* personally constructs understanding.

Inquiry Learning Models

Constructivists believe that effective instruction depends on our ability as teachers to understand how students make sense of experiences and information rather than how we make sense of those same experiences ourselves. The ideas of Dewey, Bruner, Vygotsky, and Piaget on how children develop an understanding of their world have a common thread. Each of these researchers suggests that effective learning involves an interesting problem or situation that engages students through reflection on what they already know about the event. If the problem is unique, the students' prior knowledge does not help provide a satisfactory explanation. Piaget proposed that such discrepant events cause learners to experience disequilibrium. There is a discrepancy between what they think they know and what they are observing. "To bring their thinking back into equilibrium they must adapt or change their cognitive structure through interaction with the environment" (National Research Council, 2000, p. 34). In classrooms, this interaction with the environment is facilitated by investigations designed to gather evidence that supports a newly discovered explanation. This approach is central to teaching and learning through inquiry. Contemporary science educators support the premise that inquiry approaches to learning are more effective in promoting the understanding of concepts (Loucks-Horsley et al., 1990).

The Learning Cycle. Instructional models provide a consistent framework to help teachers become more effective in using inquiry approaches. One widely accepted model of learning and teaching has evolved over the past 40 years. This model is referred to as the *Learning Cycle*. Influenced by the work of Jean Piaget, Professor Robert Karplus, at the University of California–Berkeley, began looking at how one might apply cognitive development theory and discovery learning to instructional strategies in elementary science. Karplus and his colleague, J. Myron Atkin, with the support of the National Science Foundation, developed a three-phase Learning Cycle that served as the central teaching/learning strategy in the newly introduced Science Curriculum Improvement Study (SCIS) program (Atkin & Karplus, 1962).

Originally, the three phases of the cycle were referred to as *exploration*, *invention*, and *discovery*. Later, Karplus referred to them as *exploration*, *concept introduction*, and *concept application*. The Learning Cycle (Figure I.4) has been promoted widely by science educators since its introduction by Karplus. The cycle has evolved through modification to include additional phases such as *engage, explore, explain, elaborate, extend,* and *apply* and is used to frame single guided discovery lessons as well as extended experiences such as chapters and units (Barman & Kotar, 1989; Hackett & Moyer, 1991). A fifth phase, *evaluate*, was incorporated into an elementary science program developed by the Biological Sciences Curriculum Study (Biological Sciences Curriculum Study, 1992). The learning cycle approach to discovery learning (see Figure I.4) is developed more thoroughly in Investigation 1.

Figure I.4 The Learning Cycle

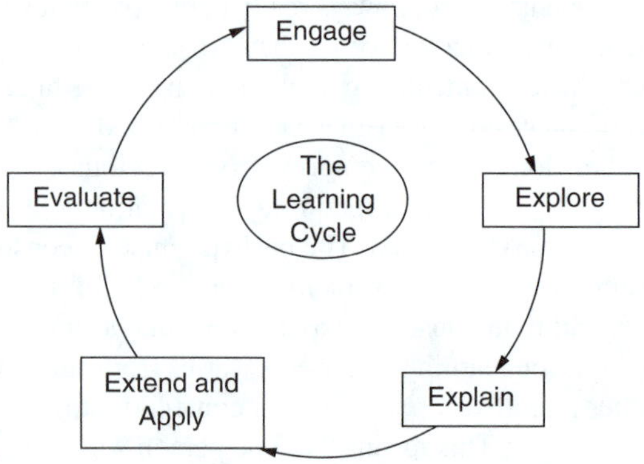

The Learning Cycle
Engage
Explore
Explain
Extend and Apply
Evaluate

Teaching for conceptual change. The Learning Cycle has been further modified to address student misconceptions (Driver, Guesne, & Tiberghien, 1985). Rosalind Driver, in her work with elementary students, has investigated methods of instruction designed to help children confront previously developed misconceptions by comparing them with new experiences. She places great emphasis on providing opportunities for children to express what they already know—their prior understanding. The teacher must then structure new student experiences for situations in which the prior conception or explanation results in learner disequilibrium.

Discrepant events. One effective way to challenge student misconceptions is through the use of discrepant events (Friedl & Koontz, 2005). Discrepant events, as the name implies, are activities or demonstrations whose results are counterintuitive. Imagine the two balloons depicted in Figure I.5. What will happen if the valve is opened between the two balloons? Most people conclude that, because the pressure must equalize, air will then flow from the larger balloon to the smaller balloon, resulting in the two balloons becoming approximately the same size. But this is not what occurs! The pressure does indeed become equal, but air flows from the *smaller to the larger*

Figure I.5

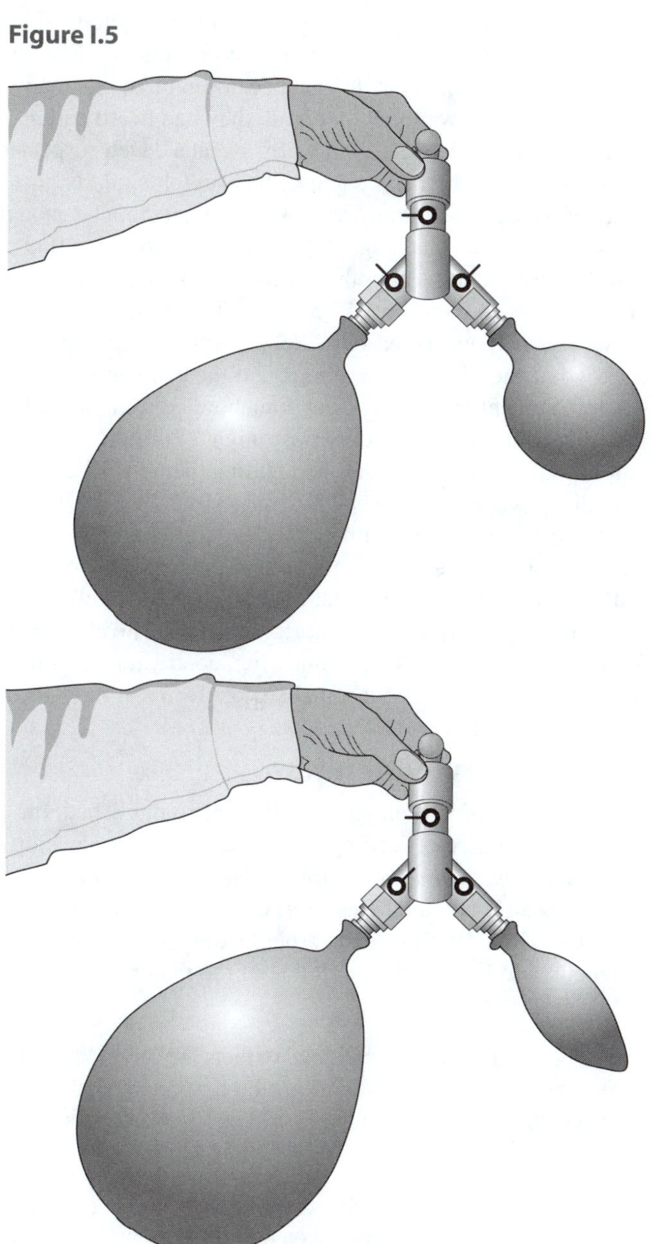

balloon![2] At this point learners may well experience disequilibrium. The learners are motivated intellectually to investigate further.

Through further exploration, exchanging ideas with others, and restructuring thought through assimilation and accommodation, the learner constructs new understanding.

Using the Learning Cycle to address misconceptions. Identification of learner misconceptions becomes an important part of the *Engage* phase of the Learning Cycle. Student investigations designed to assist the learner in restructuring new understanding are the focus of both the *Explore* and *Explain* phases of the Learning Cycle. The intent of the *Extend* and *Apply* phase is to provide students with opportunities to transfer their reconstructed understanding of concepts to different situations. Emphasis should be on applications to situations and events in everyday living. This approach Driver calls *teaching for conceptual change*.

Conceptual change in a classroom. Following is an excellent example of a classroom teacher applying strategies of teaching for conceptual change. Deb O'Brien, a fourth grade teacher in Massachusetts, was about to begin a unit on heat (Watson & Konicek, 1990). Her original plan called for studying major heat sources and learning to use thermometers. Students were to finish the unit in about two weeks. O'Brien began by asking, "What is heat?" She and the students kept record of what they already knew about heat. It soon became evident that many of the children believed that sweaters, coats, and hats were hot. After all, they had heard parents repeatedly say, "It is going to be cold today, so be sure to wear your warm sweater." Deb suspected this was just one of several "naive conceptions" held by her students. She also felt sure that just telling them about the insulative properties of hats, coats, mittens, and sweaters would not be enough to alter their perceptions. So, she responded with the challenge, "Well, let's see if we can find out!"

Ms. O'Brien's students set about testing their ideas with simple experiments. They wrapped a thermometer inside a sweater and left it for 15 minutes. To the surprise of the students the temperature on the thermometer had not increased. "Well, it would have gone up if we had left it in there longer!" Next, they left their tests overnight. Again there was no temperature change. Puzzled by the results, some students suggested that somehow cold air must have gotten into the sweater. After all, the thermostat is turned down overnight! Further testing was performed, including sealing sweaters and hats in plastic bags and putting them in closets and drawers. One student even suggested sealing a sweater in a metal box for one whole year. That would make it heat up! Test data continued to be consistent with earlier experiments. After three days of testing, O'Brien felt the children had begun to face the idea that their old theory just didn't work. Now they were ready for discussions of where the heat in "hot" sweaters really comes from, heat flow from the source to a receiver, properties of insulators, and so on. The children had a series of new experiences that promoted reflective thinking, comparing, contrasting, and restructuring explanations. This approach actually resulted in conceptual change for most of O'Brien's students.

Findings from the Inquiry Addendum

After the National Science Education Standards (NSES) were published, the National Research Council formed a special committee of leading science educators to develop an addendum that focused on inquiry entitled *Inquiry and the National Science Education Standards* (2000). This document is based, in part, on a National Research Council report entitled *How People Learn* (Bransford, Brown, & Cocking, 1999), which brought together research results on cognition studies, child development, and brain function. Some of the major findings of the addendum are discussed below.

1. "Understanding science is more than knowing facts" (National Research Council, 2000, p. 116). Recent research has focused on learning for understanding. Learners who understand concepts can apply them in new situations. To do this learners must have a

[2] The reason is that the pressure on the air in the balloons is caused by the elasticity of the balloons. Because the latex is thicker in the smaller balloon, the pressure on the air is greater. For this reason the first puff of air one blows into a balloon takes the most effort.

foundation of facts organized in a particular context in a manner that allows them to retrieve and apply them. In addition to understanding concepts, students need to develop abilities and understandings of scientific inquiry as described in the *NSES*.

2. "Students build new knowledge and understanding on what they already know and believe" (National Research Council, 2000, p. 117). This finding is supported by research related to how prior knowledge and conceptions influence learning. If these understandings are not engaged by investigations that provide evidence to help students restructure their reasoning, learners may hold fast to their old ideas and rely on memorization to help them pass tests.
3. "Students formulate new knowledge by modifying and refining their current concepts and by adding new concepts to what they already know" (National Research Council, 2000, p. 118). Research on conceptual change shows that students are more apt to change their explanations when they find that their initial ideas do not help explain what happened in a given event (from Driver et al., 1985).
4. "Learning is mediated by the social environment in which learners react with others" (National Research Council, 2000, p. 118). A classroom learning environment where students defend explanations that they have derived from evidence enhanced learning. This environment is consistent with learning science through inquiry.
5. "Effective learning requires that students take control of their own learning" (National Research Council, 2000, p. 119). Learning through inquiry can help students recognize when they do not understand and need additional information or evidence. Teachers can assist students in these processes by consistently helping them reflect on the processes involved in constructing understanding.
6. "The ability to apply knowledge to novel situations, that is, transfer of learning, is affected by the degree to which students learn with understanding" (National Research Council, 2000, p. 119). Students who are very successful at learning through acquisition are not necessarily good at applying this knowledge to other situations. Memorizing terms such as *heat*, *evaporation*, or *photosynthesis*, for examples, does not guarantee that the learner can apply them to events in the natural world. This fact may be especially evident to science teachers who can easily define such terms, but find it difficult to answer students' questions regarding application of the concepts in nature.

Summary

How effectively we teach children science is linked to our understanding of how children learn. Ideas proposed by early cognitive researchers like Dewey, Vygotsky, Piaget, and Bruner provide us with insight into teaching and learning through inquiry. Children are ruled by their perceptions, and so our ability to help them construct meaningful explanations for events in their world is critical. Children, as well as adults, appear to derive meaning from experiences by reflecting and constructing on what they already know. Learning proceeds by fitting new information into an existing schema (assimilation), and modifying or forming a new schema (accommodation). Because an existing schema may either help or hinder new learning, teachers must be aware of such knowledge so they can plan suitable lessons to help students develop explanations consistent with accepted scientific knowledge. Skillful teaching can help children build organized structures of related information in their

Teaching Tip

Inquiry Teaching

In the following Investigations you may want to refer back to this introduction as you learn more about inquiry pedagogy. As you do so, you may also wish to consider how the authors chose to organize this section. Note that it begins with two vignettes describing classroom teaching. Based on these examples, we have developed some understandings regarding inquiry science teaching and the *National Science Education Standards* (NSES). This was a conscious choice to reflect the constructivist philosophy of this book rather than a more traditional didactic pedagogy. We chose not to begin with a definition of constructivist learning or inquiry followed by a listing of the NSES Inquiry Abilities and Teaching Standards, but rather developed those from the teaching examples. You will have additional opportunities to experience this model as you proceed through the text.

memories that improve their ability to retrieve and apply knowledge. It is fitting to close with the following quote:

> Learning science is something that students do, not something that is done to them. In learning science, students describe objects and events, ask questions, achieve knowledge, construct explanations of natural phenomena, test those explanations in many different ways, and communicate their ideas to others. (National Research Council, 1996, p. 20)

References

American Association for the Advancement of Science. (1990). *Science for all Americans*. New York: Oxford University Press.

Atkin, J. M., & Karplus, R. (1962). Discovery or invention. *The Science Teacher, 29*(2), 121–143.

Barman, C., & Kotar, M. (1989). The learning cycle. *Science and Children, 26*, 30–32.

Bell, B. F. (1981). What is a plant: Some children's ideas. *New Zealand Science Teacher, 31*, 10–14.

Biological Sciences Curriculum Study. (1992). *Science for life and living.* Dubuque, IA: Kendall/Hunt.

Bodner, G. (1991). I have found you an argument: The conceptual knowledge of beginning chemistry graduate students. *Journal of Chemical Education, 68*(5), 385.

Bransford, J. D., Brown, A. L., & Cocking, R. (Eds.). (1999). *How people learn: Brain, mind, experience, and school.* Washington, DC: National Academy Press.

Bredderman, T. (1982). *Elementary school science process programs: A meta-analysis of education studies*. (Final report of NSF-RISE: Grant SED 18717)

Bruner, J. S. (1960). *Process of education*. Cambridge, MA: Harvard University Press.

Bybee, R., & Sund, R. (1982). *Piaget for educators*. Columbus, OH: Charles E. Merrill.

Dewey, J. (1910). *How we think.* Lexington, MA: DC Heath.

diSessa, A. (1982). Unlearning Aristotelian physics: A study of knowledge-based learning. *Cognitive Science, 6*(2), 37–75.

Driver, R., Guesne, E., & Tiberghien, A. (1985). *Children's ideas in science*. Philadelphia: Open University Press.

Friedl, A., & Koontz, T. (2005). *Teaching science to children: An inquiry approach,* 6th ed. New York: McGraw-Hill.

Hackett, J., & Moyer, R. (1991). *Science in your world.* New York: Macmillan.

Hapkiewicz, A. (1992). Finding a list of science misconceptions. *Michigan Science Teachers Association Journal*, 11–14.

Harms, N., & Kahl, S. (1980). *Project synthesis: Final report to the National Science Foundation*. Boulder: University of Colorado.

Inhelder, B., & Piaget, J. (1958). *The growth of logical thinking.* New York: Basic Books.

Loucks-Horsley, S., Brooks, J. G., Carlson, M. O., Kuerbis, P., Marsh, D. P., Pakilla, M., et al. (1990). *Developing and supporting teachers for science education in the middle years.* Andover, MA: The National Center for Improving Science Education.

Meltzer, D. (2004). Investigation of students' reasoning regarding work, heat, and the first law of thermodynamics in an introductory calculus-based general physics course. *American Journal of Physics, 72*(11), 1432–1446.

National Research Council. (1996). *National Science Education Standards*. Washington, DC: National Academy Press.

National Research Council. (2000). *Inquiry and the National Science Education Standards*. Washington, DC: National Academy Press.

Pratt, H., & Hackett, J. (1998). Teaching science: The inquiry approach. *Principal, 78*(2), 20–22.

Pyramid Film and Video. (1988). *A private universe*. Santa Monica, CA.

Shymansky, J. A., Kyle, W. C., Jr., & Allport, J. M. (1983). The effects of new science curricula on student performance. *Journal of Research in Science Teaching, 20*(5), 387–404.

Stevenson, R. L. (1906). *A child's garden of verses and underwoods*. New York: Current Literature Publishing Co.

Vygotsky, L. S. (1966). Development of the higher mental functions. In A. Leontiev, A. Luriya, & A. Smirnov (Eds.), *Psychological research in the USSR,* Vol. 1 (pp 11–45). Moscow: Progress.

Vygotsky, L. S. (1978). *Mind in society.* Cambridge, MA: Harvard University Press.

Watson, B., & Konicek, R. (1990). Teaching for conceptual change: Confronting children's experience. *Phi Delta Kappan, 71*, 680–685.

UNIT I

Physical Science

INVESTIGATION 1 Light (K–4)

Teaching Focus: The Learning Cycle

Lesson 1.1 See in the Dark?
Lesson 1.2 Filtering Colors
Lesson 1.3 Rainbow Colors

INVESTIGATION 2 Solubility (5–8)

Teaching Focus: Using Guided and Open Inquiry

Lesson 2.1 How Long Does It Take?
Lesson 2.2 How Much Will Dissolve?
Lesson 2.3 Dissolving Different Substances

INVESTIGATION 3 Density (5–8)

Teaching Focus: Assessing Science

Lesson 3.1 Which Is More Dense?
Lesson 3.2 Do Raisins Sink or Float?
Lesson 3.3 Comparing Densities

INVESTIGATION 4 Energy (5–8)

Teaching Focus: Integrating Mathematics in Science Learning

Lesson 4.1 How Far Can Your Bike Roll Uphill?
Lesson 4.2 How High Will It Bounce?
Lesson 4.3 How Does the Kind of Floor Affect the Bounce?

INVESTIGATION 1

LIGHT

(K–4)

Teaching Focus: The Learning Cycle

Lesson 1.1
See in the Dark?

ENGAGE

How well do you see in the dark? Think about when you wake up at night. Are you able to see? How much light is there in your room at night? How could you do an experiment to find out if you can see in the dark? We will investigate the following question: **Can you see objects inside a dark box?**

EXPLORE

1. Your teacher will give you a box that has a small peephole. Look in the hole and tell what you see.

2. Trade boxes with another group and look in the peephole again. What do you see? Trade again until you have seen all of the boxes.

3. How well could you see in the dark boxes?

EXPLAIN

1. Discuss with your classmates what you thought you saw in each of the boxes.

2. Open the hole on the top of the box. Shine a light into the hole and look through the peephole again. Now what do you see?

3. Compare what you saw in the lighted and the dark boxes.

EXTEND

1. Put a colored sticky note inside one of the boxes as shown in Figure 1.1.1. Don't let your partner see what color you have chosen.

2. Can your partner see the color of the sticky note by looking in the peephole?

3. Have your partner open the top hole and try to identify the color. If it is not possible, have your partner shine the light in the hole.

4. Switch with your partner and see if you can tell the color of the sticky note.

Figure 1.1.1 Place a colored sticky note inside the box

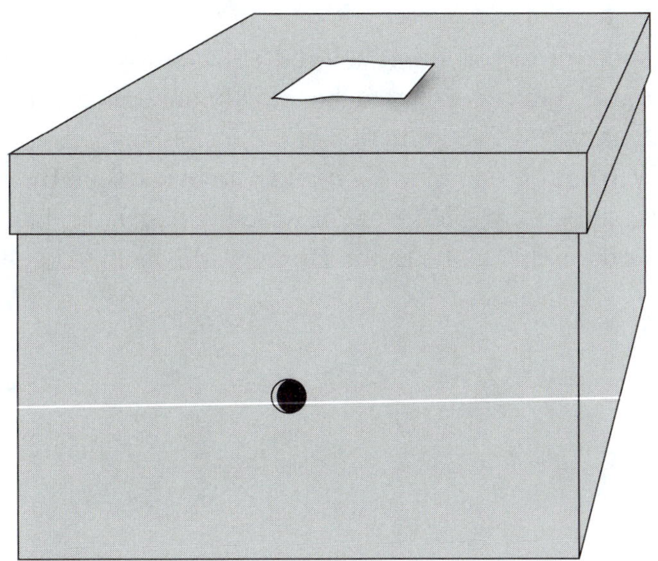

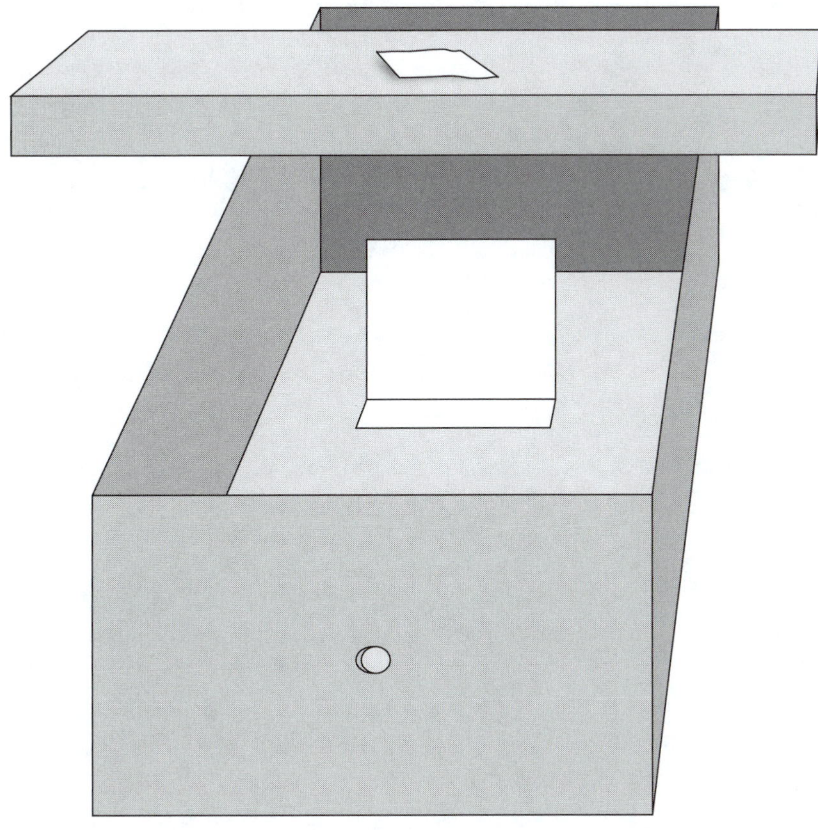

APPLY

Make a list of some of the different colored objects in your room. Predict what will happen to these colors as your teacher slowly darkens the room. Then watch what happens. Compare your prediction and the results.

Have you ever put on one blue sock and one black sock by mistake in your dark bedroom? Compare two pieces of construction paper, one black and the other dark blue. Lower the lights in the room. Do they still seem to be different colors?

Lesson 1.1

See in the Dark?

Teaching Focus: The Learning Cycle

A Learning Cycle comes from the discipline itself; it represents science. If science is to be taught in a manner that leads students to construct knowledge, they must make a quest. The Learning Cycle leads students on that quest for knowledge.

Renner and Marek (1988, p. 170)

NSES CONTENT STANDARD, K–4: LIGHT, HEAT, ELECTRICITY, AND MAGNETISM

"Light travels in a straight line until it strikes an object. Light can be reflected by a mirror, refracted by a lens, or absorbed by the object" (National Research Council, 1996, p. 127).

DESCRIPTIVE OBJECTIVE

Students will investigate to determine how much light is needed to see objects and how much is needed to see color.

MATERIALS

Provide each group of students with a shoebox, flashlight, and colored sticky notes. The shoebox should have a hole-punch-sized hole in one end. A second hole should be made in the top of the box but covered with a flap of heavy, dark paper so it can be opened and closed. You can place various small objects in the boxes. The objects should be taped so they do not move as the boxes are manipulated. Colored construction paper is needed for the Apply section of the lesson.

SCIENCE BACKGROUND

We can see only two types of objects—those that reflect light and those that produce their own light. The vast majority of the objects we perceive reflect ambient light to our eyes.

As you are probably aware, white light is made up of all of the colors of the spectrum, which are usually designated as red, orange, yellow, green, blue, indigo, and violet. When white light falls on a colored (let's say red) object, all of the spectral colors are absorbed except for red, which is reflected. Thus, an observer perceives the object as red.

The retina of the eye contains special cells known as rods and cones (because of their shape). Rods are more sensitive to lower levels of light. Cones, however, are responsible for our ability to perceive color. Thus, our ability to see colors is reduced in lower levels of illumination.

MISCONCEPTION INFORMATION

Although much research has been conducted on the topic of optics, there is limited information on the misconceptions students have about colors of light. Some examples of misconceptions include:

- White light is pure and colorless.
- A color filter adds color to white light.
- Mixing colored light has the same results as mixing paint.

For additional information, you may wish to refer to:

Stepans, J. (1996). *Targeting students' science misconceptions.* Riverview, FL: Idea Factory, Inc.

Teaching Focus

Begin with Students' Ideas

In the Engage phase of a learning cycle lesson, you should use the students' initial ideas to develop an explorable question or questions. In this lesson, we want to lead the students to wonder about how they might test to determine whether or not they can see anything in the dark. It is important that the students be aware of what the question is before they start the activity. Otherwise, they are merely following some sort of recipe and are not doing science. Science is a process by which we pose and try to answer questions about the natural world.

CLASSROOM SAFETY

There are no special safety concerns. You may, however, have a color-blind student in your class. Approximately 8% of males and 1% of females are color-blind.

ENGAGE

Initiate a discussion about seeing in a darkened room. Students will likely report that they are able to see in their bedrooms if they wake up during the night. At this point they are probably unaware that their rooms are not totally dark.

Discuss the students' ideas about how to test whether they can see in the dark. Show them the box and determine whether they know how to use it to answer the investigation question: **Can you see objects inside a dark box?**

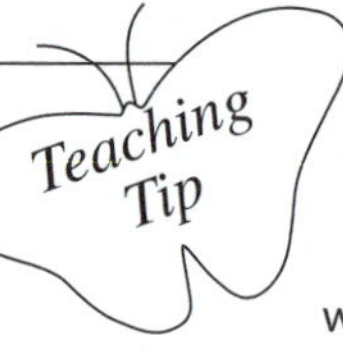

Making Centers

With younger students, you may wish to put the boxes in separate centers. This way, the children move from one box to another rather than passing the boxes among their groups.

EXPLORE

1. Prepare several boxes ahead of time with a familiar object in each. Check the boxes to make sure the object is not visible through the peephole. Students should not be able to determine (due to lack of light) what object is in each box at this point.
2. Students should trade boxes with other groups. This enables them to look at several boxes and reinforce their observation that they are unable to see without sufficient light.
3. It is not possible to see in total darkness. Although the inside of the box is not totally dark (some light will enter through the peephole), there is insufficient light to see the objects.

Teaching Focus

Explorations Must Answer a Question

Most activities that you will find on the Web or in activity books are demonstration or verification activities. That is, they do not really answer any question for the student, but rather simply verify that something is so. The Learning Cycle is an inquiry teaching method. Therefore, student activities must answer some question. In this lesson, the activity clearly answers the question: Can you see objects inside a dark box?

EXPLAIN

1. Younger students may offer a variety of guesses. Encourage them to report on their actual observations. Students should conclude that they only observed darkness inside the box and were not able to perceive any actual objects.
2. When more light enters the box through the additional opening, students should easily be able to identify the objects.
3. Depending on the ambient light in the room, students may be able to identify the objects when the hole is uncovered. If the room is rather dim, they may need more light from the flashlight in order to see in the box. Help students infer from their observations that the reason they can see objects is because the objects reflect light to our eyes. When the box was dark the object did not reflect enough light to make it visible.

> **TEACHING FOCUS**
>
> **Constructing Understanding**
>
> In the Learning Cycle, the Explain phase uses the results of the students' investigations to help them develop conceptual understanding. Furthermore, this understanding can "serve as a framework from which further discoveries can be made—not a conclusion or wrapping up of the Exploration Phase's observations" (Beisenherz & Dantonio, 1996, p. 5).

EXTEND

1. Here we ask students to continue their investigation by trying to identify color in reduced light. Use a variety of different colored objects. We suggest that you use colored sticky notes. These can be easily attached to the bottom of the boxes.
2. This activity should reinforce what the students discovered in the exploration. Students will not be able even to see the paper, let alone determine its color.
3. Students will discover that they need more light to perceive the color than they do to merely see the object. They may be able to perceive the color from the ambient light entering through the hole. If this is the case, have the students partially cover the hole until they can see the object but cannot identify the color. Likewise, students may need the additional light of the flashlight to determine the color of the object.
4. Have students trade one or more times until they seem to understand the concept—more light is required to perceive color than to identify an object in black and white.

APPLY

Have students identify a number of colored objects in the classroom. Explain that you are going to gradually darken the room (by pulling shades, turning off lights, etc.). Ask them to predict whether they will still be able to see the colors. They should be able to observe that as the lighting is reduced, so is their ability to perceive color (even though they can still see the objects). This is particularly noticeable if you compare a dark blue and a black piece of construction paper. (One of the authors has been spotted wearing one black and one navy blue sock on several occasions.)

> **TEACHING FOCUS**
>
> **Rejecting Misconceptions**
>
> In the Learning Cycle, students often make a conceptual change in their thinking by rejecting a misconception for a scientifically accurate idea. In this lesson, the likely misconception is "I can see in the dark." In the Explore phase the students were confronted with evidence contrary to this misconception. In the Explain phase, the teacher helps the students make sense of the new understanding so that it becomes a part of their mental structure. The Extend and Apply phases of the Learning Cycle enable students to build new mental connections as well as to reorganize prior knowledge to "fit" with their new understandings.

Note that the purpose here is not to totally darken the room but to reduce the light until it is impossible to perceive color. As we noted above, however, students may not realize that it is very difficult to totally darken a room. To that end, you might *try* to totally darken your classroom. Students will then be able to conclude that some light must be present because they are still able to see some objects and shadows (but most likely not color). Encourage students to go home and observe how well they can see in their bedrooms at night. They will probably report that they can see objects and shadows.

Lesson 1.2
Filtering Colors

ENGAGE

Have you ever seen a rainbow? What colors did you see? Where else have you seen something like a rainbow?

You can make rainbow colors with a prism and a white light. Watch as your teacher makes rainbow colors with a prism and the sun. What colors do you see? What color is sunlight? What does the prism do to the sunlight?

Your teacher will hold a flashlight. What color of light do you see? What color would you see if you looked at the flashlight through a blue filter? A red filter? Green?

Let's think about looking at objects. Your teacher has a glass of milk. What color is the milk? What color will it seem to be if you look at it through colored filters?

What if you look at something that is not white like milk? What about colored objects? We will investigate the following question: **What will you see if you look at colored objects through colored filters?**

EXPLORE

1. Look at the different colored paper squares you have. What color will they seem to be if you look at them through the blue filter? Test your predictions by laying the filter right on top of the paper. Record your results in the table below.

2. What do you think will happen if you look through the green filter? The red? Test your predictions and fill in the chart below.

Paper Color	Blue Filter	Green Filter	Red Filter
White			
Blue			
Green			
Red			
Yellow			
Black			

EXPLAIN

1. Compare your predictions with your observations.

2. When you used the blue filter, what colors of paper looked blue? What did the other colors of paper look like?

3. When you used the green filter, what colors of paper looked green? What did the other colors of paper look like?

4. When you used the red filter, what colors of paper looked red? What did the other colors of paper look like?

5. White light was shining on each piece of paper. What color of light reflected off each colored piece of paper? What color passed through the blue filter? Through the red filter? The green?

6. What pattern do you see from your results?

EXTEND

1. Predict the color you will see when you look at each piece of paper through a yellow filter.

2. Test your predictions. Record your findings in the table below.

Paper Color	Yellow Filter
White	
Blue	
Green	
Red	
Yellow	
Black	

3. When you used the yellow filter, which colors of paper looked yellow? What did the other colors of paper look like?

4. White light was shining on each piece of paper. What color of light reflected off each colored piece of paper? What color passed through the yellow filter?

APPLY

All of the colors can be made from the three primary colors of light: red, green, and blue. Look at a colored page from a newspaper with a hand lens. What do you observe? In addition, look at a computer monitor or a television picture. What do you observe? What do you think you would see if you looked through both a hand lens and a colored filter?

Lesson 1.2

Filtering Colors

Teaching Focus: The Learning Cycle

NSES CONTENT STANDARD, K–4: LIGHT, HEAT, ELECTRICITY, AND MAGNETISM

"Light travels in a straight line until it strikes an object. Light can be reflected by a mirror, refracted by a lens, or absorbed by the object" (National Research Council, 1996, p. 127).

DESCRIPTIVE OBJECTIVE

Students will investigate to determine the following: White light is made up of colors, and a filter of a primary color of light filters out everything except that primary color. Complementary colored filters block one color—yellow filters block blue, cyan filters block red, and magenta filters block green.

MATERIALS

Provide each group of students with small pieces of colored paper (white, black, red, green, blue, and yellow) and four transparent filters (red, green, blue, and yellow). You may want to use cyan and magenta filters as well if you have them. You may be able to use colored report covers. Inexpensive optical quality filters are available in science supply catalogs. Also, in the Engage phase, the teacher will need a prism, a flashlight, and a clear glass of milk. A hand lens and a colored newspaper are needed for the Apply phase.

SCIENCE BACKGROUND

You may wish to use the more familiar term *rainbow* when referring to the spectrum. Technically, the spectrum formed by a prism is not a rainbow. Rainbows are formed by the reflection and refraction (bending) of light by tiny water drops in the atmosphere. Prisms simply refract light.

White light is a combination of all the spectral colors—each having a different wavelength and frequency. Each frequency is refracted a different amount by the prism, which separates the colors into the spectrum. As originally defined by Isaac Newton, there are seven spectral colors: red, orange, yellow, green, blue, indigo, and violet.

Note at the outset that mixing colors of light is not the same as mixing pigments. The primary colors of light are red, green, and blue. Mixing these three primary colors in different ratios produces all the other colors. White light results when all three are mixed together in equal proportions. Red and green light produce yellow, which is known as a secondary color. Magenta and cyan are the other secondary colors. Magenta is made by combining blue and red light, and cyan by combining green and blue light. If the three secondary colors are mixed together they, too, result in white. Televisions and computer monitors use red, green, and blue light to produce their images (a so-called RGB system). Cyan, magenta, and yellow are often used in color printing processes.

Because we can produce white light by combining red, green, and blue, we can also produce white light if we combine red with cyan because cyan is made up of green and blue. For this reason, red and cyan are called *complementary* colors. Complementary colors are any two colors that

Figure 1.2.1 Mixing colored light

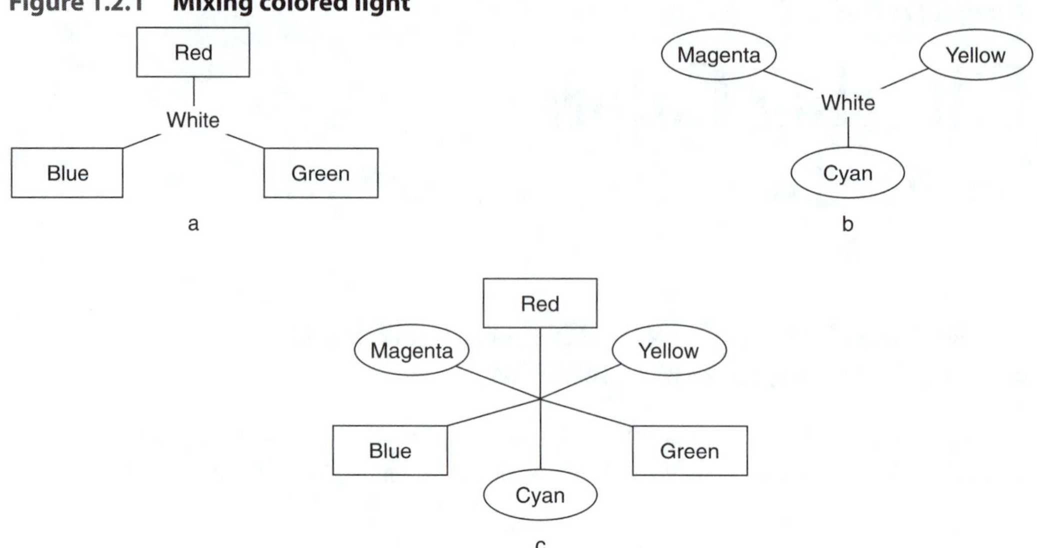

produce white light when they are combined. Consequently, blue and yellow are also complementary colors—they produce white light when they are combined (yellow is the secondary color formed by combining red and green). Notice that complementary colors always consist of a primary and a secondary color. Figure 1.2.1 shows these relationships and how colored lights can be added.

If you look at a white light source through a red filter, you will, of course, see red light. This is because only red light passes through a red filter. The other colors are absorbed. If you look at a red light source through a red filter, it will still look red. But if you look at another primary color through a red filter, it will appear to be black. For example, a blue light shining through a red filter appears black because the filter absorbs the blue light (and no red light emanates from the blue light source).

From the above we see that each of the primary filters removes two colors—red removes blue and green, blue removes red and green, and green removes red and blue. Secondary filters work the same way, except they remove only one color—cyan removes red, yellow removes blue, and magenta removes green. So, if you look at a spectrum through a cyan filter you will see cyan and its two components, blue and green. Through a magenta filter you will see magenta and its components, red and blue. Finally, as we suggest in this lesson, if you look at a spectrum through a yellow filter, you will see yellow and its components, red and green.

TEACHING FOCUS

Using a Demonstration in the Engage Phase

In the Engage phase above, we suggested that the teacher perform a demonstration with a prism. Here, the demonstration helps students recall their prior experiences and understandings about rainbows or other examples of visible spectra (soap bubbles, CDs, cut glass, etc.). Demonstrations can also arouse students' curiosity, motivate them to participate, develop the question to be explored, and cause cognitive dissonance (discrepant events).

CLASSROOM SAFETY

There are no special safety concerns other than cautioning students not to look directly at the sun. You may, however, have a color-blind student in your class.

ENGAGE

Initiate a discussion about seeing rainbows. Because not all students may have the same experiences with rainbows and the spectral colors, the prism demonstration may be important. Remind students that white light is composed of the seven colors of the spectrum—red, orange, yellow, green, blue, indigo, and violet. Students should keep this in mind as they complete the next two investigations.

EXPLORE

1. Encourage students to make predictions. You may wish to have them make another data table of their predictions.
2. The students' predictions should improve for the green and red filters. Make sure the students place the filter directly on top of the sheets of paper. Due to variations in the intensity of the filters, some objects that should appear black may not appear black if the filter is held away from the paper. (See Table 1.2.1 below.)

What Do We Mean by Demonstration?

Teaching Tip

The word *demonstrate* has two distinct meanings to science educators. In one sense it means that the teacher (and not the students) performs some activity as the students observe. This is often an effective strategy when safety, cost, or time is a factor (all three of these reasons prompted us to suggest a demonstration above).

The second meaning of *demonstrate* is "to confirm" or "to verify." Inquiry activities attempt to answer a question for the student. Demonstration activities verify that something is so for the students. Making a spectrum is an example of a demonstration. Exploring what parts of the spectrum you can see with different filters is an inquiry activity and not a demonstration.

EXPLAIN

1. The students' predictions probably will not be correct, especially when black is the resulting color. Students may be influenced by their prior knowledge of mixing paints and pigments.
2. As noted in the chart below, both the white and the blue papers will look blue when viewed through a blue filter. Because blue filters allow only blue light to pass, all of the other papers will appear black.
3. Similarly, with a green filter the white and green papers will appear green and all other colors will appear black.
4. The red and white papers will appear red and all the others will appear black.
5. Because the blue filter allows only blue light to pass through, the paper is illuminated only by blue light. Green paper, however, absorbs all colors of the spectrum *except* for green. There is no green light to be reflected, however, so the paper appears to be black. Note that if students simply look through blue filters they will probably not see all yellow, green, and red objects as black. This is due to the low intensity of the filters you are using. If this situation confuses the students, have them fold the filters in halves (or fourths) to increase their intensity. The explanation here is slightly different from the one above. Here white light strikes a sheet of green paper. The paper absorbs

Table 1.2.1 Correct Responses for Table

Paper Color	Blue Filter	Green Filter	Red Filter
White	Blue	Green	Red
Blue	Blue	Black	Black
Green	Black	Green	Black
Red	Black	Black	Red
Yellow	Black	Black	Black
Black	Black	Black	Black

all of the colors except for green, which is reflected. The blue filter, however, allows only blue (not green) light to pass on to the eye. Therefore, the paper appears black.

6. Students should notice that the primary filters remove all colors except for the filter color. They could also conclude that black is the absence of color. The black paper absorbs all of the spectral colors and reflects virtually none.

EXTEND

1. Student predictions will probably follow the above pattern.
2. Students will probably be surprised when they discover that the yellow filter does not follow the above pattern. See Table 1.2.2 for sample data.
3. Students will discover that the white and the yellow papers appear yellow. The students may expect all other colors to appear black, as was the case with the primary filters. The green and red papers, however, will appear to be green and red when viewed through the yellow filter, while only the blue and black papers will appear to be black.
4. The results in this case are different because secondary color filters remove only one color—their complementary color. Thus, the yellow filter removes only blue (its complement) light, allowing red, yellow, and green light to pass through it. The white, yellow, black, and blue papers all appear as you would expect. The green paper, however, will not be black but green when viewed through the yellow filter. This is because the green paper reflects green light, and the yellow filter allows green and red light to pass through (because yellow light is made up of green and red light). Similarly, the red paper will not appear black because it reflects red light, and the yellow filter allows green and red light to pass through.

TEACHING FOCUS

Purpose of the Extend Phase

Students used the knowledge gained from the Explore and Explain phases by conducting deeper investigations. Here, we ask students to continue the investigation of filters they began in the Explore phase, where they used primary color filters (red, green, and blue). The mechanism of secondary color filtering is more complex and thus more difficult to understand. For that reason we chose to do the primary filters first and then extend the lesson to secondary filters.

Table 1.2.2

Paper Color	Yellow Filter
White	Yellow
Blue	Black
Green	Green
Red	Red
Yellow	Yellow
Black	Black

APPLY

When students observe a colored page from a newspaper with a hand lens, they will notice that colored objects are not solid but are composed of many small dots of different colors. This is also the case when viewing a television picture or computer monitor. The dots will likely be made up

TEACHING FOCUS

Value of Real-World Applications

Just as it is helpful to begin a learning cycle lesson with some real-world context (to activate students' prior knowledge), it is also beneficial to relate a newly learned concept with students' existing understandings. One way to accomplish this is to involve students with applications of the new concept. This is the major function of the Apply phase of the Learning Cycle. One can think of the Learning Cycle as a spiraling one. The initial real-world context of the Engage is rather simple. Then, after students learn more about the concept through explorations and explanation, they can apply their learning at a more abstract and richer level.

In this lesson, the opening real-world context in the Engage phase was a discussion of students' experiences with rainbows and other spectral phenomena. After explorations and explanations related to the concept of color mixing and filtering, we ask the student to apply this new knowledge to the processes of color printing, televisions, and monitors.

of either the primary colors (red, green, and blue) or the secondary colors (cyan, magenta, and yellow). They will also observe black dots. All colors can be produced by mixing various amounts of these colors.

You may wish to have students explore mixing colors of light. It is very difficult to do this with flashlights. Floodlights and theatrical gel filters, however, work quite well. You can wrap the filters around the floodlight after it has been screwed into a socket and attach them around the socket with a rubber band. Students can shine the lights onto a white ceiling or wall to experiment mixing the different colors.

Students can also use a computer to investigate color mixing. Many word processing programs have color options on a palette that can be altered. Many Web sites also allow you to perform this investigation. For example, students can experiment mixing the primary colors of light at the following NASA Web site: http://imagers.gsfc.nasa.gov/color/

Students should get the same results looking at the dots with a lens and a filter as they did in the Explore activity above.

Lesson 1.3
Rainbow Colors

ENGAGE

What examples of rainbow colors have you noticed since the last explorations?

You can make a prism out of a cup of water. Put about an inch of water into the cup. Carefully place the cup on a table so that it hangs a little bit over the edge. See Figure 1.3.1.

Shine the flashlight up through the bottom of the cup of water. What colors do you see on the wall behind the cup?

What do you think will happen to the colors on the wall if you dye the water in the cup? We will investigate the following: **What effect does dyeing the water in the cup have on the rainbow?**

Figure 1.3.1 Making a rainbow

EXPLORE

1. Record the colors you see when the light shines through the colorless water.

Color of Water	Predictions	Rainbow Colors You See
Colorless		
Blue		
Green		
Red		

2. Predict what the rainbow will look like if you dye the water blue. Get some blue-colored water from your teacher and test your prediction.

3. Now predict what you will see if you use green- and red-colored water. Then test your prediction.

EXPLAIN

1. Compare your predictions with your results.

2. What happened to the rainbow colors when you used a cup of blue water? Green? Red?

3. Think about the filter investigation. Did the filters do the same thing as the colored water? Explain.

EXTEND

1. Predict what the rainbow will look like if you dye the water yellow.

2. Get some yellow-colored water from your teacher and test your prediction.

3. How is the yellow filter like the yellow-colored water? Explain.

APPLY

The lenses in sunglasses come in several different tints. Design a test to find out how the color of a lens affects the colors you can see through it.

Lesson 1.3

Rainbow Colors

Teaching Focus: The Learning Cycle

NSES CONTENT STANDARD, K–4: LIGHT, HEAT, ELECTRICITY, AND MAGNETISM

"Light travels in a straight line until it strikes an object. Light can be reflected by a mirror, refracted by a lens, or absorbed by the object" (National Research Council, 1996, p. 127).

DESCRIPTIVE OBJECTIVE

Students will investigate to determine that water can refract light into its spectral colors and that colored water can act like a colored filter.

MATERIALS

Provide each group of students with clear, colorless plastic cups (9 oz party cups work well), flashlights, water, and colored water. Assorted sunglasses (or lenses) are required for the Apply phase of the lesson. If you have six groups consisting of four students each, you will need about one or two quarts of each of the colored water solutions (red, green, blue, and yellow). You may also need newspaper to cover the work area and a smock for students because food dyes can stain.

SCIENCE BACKGROUND

A cup of water can act like a prism because light slows as it passes through the water and thus can be refracted (if it passes through at an angle). Different colors of light are slowed to different speeds and thus are refracted by different amounts. You will need to experiment with the angle of the flashlight to project a spectrum on a wall or a screen behind the cup.

The colored water will act just like the colored filters from the previous lesson. You can refer to the Science Background in Lesson 1.2 for an extensive discussion on colored filters.

CLASSROOM SAFETY

No special safety concerns exist other than cautioning students to be careful if water spills on the floor. Advise students not to drink the water.

ENGAGE

Review the discussion of where students have seen the spectral colors. Perhaps they have noticed some additional occurrences since the last lesson. Demonstrate how to create a spectrum using a cup of water and a flashlight. The cup must stick out a bit over the edge of the table to form a spectrum. Caution students to take care not to spill water from the cup.

After you have discussed the spectrum on the wall, ask students what they think would happen to the colors if we dyed the water in the cups with the primary colors red, green, and blue.

EXPLORE

1. Students will construct a water prism.
2. The students should see only blue on the wall when the water is dyed blue. All of the other colors have been filtered out. See the sample data below.

Teaching Focus

Obtaining Evidence

In the Learning Cycle—in all inquiry learning—students must base all conclusions on evidence. This is also how scientists come to conclusions. Indeed, this is what sets science apart from other ways of thinking. Rather than simply accept information from an authority figure like the teacher, students can draw conclusions and make sense of the world based on the evidence they obtain. To this end, students have gathered evidence in the Learning Cycle before the teacher conducts the explanation and, we hope, used it to draw some conclusions of their own.

Teaching Focus

The Importance of Exploration

Student exploration is the core of the Learning Cycle. Professor Anton Lawson at Arizona State University is a leading researcher in learning cycle theory. He states that "the most appropriate way, perhaps the only way . . . to teach [is] in a way that allows students to reveal prior conceptions and test them in an atmosphere in which ideas are openly generated, debated and tested, with the means of testing becoming an explicit focus of classroom attention" (Lawson, 2002, pp. 59–60).

3. Students will see green only when the water is dyed green and see red only when the water is dyed red. (See Table 1.3.1.)

Table 1.3.1

Color of Water	Predictions	Rainbow Colors You See
Colorless		All the colors of the spectrum
Blue		Only blue
Green		Only green
Red		Only red

EXPLAIN

1. If students thought of the colored water as filters, their predictions should be accurate. Many students, however, will not realize that colored water acts like a filter.

TEACHING FOCUS

When Do You Read?

If you are using a textbook, the students should read it only after they have completed the exploration. This way, the concrete experience of the exploration sets up the reading for the student. The students then have a reason to read and are able to make sense of the reading.

Most of us probably learned science with a pedagogy where we read first and then, perhaps, conducted a laboratory activity (which probably was a verification of what we had read). Thus, we may teach in that same manner. Consider, however, how we actually learn new material ourselves. As an example, one of the authors recently purchased a new cell phone and, upon talking to other cell phone purchasers, realized that most of them had learning experiences similar to his. Most cell phones (or almost any electronic gadget) have lengthy user's manuals. Consequently, almost no one reads the entire manual before attempting to use the phone. Indeed, most experiment a bit to see what different buttons do and then read the manual when they need some specific information. This example of how we learn shows that it is more "natural" to read following the concrete experiences. Indeed, as Lawson indicates, the Learning Cycle is "a method of instruction consistent with the way people spontaneously construct knowledge" (Lawson, 2002, p. 60).

2. The dyed water acts like a filter. In the first step of the Explore phase, students separated white light into the spectral colors with a cup of water. When the water is dyed it acts like a filter. For example, when white light enters blue water, all of the colors except for blue are filtered out. Thus, only blue is seen on the wall. Similarly, students will see only green when the water is dyed green, and only red when it is dyed red.
3. Yes. As noted above, the colored water acts like colored filters.

EXTEND

1. Again, if students relate this question to what they learned in the previous investigation they may predict correctly.
2. Students may be surprised to observe that in this case they see the red, yellow, and green portions of the spectrum.
3. The yellow water acts as if it were a yellow filter. Recall that yellow is a secondary color and that yellow filters allow red, yellow, and green light to pass through and filter out the other colors. So, only those three colors are refracted by the water and travel on to the wall.

TEACHING FOCUS

Misuse of the Extend Phase

Do not introduce new concepts during the Extend phase of a learning cycle lesson. Many teachers who are new to the Learning Cycle try to deal with a concept quite apart from the main idea in the Extend phase. For example, they may try to have the Extend phase of this lesson deal with the reflection of light. While reflection is often taught in a unit on light, it is really a quite distinct construct. Reflection should have several lessons devoted to it alone.

Remember, the purpose of the Extend phase is to help students construct meaningful understandings of the main concept. It enables the students to interact with the concept after the explanation—thus at a deeper and perhaps more abstract level.

APPLY

You will probably need to use a prism and sunlight to obtain a bright spectrum. Caution students not to look at the sun. They should find that sunglass lenses operate much like the filters they have been using. That is, blue lenses will remove the red portion of the spectrum while yellow lenses will remove the blue portion. Some sunglasses are marketed as so-called blue blockers. Some people feel that this is an advantage because blue light scatters so much (which is why the sky is blue as well). Aviator glasses are usually yellow or amber for a similar reason. Gray sunglasses, on the other hand, simply reduce glare and light intensity with little color change.

Teaching Focus Summary: The Learning Cycle

- Use students' ideas in the Engage phase to develop and plan ways to answer the explorable question.
- The Explain phase enables students to use the results of their investigations to develop an understanding of the concept.
- Students may reject a misconception and accept a scientifically accurate one with learning cycle lessons.
- Demonstrations in the Engage phase serve to arouse students' curiosity, to create cognitive dissonance, or to develop an explorable question.
- During the Extend and Apply phases, students should relate the new information they have learned to real-world contexts.

References

Beisenherz, P., & Dantonio, M. (1996). *Using the learning cycle to teach physical science.* Portsmouth, NH: Heinemann.

Lawson, A. E. (2002). The learning cycle. In R. G. Fuller (Ed.), *A love of discovery: Science education—the second career of Robert Karplus* (pp. 51–62). New York: Kluwer Academic/Plenum.

National Research Council. (1996). *National Science Education Standards.* Washington, DC: National Academy Press.

Renner, J. W., & Marek, E. A. (1988). *The learning cycle and elementary school science teaching.* Portsmouth, NH: Heinemann.

INVESTIGATION 2

SOLUBILITY

(5–8)

Teaching Focus: Using Guided and Open Inquiry

Lesson 2.1
How Long Does It Take?

ENGAGE

You want to make some lemonade for your friends. Some like it sweet, so you need to add more sugar. You want to find the quickest way to add sugar to the lemonade. To find out what will happen, you put a sugar cube in a glass of water. What happens? How long does it take? Make your prediction and try it. Record your observations and results.

Here are some questions for you: What could you do to make the sugar cube dissolve faster? Why do you think it will increase the dissolving rate? List your ideas and explanations:

____

____

Now that you have several ideas, let's begin the investigation by testing the idea of stirring: **How does stirring affect how fast sugar dissolves?** Later in the lesson you will try one of the ideas you have listed above.

EXPLORE

1. Design a science investigation to answer the question, "How does stirring affect how fast sugar dissolves?" Be sure your plan results in a fair test. Think about these questions as you make your plan:
   - What materials will you need? Why will you need each item?
   - What observations and measurements will you need as evidence?
   - How might you organize your observations and measurements?

2. After your teacher approves your plan, carry out your investigation. Gather and record your evidence.

EXPLAIN

1. Write a statement to answer your explorable question.

2. Use observations and measurements to try to explain your results. Discuss with your classmates and your teacher why you think this happens.

EXTEND

1. Choose one factor from the list you made earlier and investigate its effect on how fast sugar dissolves. What is the question you will investigate?

2. Design a plan. After your teacher approves your plan, gather, record, and organize your observations and measurements.

3. Use your evidence to answer your question and explain your results.

4. Find out the results obtained by other student groups and record them in the chart below.

Factor Tested	Results

5. Write a statement summarizing your new knowledge about the factors that affect how sugar dissolves.

6. How does this statement compare with your ideas and explanations from the Engage phase?

APPLY

Suppose that you and a friend have discovered a special yummy-flavored tablet. The tablet, when dissolved in water, makes a delicious and healthy soft drink. Other students would like to buy your new soft drink. The faster you can make the drink, the more money you can make. What will you do? Write out your plan for making your new soft drink.

Lesson 2.1

How Long Does It Take?

Teaching Focus: Using Guided and Open Inquiry

Inquiry into authentic questions generated from student experiences is the central strategy for teaching science.

National Science Education Standards

NSES CONTENT STANDARD, 5–8: PROPERTIES AND CHANGES OF PROPERTIES IN MATTER

"A substance has characteristic properties, such as density, a boiling point, and solubility, all of which are independent of the amount of the sample" (National Research Council, 1996, p. 154).

DESCRIPTIVE OBJECTIVE

Students will design and carry out investigations to determine that different factors such as temperature and surface area affect the rate at which sugar dissolves.

MATERIALS

For each group of students provide sugar cubes, plastic cups, plastic spoons or stir sticks, water of different temperatures (a cold refrigerated pitcher of water [about 5°C]; a warm pitcher of water at room temperature [about 20°C]; hot tap water, but NOT hot enough to burn one's hands [about 45°C]), measuring cups or graduated cylinders, and a stopwatch or clock for keeping time. Students may request additional items when testing their ideas.

SCIENCE BACKGROUND

The substance in greater concentration is known as the solvent and the one that is being dissolved is the solute. Dissolving occurs because of electrostatic attractions between atoms, ions, or molecules—in this case, between water (solvent) and sugar (solute) molecules. The attraction between sugar and water molecules is rather strong, which is why you can dissolve so much sugar in water. The water molecules essentially pull the crystal lattice of the sugar apart, which brings more sugar molecules into contact with water molecules. Increasing the contact between the water and sugar serves to increase the rate at which the dissolving takes place. Thus, stirring increases the rate of dissolving as does crushing the sugar into smaller pieces.

Figure 2.1.1 Solubility for salt and sugar in water

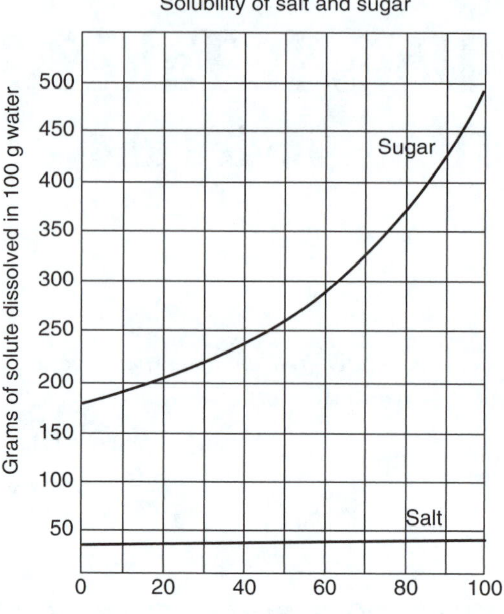

Increasing the temperature adds to the kinetic energy of the molecules and thus increases their motion. The faster the water molecules move, the more often they come in contact with the sugar molecules. This results in more sugar being dissolved. In general, a greater amount of solute will dissolve at higher temperatures. Not all solutes dissolve as readily at higher temperatures as sugar, however. For example, while more salt (NaCl) will dissolve at higher temperatures, the difference is less noticeable. In other words, the solubility curve, as shown in Figure 2.1.1, is flatter for salt than it is for sugar.

MISCONCEPTION INFORMATION

Solubility can be a difficult topic for students because they cannot observe what is happening at the microscopic level. Therefore, you may find many misconceptions including:

- Sugar melts when mixed with water.
- In general, melting is the same as dissolving.
- Sugar transforms into water when it dissolves.

For additional information, you may wish to refer to:

Stavy, R. (1991). Using analogy to overcome misconceptions about conservation of matter. *Journal of Research in Science Teaching, 28*(4), 305–313.

Taylor, N., & Coll, R. (1997). The use of analogy in the teaching of solubility to pre-service primary teachers. *Australian Science Teachers Journal, 43*(4), 58–64.

CLASSROOM SAFETY

Students should be cautioned not to ingest any of the materials. Check the temperature of the hot tap water yourself before allowing students to use it.

TEACHING FOCUS

Defining Inquiry

"Scientific inquiry refers to the diverse ways in which scientists study the natural world and propose explanations based on the evidence derived from their work" (National Research Council, 1996, p. 23). In short, inquiry is asking and answering a question about the natural world. It is not the scientific method or any other step-by-step process that scientists or students follow.

Guided inquiry usually refers to a method of investigation that begins with a specified question and some suggestions or guidelines for answering the question. Open inquiry, or full inquiry as noted in the NSES (National Research Council, 1996, p. 122), usually refers to students developing a question and a process for finding the answer as well as carrying out the investigation by collecting evidence, formulating the answer, and sharing the results with others.

It is interesting to discuss individual definitions of inquiry with fellow educators. In 2002 the National Science Teachers Association and Charles Barman asked teachers to do exactly that. They found that teachers held a wide range of different views as to the meaning of inquiry. "Common responses included involving students in activities or investigations, engaging students in problem solving, and having students ask questions about the world in which they live" (Barman, 2002, p. 8).

ENGAGE

Display the materials. Ask the following question: **How does stirring affect how fast sugar dissolves?** Collect and display the students' predictions. Conduct the activity as a demonstration if desired.

Help the students as a class list factors that might affect how fast sugar dissolves. Ask students to tell why they think each factor will change the rate at which the sugar cube dissolves. Record explanations for each factor. Some ideas that students might generate are stirring, different temperatures, crushing the cube, different amounts of water, or different liquids. Save the explanations until the end of the lesson and have the students compare them to the results of their investigations.

TEACHING FOCUS

Inquiry Begins with Ideas for Investigations

To learn how to conduct scientific inquiry, students must move away from confirmation lab activities that demonstrate the information they already know. Have students generate their own ideas before performing a lab activity so that they will be more likely to investigate a question to which they don't know the answer. Also, having students generate ideas will enable you to access and assess their prior knowledge on the topic.

Be sure to focus the students' thinking on the question as they begin this section of the lesson. Remind students that the purpose of the investigation is to find evidence that they can use to answer this question.

TEACHING FOCUS

Starting a Lesson with Guided Inquiry

Martin notes that in guided inquiry, "teachers facilitate children in their investigations of teacher established topics in ways that are comfortable to the children and that also stimulate children to ask and investigate additional questions suggested by the original explorations" (Martin, 2003, p. 207). Because teachers tend to teach in the way that they were taught, and most were not taught with inquiry, they are often uncomfortable teaching science in this way. One way to help ease this transition for both teachers and students is to start a lesson with guided inquiry. Guided inquiry makes teachers and students more adept at generating appropriate inquiry questions and investigations.

TEACHER: Grades 5–8

EXPLORE

1. Ask the students to identify materials they will need for their investigation. Talk about units of measurement that they will use. For the Explore phase, students will probably use the units of seconds to measure time. The sugar is measured in units of cubes. Emphasize accuracy and organization of data. Help the students design a table which to record their measurements. Table 2.1.1 shows a typical data table.

Table 2.1.1 Effect of Stirring on Solubility Time

	Trial 1 Time	Trial 2 Time	Trial 3 Time	Average Time
Stirring				
No stirring				

2. Circulate among the student groups. Ask them questions about their investigation: What question are you investigating? What parts of this investigation are the same as the one in the Engage activity? What is different? Why? Compare the results and explanations of the groups. Ask the students to justify their conclusions using evidence.

Teaching Tip

Organizing Data

Often lab activities have sample charts that students will fill in as they collect their data. Although these can help structure an activity, they also limit students' thinking. Create opportunities for students to think through the processes of deciding what observations and data to collect, how to organize the data, and also how to best represent it. Until students become proficient these processes will take considerable time. The benefits for students' higher order thinking abilities are significant, however.

EXPLAIN

1. Students should write a concluding statement to answer their explorable question, using the evidence they have collected.
2. The stirred sugar solution will dissolve faster than the unstirred solution. Discuss these results and explanations with the class. Stirring continually replaces saturated water near each particle of sugar with unsaturated water, thus increasing the rate of dissolving. An interesting question to ask at this time would be whether the rate of dissolving would change if you varied the speed of the stirring. You may want to have students investigate this idea.

TEACHING FOCUS

Focusing Students on the Explorable Question

One of the authors recalls asking a fourth grader engaged in a science investigation to "tell me a little about what you're doing" and getting the response, "step three." No amount of probing gave the student any idea what question she was trying to answer. For this reason it is important to be sure students are focused on the purpose of the investigation before they begin. They should know that they are trying to answer some question(s).

EXTEND

1. Have the student groups choose another from their original list of factor that might affect how fast a sugar cube dissolves. The rate at which sugar dissolves in water is determined by such factors as the amount of water, water temperature, stirring the water, and surface area of the sugar (cube vs. crushed). You can eliminate the need for thermometers by preparing pitchers of hot, warm, and cold water ahead of time. Test the hot tap water yourself to make sure it is not too hot.
2. Question students about their plan. Ask them about the evidence they are seeking. How will they observe, measure, record, and organize their data? Check to see that they are manipulating only one variable at a time.
3. Each group can report their findings and conclusions to the class. Encourage the use of evidence to support conclusions.
4. Students should find out the results of other groups and record this information. Sample results are given in Table 2.1.2.
5. Have students write a statement that summarizes all of their knowledge about the different factors that affect how sugar dissolves. This will help them organize all of their information on the solubility of sugar.
6. Have students compare their new knowledge with their prior knowledge from the beginning of the lesson to see which ideas they have modified and which they have kept the same.

TEACHING FOCUS

Follow Guided Inquiry with Open Inquiry

As previously stated, open inquiry refers to investigations in which students generate the questions that they investigate. Guided inquiry can help students develop the skills needed to do open inquiry. When open inquiry follows a guided inquiry, students continue to use some of the same processes, materials, and thinking that they used in the guided inquiry. This method allows the open inquiry investigation to run more smoothly with fewer classroom management concerns for the teacher.

TEACHER: Grades 5–8

Table 2.1.2 Sample Student Results

Factor Tested	Results
Amount of water	More sugar will dissolve faster as the amount of water increases.
Water temperature	More sugar will dissolve faster as the temperature of the water increases.
Surface area	Sugar will dissolve faster as surface area increases.

APPLY

Discuss individual plans. Make sure student plans for investigations are consistent with what they learned in the lesson. Look for proper use of variables such as stirring, water temperature, and crushing the tablet. This application activity can also be used as an authentic assessment.

Lesson 2.2

How Much Will Dissolve?

ENGAGE

Lemonade is a yummy summer drink. But sometimes it can make you pucker. If you made a pitcher of lemonade that was too sour, you might add more sugar. Could you continue to add more and more sugar, or is there a limit?

How much sugar do you think will dissolve in a glass of lemonade? Set up a test and try it. Use half a glass of cold water. Predict how many spoons of sugar will dissolve. Predict what will happen to the volume of lemonade in the glass when you add the sugar. Keep a record.

What if you used hot water instead of cold? Will hot water dissolve more sugar or the same amount? We will investigate the following question: **How does water temperature affect the amount of sugar you can dissolve?**

EXPLORE

1. Design a science investigation to determine whether water temperature affects how much sugar will dissolve. Think about these questions as you make your plan:
   - What materials will you need?
   - What observations and measurements will you need as evidence?
   - How might you organize your observations and measurements?

2. After your teacher approves your plan, carry out your investigation and record your measurements.

EXPLAIN

1. Graph the data you collected to show the relationship between water temperature and the amount of dissolved sugar it can hold.

The Effect of Water Temperature on the Amount of Dissolved Sugar

2. Write a statement that explains the relationship between water temperature and the amount of dissolved sugar the water can hold. Use evidence to support your statement.

3. Suppose the water is even hotter than what you used in your investigation. Would the number of spoons of sugar that would dissolve increase, decrease, or stay the same? Why do you think so?

4. How many spoons of sugar do you estimate would dissolve in water that is between warm and cold?

EXTEND

1. You have been making sugar solutions. Did you notice what happened to the amount of each ingredient when you mixed them? What happened to the total amount of mass? What happened to the volume?

2. If you dissolve a cup of sugar in a cup of water, what volume of sugar solution will you have? Measure out 250 mL of water into a plastic cup. Measure the same amount of sugar into a cup. What is the mass of the sugar? What is the mass of the water? How do you account for the mass of the cup?

3. What will happen when you mix the sugar and the water together? Predict the total mass of the sugar solution. Predict the total volume of the sugar solution.

4. Test your predictions. What did you find out? Record the mass and the volume of the sugar solution. Try to explain your results using a drawing that shows the molecular particles.

APPLY

What will happen to a sugar solution if you allow it to sit for a few days? Pour some of your sugar solution into a petri dish and set it aside in a place where you can observe it.

Lesson 2.2

How Much Will Dissolve?

Teaching Focus: Using Guided and Open Inquiry

NSES CONTENT STANDARD, 5–8: PROPERTIES AND CHANGES OF PROPERTIES IN MATTER

"A substance has characteristic properties, such as density, a boiling point, and solubility, all of which are independent of the amount of the sample" (National Research Council, 1996, p. 154).

DESCRIPTIVE OBJECTIVE

Students will be able to design and conduct investigations to determine the effect of water temperature on sugar solubility.

Note: The previous activity investigated the relationship between water temperature and the rate at which sugar dissolves. This activity studies the effect of water temperature on the amount of sugar that will dissolve. Linking these two activities helps strengthen the students' understandings of solubility.

MATERIALS

For each group of students provide granulated sugar (a 10 lb bag of sugar will provide approximately 20 cups of sugar), plastic cups, plastic spoons or stir sticks, measuring spoons, pitchers of water at different temperatures (cold or refrigerated water [about 5°C], warm or room-temperature water [about 20°C], hot tap water [about 45°C, NOT hot enough to burn one's hands]), and measuring cups or graduated cylinders. For the Extend and Apply phases you will need petri dishes (margarine lids could be substituted), and a balance.

SCIENCE BACKGROUND

Increasing the water temperature adds to the kinetic energy of the water molecules and thus increases their motion. The faster they move, the more often they come in contact with the sugar molecules. This increases not only the rate at which the sugar dissolves but also the amount of sugar dissolved or the solubility. Eventually, a solution reaches the point at which no more solid material will dissolve in the liquid. Then the solution is saturated. Any additional material settles at the bottom of the container. Heating sometimes makes it possible to supersaturate a solution. When the heated solution cools, the additional solute will crystallize out of the solution. Essentially, this is the process that is used to grow crystals (including rock candy).

The solubility of most solutes increases with an increase in temperature. Not all solutes increase solubility by the same amount, however. The amount of sugar that dissolves in water increases a great deal as the temperature increases. On the other hand, only a relatively small amount of additional salt (NaCl) will dissolve as the temperature of the water solvent increases.

The amount of a gas, however, that can dissolve in a liquid *decreases* as the temperature increases. You may have noticed that a warm bottle of soda gets "flat" quicker than a cold one. The greater energy in the warm soda increases the likelihood of a gas molecule escaping from the surface of the liquid.

When substances are combined in solutions, their mass is conserved—that is, the sum of the masses of the solute and the solvent will equal the mass of the solution. Their volume, however, is not conserved—the volume of the solution is less than the sum of the volumes of the solvent and solute. This happens because space between the molecules of the solvent (in this case water) is filled with the sugar molecules.

Volume is also not conserved in many mixtures that are impure solutions. Consider, for example, a cup of sand mixed into a cup of coarse gravel. The resulting mixture would clearly be less than 2 cups. (Here, of course, the sand is not in intermolecular spaces but in between the individual pieces of gravel.)

CLASSROOM SAFETY

Students should be cautioned not to ingest any of the materials. Check the temperature of the hot tap water yourself before allowing students to use it.

Teaching Tip

Connecting Lessons

Students should spend a minute or two connecting lessons to one other, as this will aid the learning process. It may seem obvious to teachers that the lessons build upon one another, but this fact often escapes students unless it is made explicit. Help them focus on the "big picture" of the unit on a regular basis.

Teaching Focus

Scaffolding Inquiry Investigations

As the *NSES* state: "Teachers of science guide and facilitate learning. In doing this, teachers focus and support inquiries while interacting with students" (National Research Council, 1996, p. 32). One benefit of inquiry teaching is that you gain insight into students' thinking as you interact with them during their investigations. Students do not automatically plan and conduct inquiry investigations if they are used to lab activities that only require them to follow directions. With continued encouragement and support, however, students will become more independent as they learn to think through investigations and become better problem solvers.

ENGAGE

This can be done as an activity or a demonstration using lemonade or cold water. Make sure the students predict the amount of sugar they think will dissolve. This will induce them to think about solubility, to make comparisons to the previous activity, and to think about the question they will investigate in the Explore phase. Here you may also ask what happens to the volume of the solvent as the solute is added—is the volume conserved or not? (That question will be investigated in the Extend phase.) Ask the students to think about the explorable question of the previous activity, "How does water temperature affect how fast sugar dissolves?" In this investigation we examine the following question: **How does water temperature affect the amount of sugar you can dissolve?**

EXPLORE

1. Emphasize the question that is to drive the investigation: **How does water temperature affect the amount of sugar you can dissolve?** Talk about the observations and measurements the students must make in the investigation. Ask them how they will know when a spoonful of sugar has dissolved completely. How will they know if it does not completely dissolve? (They will see particles of sugar suspended in the solution. At first, sugar crystals appear on the bottom of

the cup. With stirring, they dissolve. As more and more sugar dissolves, the solution becomes rather thick and syrupy and it becomes more difficult to tell whether or not additional sugar is dissolving. At this point the students should observe a spoonful of solution and look for undissolved particles.)

2. Circulate among the groups as they work. Ask the following questions: What question are you investigating? How is this like the earlier activity you did? How is it different?

TEACHING FOCUS

Approving Inquiry Investigations

Students must have your approval for an investigation before they conduct the lab activity. Setting up this type of routine enables you to avoid possible problems such as safety issues. In addition, it allows you to ensure that students focus on an appropriate question as well as a procedure that might provide an answer to that question.

EXPLAIN

1. Students will make line graphs of the data they collect in the investigation. The graphs should show increased solubility with increasing temperature. Sugar is very soluble in water. Expect some variation in results based on the extent of stirring.
2. The summary statement should answer the question being investigated. For example: "As the temperature of the water increases, the amount of sugar dissolved also increases."
3. More spoons of sugar will dissolve in hotter water.
4. Student answers about the number of spoons dissolved should be approximately halfway between the values for warm and cold water.

EXTEND

1. Initiate a discussion about the conservation of mass and volume of the sugar and the water. Some students may notice that the volume of solution increases as sugar is added to the water while others may not notice. Ask students to predict the mass and volume of the sugar solution.
2. The mass of the sugar is about 220 g and the mass of the water is 250 g. Students should account for the mass of the cup by massing the empty cup and subtracting that mass from the mass of the cup of sugar.
3. Students should predict the mass and volume of the sugar solution.
4. The mass of the sugar solution is about 470 g and the volume of the solution is 380 mL. The total volume is remarkably less than the 500 mL that students might have expected if the volume was conserved. The total volume is only about 76% of this amount. Students will discover that mass is conserved when a solution is made, but volume is not. (See Figure 2.2.1.)

Teaching Tip

Cognitive Disequilibrium

As we noted in the introduction, students sometimes find that their expectations, which are based on prior understandings, are quite contrary to the results they obtain. This situation is known as cognitive disequilibrium or cognitive dissonance. This mental conflict may lead students to reorganize their thinking, resulting in conceptual change and, thus, a new more scientifically accurate understanding.

Figure 2.2.1 Sample student drawings

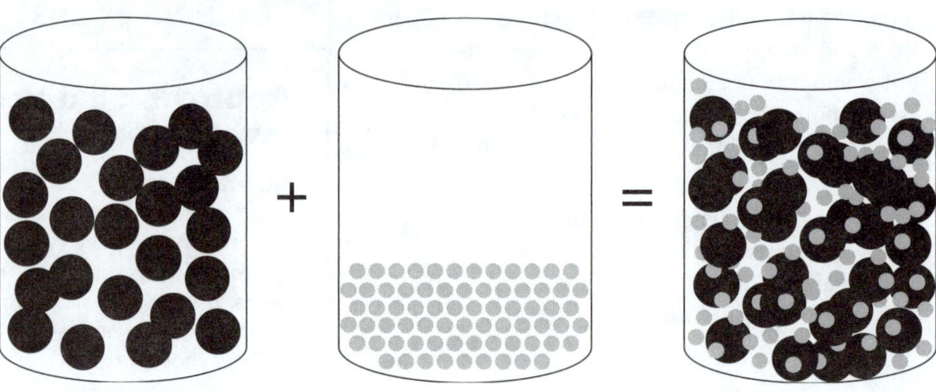

APPLY

The water will evaporate in a day or so, depending on humidity and temperature, leaving behind crystalline sugar.

An interesting additional investigation would be to take one student's solution (250 mL of water and 250 cm^3 of sugar), allow all the water to evaporate, and then determine the mass of the remaining sugar—it should, of course, be approximately 220 g, the mass of the sugar originally added to the water. Evaporating the water in a beaker may take some time. As an alternative you could pour the solution into an aluminum pie pan to speed the rate of evaporation. Another option would be to use a hot plate on very low heat to drive off the water and simultaneously avoid scorching the sugar. Find the mass of the container prior to filling it with solution. (**Caution:** If an appropriate neat sink is available you can heat Pyrex glassware on a hot plate (or on a rubberized hot plate). Otherwise, use a sauce pan.)

Lesson 2.3

Dissolving Different Substances

ENGAGE

In earlier activities you learned about factors that affect the rate at which sugar dissolves in water. Then you investigated how water temperature affected the amount of sugar that would dissolve. How do you think other household chemicals, like salt or baking soda, will dissolve in water? Is the amount of salt or baking soda that dissolves in a glass of water the same as that of sugar? Write down your prediction. How could you answer this question? We will investigate the following question: **How does the amount of salt or baking soda that will dissolve in water compare to the amount of sugar that dissolves?**

EXPLORE

1. Design your investigation to answer this question:
   How does the amount of salt or baking soda that will dissolve in water compare to the amount of sugar that dissolves?

2. This is your third activity about dissolving solids in water. In the first activity, you looked at different variables (one at a time) to find out the influence of each on *how fast* sugar dissolved in water. In the second activity, you investigated the effect of water temperature on the *amount* of sugar that would dissolve. What is the variable in this third investigation?

3. Design a science investigation to answer your question. Because you will compare the results of this investigation with those of the previous investigation, what factors will you keep the same? Think about these questions as you make your plan:
   - What materials will you need?
   - What observations and measurements will you make and record as evidence?

- How will you organize your observations and measurements so that they are most helpful in answering your question?

4. After your teacher approves your plan, carry out your investigation. Gather and record your evidence.

EXPLAIN

1. Fill out the chart below with the data collected from your investigation, other student's investigations, and your previous investigation with sugar.

Type of Substance	Amount Dissolved
Sugar	
Salt	
Baking soda	

2. Graph the data you collected to show the relationship between the amounts of each of the different substances that dissolved in water.

3. When you compare sugar, salt, and baking soda, which is most soluble in water? Which is least soluble?

4. Summarize what you have learned about the solubility of different substances in water. Use evidence from each of your three investigations.

EXTEND

1. You know what happens to a sugar solution when it is left in a Petri dish for a few days. What do you think would happen to solutions of salt and baking soda?

2. If a solution is not perfectly clear, filter out the undissolved solute from the liquid. Then pour some solution into the Petri dishes and observe it for several days.

APPLY

Does every substance dissolve in water? Get some cornstarch from your teacher. Put a very small amount into 250 mL of water and try to dissolve it. How can you prove whether or not any has dissolved?

Lesson 2.3
Dissolving Different Substances
Teaching Focus: Using Guided and Open Inquiry

NSES CONTENT STANDARD, 5–8: PROPERTIES AND CHANGES OF PROPERTIES IN MATTER

"A substance has characteristic properties, such as density, a boiling point, and solubility, all of which are independent of the amount of the sample" (National Research Council, 1996, p.154).

DESCRIPTIVE OBJECTIVE

Students will design and conduct investigations to determine that different solids have different solubilities.

MATERIALS

For each group of students provide salt, baking soda, plastic cups, plastic spoons, a pitcher of room-temperature water, measuring cups or graduated cylinders, and petri dishes. For the Apply phase you will also need cornstarch, filter paper, and funnels. (Regular coffee filters are not fine enough to filter suspended cornstarch from water.) Tincture of iodine is an optional material.

SCIENCE BACKGROUND

Different solutes have different solubilities. That is, the amount that will dissolve is different for different substances.Table 2.3.1 lists the solubilities of sugar, baking soda, and table salt in cold and hot water. Recall from the last lesson that, in general, solubilities of solids in liquids increase with temperature.

All solutions are clear (although they may be colored). In solutions of a solid in a liquid, the solute can be recovered via evaporation because the solid stays behind as the solvent evaporates.

Table 2.3.1 Solubility and Temperature

Substance	Cold (grams/100 mL @ 0°C)	Hot (grams/100 mL @ 100°C)
Sugar	179.2	487
Salt	35.7	39.1
Baking soda	6.9	16.4 (@ 60°C)
Cornstarch	0*	0*

*Cornstarch is virtually insoluble in water, although a very small amount may dissolve.

The students probably should filter any undissolved solute (on the bottom of the cup) to be sure about the source of the crystals that form in the petri dish after the water evaporates. Cornstarch forms a suspension in water. Unlike the solutions, the cornstarch suspension appears cloudy or milky due to tiny undissolved particles of starch. Cornstarch takes about 6 hours to settle while undissolved salt settles in minutes. To use evaporation as a test to see if any cornstarch has dissolved, the students must filter the suspension using filter paper. (As mentioned earlier, ordinary coffee filters are not fine enough to filter the suspended particles of cornstarch.)

CLASSROOM SAFETY

Caution students not to ingest any of the materials. Iodine is used in the Apply phase of this lesson. Mix a few drops of tincture of iodine (iodine crystals dissolved in alcohol) in water to dilute it for safety. The resulting iodine solution is quite safe, but still should not be consumed.

ENGAGE

Discuss the first two solubility lessons and their results. Use the questions in this section to focus students' thinking on how different substances compare in solubility and to set the question to be investigated.

TEACHING FOCUS

Providing Structure for Inquiry

Notice that the formats for Lessons 2.1 and 2.3 are similar. The types of planning questions are the same and the guided inquiry in the Explore phase is followed by an open inquiry in the Extend or the Apply phase. If inquiry is new for your students, then you should provide a similar format. As in anything else, following a pattern can help provide structure. Although "messing about" sometimes is valuable, inquiry isn't simply turning students loose to explore without a purpose.

EXPLORE

1. Students will probably design a procedure in which they gradually add solute to a controlled amount and temperature of water as they constantly stir.
2. Question each group about the independent variable—in this case, the type of solute (salt and baking soda). Discuss the dependent variables as well—the amount of salt and baking soda that dissolves. Finally, discuss the variables that are controlled—the amount and temperature of water, and the amount of stirring.
3. Guide students as needed as they create their investigations. Many students will be able to do this independently because they have completed this format in the two previous lessons, but a few may need assistance. Use questions such as these to guide their thinking: What is the question that you are investigating? What did you do in the second activity? How is this investigation similar? How is it different?

Teaching Tip

Diversity—Helping English Language Learners with Inquiry Science

Some of your students may be recent immigrants who have never used hands-on materials in science, conducted an experiment, or experienced inquiry–based science. Therefore, be sensitive to their backgrounds and help them adjust to a classroom culture that includes group work, making predictions, class discussions, hands-on activities, and sharing findings (Short & Their, 2006).

Teaching Focus

Modeling Scientific Inquiry

"Teachers of science encourage and model the skills of scientific inquiry, as well as the curiosity, openness to new ideas and data, and skepticism that characterize science" (National Research Council, 1996, p. 32). Be an example to students by showing through your enthusiasm that you are interested in science. Display genuine interest in their ideas and activities and your willingness to show that you don't know everything about a topic. Demonstrating that you still enjoy learning new things will help your students become lifelong learners.

Teaching Focus

Challenging Students with Inquiry

"At all stages of inquiry, teachers guide, focus, challenge and encourage student learning" (National Research Council, 1996, p. 33). One benefit of open inquiry teaching is that not all students have to conduct the exact same activity at the same time. If students ask and answer their own questions, they can work at different levels that are appropriate for their abilities and prior knowledge. You can challenge students who need it or provide opportunities for students who need more basic work.

4. Review the students' plans for their investigations. Review again the procedure that the students are to follow to determine when no more solid is dissolving. Remind your students to save their solutions for the Extend phase.

EXPLAIN

1. Table 2.3.2 gives actual classroom sample data. Your student data will vary somewhat depending on the amount of water used, the water temperature, and the rate of stirring.
2. Students should make a bar graph of the data (it is categorical data) to show the relationship among the amounts of each of the different chemicals that dissolve in water.
3. Sugar is the most soluble. Baking soda is the least soluble.
4. The amount of a solid that dissolves in water depends upon the type of solid. Factors such as water temperature, stirring, and particle size determine how fast a solid dissolves.

EXTEND

1. Review with students the results of the sugar solution left in a Petri dish from Lesson 2.2. Have them predict what will happen to the salt and baking soda solutions.
2. Students should filter their solutions to ensure that any crystals they find were indeed dissolved in the water. The crystals should be readily observable in a few days. To speed this process, place the petri dishes under a lamp or heat the water.

APPLY

Students will probably think that some amount of cornstarch will dissolve in water. Some may know that their parents use cornstarch to thicken sauces and gravies. Actually, cornstarch is almost totally insoluble in water. Particles of cornstarch, which are made up of large molecules called *polymers*, do vary in size. Most, however, do not dissolve in water although a few may be small enough to dissolve.

Students have two ways to investigate whether any cornstarch is dissolved in the water. It is likely, however, that ultimately they will not be able to answer this question. One method is the one we have been using above—filter and then evaporate the mixture in a petri dish and look for

Table 2.3.2 Sample Student Data

Type of Substance	Amount Dissolved in 250 mL
Sugar	375 cm^3
Salt	70 cm^3
Baking soda	20 cm^3

remaining particles of the starch. Because these particles are so small, it is difficult to filter all of the suspended particles of cornstarch out of the water. Thus, a slight residue (along with a few contaminants) will remain in the petri dish after the water evaporates. The other method would be to test the filtrate (the liquid obtained when the cornstarch suspension is filtered) with a drop of iodine. The iodine, a standard test for starch, turns from a yellow to a blue color in the presence of starch. The iodine will not turn completely dark, but when compared to a drop of iodine in pure water it will definitely be darker, indicating that a slight amount of cornstarch is present. This happens because the filter cannot remove all of the smaller particles of starch. If you test the residue in the petri dish in the same manner, you will obtain the same slightly positive results. It is impossible to determine whether this small amount of starch in the residue was suspended or dissolved in the water. It will be obvious to the students, however, that cornstarch is nearly insoluble compared to salt, sugar, and baking soda.

Teaching Tip

Unanswered Questions

Scientists cannot answer all of their questions about the natural world. Often this is due to a lack of technology to collect data or perform an experiment, or to ambiguous data from which they cannot draw definite conclusions. Your students may also sometimes find that they cannot draw conclusive results from their investigations to answer a question. This type of experience will enable students to appreciate how the entire scientific enterprise works. Real-life science questions may go unanswered for long periods of time. This is the nature of science.

If your students wish to study this further, have them stir a spoonful of starch in 250 mL of water. Then have them set the container aside where it can remain undisturbed for several days. The starch immediately begins to settle out of suspension. After a day, almost all of the cornstarch will be on the bottom with nearly clear water above it. The water is only nearly clear, however, indicating a suspension and not a solution. The water remains cloudy because the small particles remain in suspension indefinitely.

Teaching Focus Summary: Guided and Open Inquiry

- Inquiry is asking and answering a question about the natural world. It is not the scientific method or any other step-by-step process that scientists or students follow.
- Have students generate their own ideas before the activity to ensure that they investigate a question to which they do not already know the answer.
- Starting a lesson with guided inquiry can help both teachers and students make the transition from using directed, confirmation activities to full, open inquiry.
- Follow a guided inquiry with an open inquiry. This gives students confidence in answering their own questions while allowing them to still use some of the same processes, materials, and thinking that they used in the guided inquiry.
- When students conduct open inquiry, they must gain your approval of their plans before they conduct their investigations. This enables you to check for safety concerns, materials use, and procedures.
- Structure inquiry for students to make them comfortable and confident in planning their own investigations.

References

Barman, C. (2002). Guest editorial: How do you define inquiry? *Science and Children, 40*(2), 8–9.

Martin, D. J. (2003). *Elementary science methods: A constructivist approach,* 3rd ed. Belmont, CA: Wadsworth/Thomson Learning.

National Research Council. (1996). *National Science Education Standards*. Washington, DC: National Academy Press.

Short, D., & Their, M. (2006). Perspectives on teaching and integrating English as a second language and science. In A. Fathman and D. Crowther (Eds.), *Science for English language learners* (pp. 199–219). Arlington, VA: NSTA Press.

INVESTIGATION 3

DENSITY

(5–8)

Teaching Focus: Assessing Science

Lesson 3.1

Which Is More Dense?

ENGAGE

Make a list of some objects that you know will float and another list of those that you know will sink. How are the two lists different? Now, examine an unpopped kernel of popcorn. Can you predict whether it will sink or float in water? Write down the reasons for your prediction.

Place the kernel in a small cup of water. What happens?

Now think about a popped kernel of popcorn. How does it differ? Do you think it will it sink or float? Why? Put it in the water to test your prediction.

How do the two kernels compare? What about their mass? Volume?

We will investigate the following question: **How do the mass and volume compare for popped and unpopped popcorn?**

EXPLORE

1. Place 10 kernels of unpopped popcorn in a plastic cup on one pan of a balance, and a cup with 10 kernels of popped popcorn on the other pan. How do their masses compare?

2. How does the amount of space or volume of each group of kernels compare to that of the other?

3. Place several kernels of popped and unpopped popcorn in a cup of water and observe. Draw a picture of what you observe.

4. How can you explain what happened to the popped and unpopped popcorn? What evidence supports your explanation?

EXPLAIN

1. When corn is popped, which changes more: its mass or its volume?

2. *Dense* is a word used to compare the mass of an object and the amount of space it takes up (volume). How have you used the word *dense*? What does this word mean to you?

3. Objects that have relatively large masses and take up little space or volume are said to be dense. Objects that have about the same mass but take up lots more space or volume are less dense. Explain why popped popcorn is less dense than unpopped popcorn.

4. How do the mass and volume compare for popped and unpopped popcorn?

EXTEND

1. Which is more dense, an empty balloon or the same balloon when inflated? Before you make a guess, consider the mass and volume for each.

2. Now try to determine the mass and volume for the empty and inflated balloons. Which is more dense? What is your evidence?

3. Earlier we asked you to define what the word *dense* meant. You have been exploring the concept of density. Write below how you would explain the concept of density to one of your friends.

4. Place a can of diet soda and a can of regular soda (of the same brand) into a container of water. Record your observations. Because the two cans are the exact same volume, what can you deduce about their masses? Why? Which can is more dense?

APPLY

Several kernels of popped corn are floating in a cup of water. After some time, one of the kernels sinks to the bottom. How does the density of a floating kernel compare to that of the one that sank? What might have caused the kernel to sink?

Lesson 3.1

Which Is More Dense?

Teaching Focus: Assessing Science

If I had to reduce all of educational psychology to just one principle, I would say this: The most important single factor influencing learning is what the learner already knows. Ascertain this and teach him accordingly.

David Ausubel (1968)

NSES CONTENT STANDARD, 5–8: PROPERTIES AND CHANGES IN PROPERTIES OF MATTER

"A substance has characteristic properties such as density. The density of a substance is independent of the amount of the sample" (National Research Council, 1996, p. 154).

DESCRIPTIVE OBJECTIVE

Students will investigate the mass and volume of popped and unpopped kernels of popcorn to understand the intensive property of density.

MATERIALS

For each group of students provide approximately 25 kernels of both popped and unpopped popcorn, two clear plastic cups, a metric balance, a measuring cup or graduated cylinder, and water. Microwave popcorn works as well as regular popcorn for this activity. For the Extend and Apply phases, provide each group with several balloons, a can of regular soda and a can of diet soda (of the same brand), and a container large enough to float the soda cans.

SCIENCE BACKGROUND

The ratio of an object's mass to its volume is known as density. That is, the heavier an object is for its size, the more dense it is. For example, consider a piece of angel food cake and an equal-sized brownie. The brownie is of the same size, but is obviously much heavier and therefore is much more dense. Mathematically, this ratio is expressed as $d = m/v$ where d is the density, m is the mass, and v is the volume. In the metric system, density is usually expressed in terms of grams per cubic centimeter (g/cm^3).

Note that because density is a ratio, it is invariant. In other words, a small brownie has the same density as the entire pan of brownies (not counting the pan). The property of density, therefore, is known as an *intensive* term. The weight of an object, however, depends on the volume and therefore is called an *extensive* property.

MISCONCEPTION INFORMATION

Density is a difficult topic for most students, so many of your students will have misconceptions related to sinking and floating. Many of these misconceptions result from overgeneralizations in which students focus on only one variable rather than on the relationship between mass and volume. Some of the more common misconceptions students have about density focus only on:

- Size
- Shape
- Material

For additional information, you may wish to refer to:

Libarkin, J., Crockett, C., & Sadler, P. (2003). Density on dry land. *The Science Teacher, 70*(6), 46–50.

Stepans, J., Beiswenger, R., & Dyche, S. (1986). Misconceptions die hard. *The Science Teacher, 53*(6), 65–69.

CLASSROOM SAFETY

Caution students not to ingest any of the materials.

ENGAGE

Initiate a discussion to elicit students' prior knowledge about objects that sink and those that float. Many students will probably have the misconception that heavy objects sink and light objects float. Now let the students observe the popped and unpopped popcorn kernels. Have them predict whether the kernels will sink or float and then test their predictions.

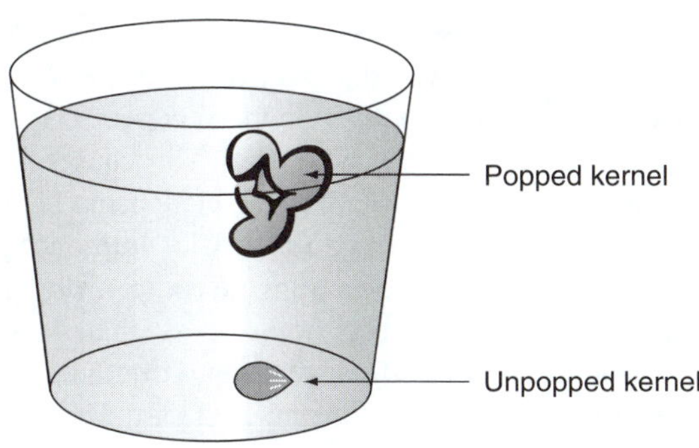

Clear cup with water

Focus students' attention on how the two kernels are different, leading them to consider the possible effect of mass and volume. Raise the question of comparing equal numbers of kernels of popped and unpopped popcorn and ask the question: **How do the mass and volume compare for popped and unpopped popcorn?**

TEACHING FOCUS

Using Pre-assessments

Pre-assessments measure students' understanding by comparing their knowledge prior to instruction with their knowledge at the conclusion of the lesson. Here the teacher can determine how this exploration alters students' knowledge about sinking and floating. At this point in the lesson, therefore, many students probably will not have accurate or complete knowledge of the topic. Resist the temptation to correct their misconceptions verbally at this stage of the lesson.

Pre-assessments also give teachers needed feedback to help them determine whether they need to adjust their lesson plan. For example, if the teacher learns that the students already understand the subject of the lesson, there is probably no need to teach the lesson, at least as planned. On the other hand, a teacher might conclude after pre-assessment that the lesson is too difficult for the students.

Using Balances

A variety of different balances is available for use in elementary classrooms. If you are using an equal-arm balance, place the cup with 10 kernels of unpopped popcorn on one pan and the cup with 10 kernels of popped popcorn on the other pan. If you are using single-arm balances or electronic balances, mass the two cups separately. This technique assumes that the two cups are equal in mass, an appropriate assumption for this exploration.

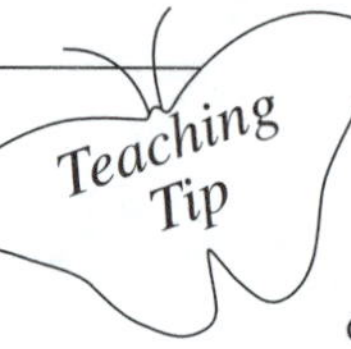

The Importance of Drawing in Science

Talk with students about the importance of their drawings in making focused and accurate observations. Often in science, students can record more information with a drawing than with words alone. This is particularly true for English language learners (ELL). Drawings, therefore, are helpful in communicating results as well as in developing explanations.

EXPLORE

1. Review the techniques for using a balance to help your students compare the masses of the two cups. The two cups should have very similar masses. Typically, a kernel of popcorn is between about 0.1 gram and 0.2 gram. The important thing to emphasize is that their masses are nearly the same while their volumes are obviously much different.
2. The volume of the popped kernels is much larger than that of the unpopped kernels—approximately 20 times larger.
3. The popped kernels should float, and the unpopped kernels should sink. Drawings are an important technique for improving observation abilities. They also serve as a record for later reference.
4. Unpopped kernels of popcorn are more dense than popped kernels. Objects that sink have a greater density than those that float. Pure water has a density of 1 g/cm^3. Objects that float in water have densities less than 1 g/cm^3, and those that sink have densities that are greater than 1 g/cm^3.

EXPLAIN

1. The volume of a popcorn kernel increases dramatically when popped. Its mass remains relatively unchanged. A slight loss of mass occurs from water vapor that escapes as the kernel pops, but this mass is probably not measurable with typical school balances.
2. You could begin a discussion on students' prior conceptions of the word *dense* and how it is used in everyday language. The dictionary defines density as marked by *compactness* or *crowding together* of parts.
3. Popped popcorn is less dense than unpopped popcorn because its mass is about the same, but its volume is much larger.
4. The masses of popped and unpopped popcorn kernels are about the same. The volume of popped popcorn is much larger than that of unpopped popcorn. This causes the popped kernel to be less dense. The relationship between mass and volume is referred to as density. Introduce the term *density* using examples from the activity. Unpopped popcorn has a higher density (more dense) than does popped popcorn (lower density). Emphasize the relationship between mass and volume in each part of the activity.

Teaching Focus

Constructing a Rubric

Creating rubrics for assessment can focus instruction as well as help students understand expectations. Luft (1997) gives four steps for constructing rubrics:

1. Determine your goals for instruction.
2. Choose the structure of the rubric—holistic (determining an overall level of performance) or analytical (selecting several different criteria with performance levels for each).
3. Select the levels of performance.
4. Share with your students.

EXTEND

1. An empty balloon is denser than the same balloon when inflated.
2. Although students may find it difficult to determine the mass and volume of the balloons mathematically, they should readily observe that

the masses of both balloons are about the same, but the volume of the inflated balloon is much larger. Blowing air into the balloon increases its mass somewhat, but very little compared to the mass of the balloon itself, whereas it does increase its volume greatly. This inverse relationship between mass and volume causes the inflated balloon to be less dense than the empty balloon.

3. Often, teachers use a scoring rubric in order to consistently apply scoring criteria. A four-point scoring rubric for the explanation of density might look like the following:

   0 points: Explanation shows little understanding of the concept—answer makes no mention of mass or volume.

   1 point: Explanation focuses on only one variable (most likely mass) and shows little understanding of the fact that density is a ratio.

   2 points: Explanation includes both mass and volume but does not clearly explain the relationship of the two.

   3 points: Explanation includes both mass and volume and indicates that density increases with increasing mass and decreasing volume.

4. For most brands of soda, the can of regular soda will sink in water while the diet soda can will float. The volumes, of course, are the same, but the regular soda is substantially more massive and, therefore, more dense as well. This is because artificial sweeteners are much sweeter than sugar and corn syrup. Saccharin is 300 times sweeter than sugar, aspartame is about 200 times sweeter, and the newest noncalorie sweetener, sucralose, is about 600 times sweeter than sugar. Have the students find the masses and the volumes (by displacement) of the two cans of soda.

APPLY

The densities of the floating kernels are less than those of the kernels that sank. The volumes of the floating and the sunken kernels are nearly the same. Therefore, the mass of the sunken kernels must have increased. The kernels of popped popcorn eventually absorb water. This increases their mass, causing them to be more dense and sink.

TEACHING FOCUS

Scoring Rubrics

Scoring rubrics like the one to the left are useful for determining different levels of student understanding in a consistent manner. They can be formulated for nearly all answers and used to assess students and assign grades.

In addition, writing a rubric prior to lesson planning can help the teacher clearly recognize desired outcomes. The value of considering outcomes in planning has been the subject of much recent professional development. Working backwards from anticipated outcomes can reveal useful teaching plans. For more information, see *Understanding by Design* by Wiggins and McTighe (1998, ASCD, Alexandria, VA).

TEACHING FOCUS

Writing Performance Criteria Descriptors for Rubrics

To make a rubric useful to both teachers and students for instructional purposes, you must be consistent when writing the performance descriptors. Often, the criteria change from level to level rather than providing a coherent, developing continuum across the levels (Tierney & Simon, 2004).

TEACHING FOCUS

Reflective Self-Assessment

Successful teachers know that students benefit from evaluating and reflecting on their own learning. For this reason, the students should compare their initial definition of the word *dense* with their later explanation of density to see how their thinking has changed. To that end, the *National Science Education Standards* include: "Guide Students In Self Assessment" as one of the Teaching Standards (National Research Council, 1996, p. 42).

Lesson 3.2
Do Raisins Sink or Float?

ENGAGE

Do raisins sink or float in water? Write down your prediction and then test it. Will the raisin sink or float? Describe what you observe.

Think about the activity where you compared popped and unpopped corn. What properties of a popcorn kernel determine its density? Now, suppose you put the raisin in a glass of clear soda. Will it sink or float? **How does the relationship between the mass and the volume of a raisin affect its behavior in clear soda?**

EXPLORE

1. Carefully observe a raisin in the glass of water. Describe its behavior. Draw a picture of the raisin.

2. Carefully observe a "raisin" in a glass of soda. (In this activity, "raisin" means the raisin itself and anything stuck to it.) Describe what happens. Draw a picture of the "raisin" when it is placed in the glass of soda and another picture each time its behavior changes.

3. Compare the differences in the raisin's behavior in the water and in the clear soda.

EXPLAIN

1. Is the raisin more or less dense than the water in the cup? What evidence supports your answer?

2. Is the "raisin" more or less dense than the soda in the cup? What evidence supports your answer?

3. What property of the "raisin" changes in the soda? Describe the change and its effect on the density of the "raisin." Refer to your drawings to form your answer. The density of the "raisin" is affected by the relationship between its mass and its volume. Explain this relationship.

EXTEND

1. Does the size of a raisin (by itself) affect its density? Suppose you cut a raisin in half. Does this affect the density of each half? Try it. Explain the results.

2. Raisins are made from grapes. When grapes dry out and shrivel up they become raisins. Do you think a grape floats or sinks in water? Try it and see. Explain the results by comparing the mass and volume of both grapes and raisins.

3. Do you think a navel orange will float or sink in water? Try it and see. Now, carefully peel the orange and try it again. Does it sink or float? What about the peel? Explain your results in terms of the mass and volume of the orange, the peel, and the fleshy part of the orange.

APPLY

How might you make a raisin float in water? Consider both the mass and the volume of the raisin. Make a list of the materials that you need. Write a paragraph explaining what you plan to do and the anticipated result. Give your plan to your teacher for approval, then test your idea. Write a summary of your results. Be sure to include drawings of what you did to the raisin.

Lesson 3.2
Do Raisins Sink or Float?
Teaching Focus: Assessing Science

NSES CONTENT STANDARD, 5–8: PROPERTIES AND CHANGES IN PROPERTIES OF MATTER

"A substance has characteristic properties such as density. The density of a substance is independent of the amount of the sample" (National Research Council, 1996, p. 154).

DESCRIPTIVE OBJECTIVE

Students will investigate raisins that rise and fall in order to infer the relationship between mass and volume in terms of density.

MATERIALS

For each group of students you will need to provide plastic cups, raisins, water, and a clear carbonated soda (such as Sprite™). To complete the Extend phase of the lesson, provide each group with a navel orange and some grapes. For the Apply phase of the lesson students will need foam plastic material, packing peanuts, toothpicks, wooden stir sticks, marshmallows, or other materials that easily float in water.

SCIENCE BACKGROUND

See the Science Background section in the previous lesson for a basic explanation of density. In this lesson, students will observe that the density of the raisin system decreases as bubbles adhere to the raisin, resulting in an increase in volume but little increase in mass. Qualitatively, you might discuss this with your students in terms of the raisin system becoming less massive for its size—because the volume has increased but not the mass. More quantitatively, you might look at the relationship $d = m/v$ and analyze what happens as v gets larger and m stays constant (or nearly constant). For example, have students consider what happens to the ratio (fraction) m/v if m stays the same but v increases. Use concrete integer examples to show them that the fraction m/v gets smaller: $1/1 = 1$; $1/2 = 0.5$; $1/4 = 0.25$; $1/10 = 0.1$. . .

> **Teaching Abstract Ideas (Part I)**
>
> *Teaching Tip*
>
> Students often have difficulty conceptualizing abstractions that involve ratios such as density. Some examples in science include Newton's Second Law, $a = F/m$; Ohm's law, $I = E/R$; and density, $d = m/v$. When focusing on volume, as in the example of density developed in this lesson, students have great difficulty visualizing the inverse nature of density getting **smaller** as the volume gets **larger**. One way to help students with this abstraction is to simply make the problem more concrete, as the above demonstrates. First, students observe the raisin/bubble system getting larger before it floats. Second, when the students look at the mathematics, the teacher might actually use whole number integers to demonstrate how the value of the fraction or ratio changes as the denominator increases.

CLASSROOM SAFETY

Caution students not to ingest any of the materials.

ENGAGE

The first part of the Engage phase can be done as a demonstration or in small groups. Ask the question: Do raisins sink or float in water? Gather predictions from the class and then put the raisin in the water. The raisin sinks. Ask the following question: Which do you think is denser, the water or the raisin? The raisin is denser because it sinks.

Focus the students' thinking on the activity with popped and unpopped corn. Ask them to think about the properties that determined whether the kernel would sink or float. Have the students focus on the behavior of the raisin in clear soda. Ask the following question: **How does the relationship between the mass and the volume of the raisin affect its behavior in clear soda?**

Teaching Focus

Diversity—Assessing English Language Learners

Consider many alternatives when assessing English language learners in science. Use options that do not depend as much upon written language such as drawings, building models, and oral explanations. Use formative as well as summative assessment including observations, homework, group work, and individual conversations to document student learning. These alternatives may provide more information on a student's understanding than would a formal end-of-unit test (Katz & Olson, 2006).

EXPLORE

1. The raisin sinks in the water.
2. Ask the students whether they can observe bubbles attaching themselves to the raisin. Explain that in this activity, the term "raisin" refers to both the raisin itself and any bubbles attached to it. You may want them to think of the raisin and its attached bubbles as a "raisin system." This becomes very important in students' drawings of the raisin in different positions in the cup. They can observe the volume of the "raisin system" changing as it moves up and down.
3. Because the water does not produce any gas bubbles, the raisins stay at the bottom and do not rise and fall as they do in the clear soda.

Teaching Focus

Assessing with Drawings

Some students may resist drawing their ideas because they think that they can't draw. Of course, the artistic value of the drawings is unimportant. Analyzing students' drawings, however, can reveal a great deal about their thinking. For example, consider the drawings in Figure 3.2.1. In the first drawing all the raisins have the same number of bubbles regardless of where they are located in the jar. Clearly this student does not understand how the bubbles change the density of the raisins, making them float. The second drawing shows rising and falling raisins, and the falling ones have fewer bubbles than the rising ones. This indicates that the student probably has a firm grasp on the concept. It is possible, however, that the student merely has accurately observed the phenomena and doesn't yet fully understand them. In this case, students should use a few words to explain their drawings. This is immensely easier for most students than only using words to describe their understanding of a complex process.

Figure 3.2.1 Sample student drawings

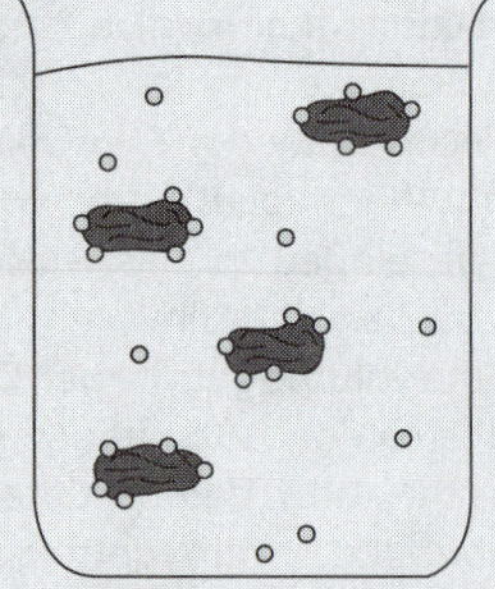

Raisins with same number of bubbles attached

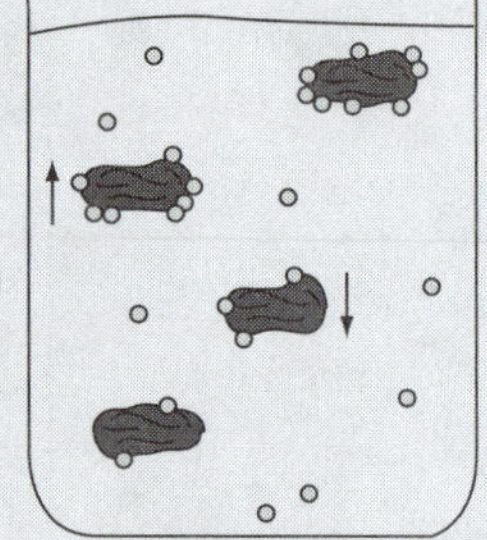

Raisins that are rising and falling

EXPLAIN

1. The raisin sinks. This is evidence that it is more dense than the water.
2. Sometimes the raisin system is more dense, and at other times it is less dense. The raisin system sinks when it is more dense than the soda, and it floats when it is less dense.
3. The mass of the raisin system stays nearly the same. The volume increases when bubbles attach to the raisin. The volume decreases as the bubbles leave the raisin. As the volume of the raisin system increases, its density becomes less. Point out to students that, with the bubbles attached, the "raisin" is less massive **for its size.** When the bubbles leave, the volume of the raisin system gets smaller and it becomes more dense.

EXTEND

1. The size of a raisin does not affect its density. When you cut a raisin in half, both halves sink in water. Both halves have the same density—greater than that of water. Recall from Lesson 3.1 that density is an intensive property.
2. Many students will predict that grapes float. They probably focus more on the volume of a grape and less on its mass. Most grapes sink. When a raisin forms from a grape, it loses both mass and volume. The mass lost is water. The relationship between the decreased mass and volume is similar to that of the original grape, thus the density of a raisin is approximately the same as the density of a grape.
3. The students will find that the orange floats. When it is peeled, however, it sinks (the peel floats). Here, the peel added a large amount to the volume of the orange without adding as significantly to its mass. This principle also explains how life jackets (flotation devices) work: They significantly increase the volume of the "person" without adding much to the mass of the system.

Including Experiences from Culturally Diverse Students

Teaching Tip

Whenever possible, use examples that are familiar to all students in your science lessons. In addition, include relevant examples from experiences that your students have to help them feel connected to the class. These will enrich the experiences of all students and possibly give another perspective.

One of the authors once taught a group of preservice teachers a density lesson involving an egg floating in salt water. A student commented that her mother floated eggs in salt water during the Muslim holiday Ramadan when they fasted from sunrise to sunset. The student's mother normally tasted a brine solution for grape leaves when preparing the evening meal, but relied on the floating egg while fasting to determine the correct amount of salt.

APPLY

Inspect the plans for each group before they begin. Make sure the students are clear about the question they are trying to answer: **How can you make a raisin float in water?** Question them about the properties of mass and volume and how these apply to their investigation. Investigations should involve significantly increasing the volume of the "raisin system" without increasing its mass too much.

Teaching Abstract Ideas (Part II)

Teaching Tip

As discussed previously, abstractions such as density are difficult for many students, especially when they are exposed to the concept for the first time. For this reason, numerous exposures and examples are often helpful. Another important technique is to use everyday examples with which students are familiar whenever possible. As we indicated in the introduction, in a constructivist learning model, students construct new meanings by combining incoming information with what they already know. This is why the above example relates the new information on the density of oranges to flotation devices with which students are likely already to have had experiences.

TEACHING FOCUS

Performance Assessment

"All performance assessment tasks have a performance that can be observed or a product that can be examined. Student performances in science assessment tasks might include measuring, observing, collecting and organizing data, constructing a graph, making a visual or audio presentation, presenting an oral defense of work, or presenting a how to explanation of a procedure. Products presented for assessment could include such tangible things as data tables, graphs, models, reports, and written explanations, and problem solutions" (Carin, Bass, & Contant, 2005, p. 164).

Lesson 3.3
Comparing Densities

ENGAGE

Have you ever played soccer or gone bowling? How do these balls compare in size or volume? How do they compare in weight or mass? The comparison of a ball's mass to its volume is called *density*. Which ball do you think is more dense?

Lots of different kinds of balls are used for different games, for example, golf balls, ping-pong balls, tennis balls, baseballs, soccer balls, and bowling balls. Let us compare their mass and volume. Compare a tennis ball and a baseball. How do their masses compare? How do their volumes compare? Which do you think has the greater density? How about the other balls? We will investigate: **How do mass and volume affect the density of a ball?**

EXPLORE

1. Arrange the balls in order of their size or volume from smallest to largest. Make a "Volume" list.

2. Heft each ball and then arrange them in order from lightest (least mass) to heaviest (most mass). Make a "Mass" list.

3. Use what you have found so far to predict the density of each ball from least dense to most dense. Number them from 1 to 8, with 8 being the most dense. Record your data in the chart below.

Type of Ball	Predicted Order of Density	Mass (g)	Volume (cm^3)	Calculated Density (g/cm^3)
Large marble				
Clay ball				
Golf ball				
Ping-pong ball				
Tennis ball				
Baseball				
Soccer ball				
Bowling ball				

4. Your teacher will provide you with the mass of the bowling ball. Find the mass of the other balls using a balance. Record the mass of each in the chart above. How does this list compare to the one you made by hefting each ball? Which ones fooled you? Why do you think you were mistaken?

5. Ask your teacher how to determine the volume of each ball. Then record the volume in the chart.

6. Ready for a challenge? The density of an object is the relationship between its mass and its volume. Density can be calculated by dividing the mass of an object by its volume.

$$\text{Density} = \text{Mass (grams)} / \text{volume } (cm^3)$$

Use the mass and volume from your chart to calculate the density of each ball. (Density = mass divided by volume.) Now, use the densities that you just calculated. Arrange the balls in order from the smallest density to the largest density.

EXPLAIN

1. Compare your two lists. How accurate were your predictions? Explain why you might have been mistaken.

2. Examine the ping-pong ball and the clay ball. How do they compare in mass? How do they compare in volume? Which has the greater density? Explain your answer.

3. Compare the golf ball and the tennis ball. How do they compare in volume? How do they compare in mass? Which has the greater density? What evidence helped you decide?

4. Write a short paragraph to explain how mass and volume affect the density of a ball.

EXTEND

1. Think about what you have learned about floating and sinking. Which of the balls do you think will float? Sink? Record your predictions.

2. Place each ball in a bucket of water to test your predictions and record the results.

3. How does the density of the balls that float compare to the density of the balls that sink? What pattern do you see?

4. Now, let's calculate the density of water. Find the mass, volume, and density of four samples of pure water.

5. Draw a graph of your water data (mass and volume) in the space below.

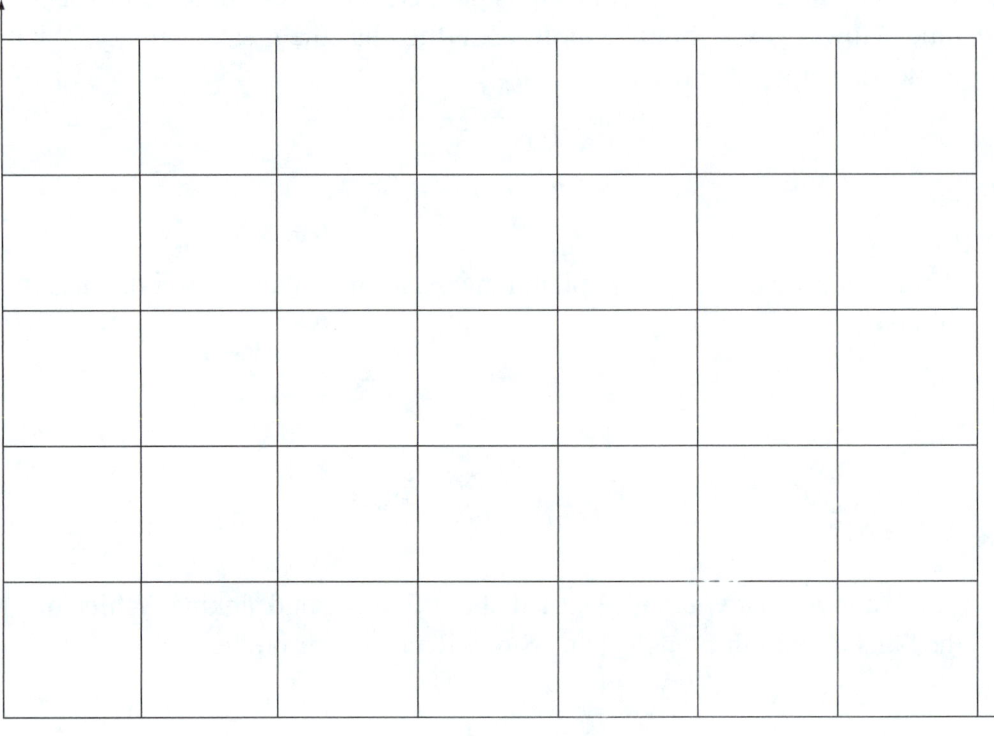

6. Now plot the mass and volume of each ball on your graph. What conclusions can you draw about the densities of the balls that sink, the balls that float, and the density of water?

APPLY

1. Examine the relationship between mass and volume again. The mass of an object divided by its volume equals its density (Density = mass / volume). Suppose you have two marbles, each made of the same kind and color of glass. One marble is twice the volume of the other. How will their masses compare?

2. If the larger marble sinks, what do you think will happen if you put the smaller marble into water? Will it sink or float? Explain.

3. Suppose you are given three new golf balls. Two of the balls are real golf balls. The third is a fake. All three look the same. How might you determine which is the fake? Explain your answer.

Lesson 3.3

Comparing Densities

Teaching Focus: Assessing Science

NSES CONTENT STANDARD, 5–8: PROPERTIES AND CHANGES IN PROPERTIES OF MATTER

"A substance has characteristic properties such as density. The density of a substance is independent of the amount of the sample" (National Research Council, 1996, p. 154).

DESCRIPTIVE OBJECTIVE

Students will determine the density of different balls by comparing the mass and volume of each.

MATERIALS

For each group of students provide a golf ball, a ping-pong ball, a tennis ball, a baseball, a soccer ball, a large marble, a ball made of modeling clay that is about the same size as the ping-pong ball, and a metric balance. Only one 8- to 10-pound bowling ball is needed as students can share information. Each group needs a large container of water (a 5-gallon bucket, perhaps) for the Extend phase.

SCIENCE BACKGROUND

Density can be calculated by dividing a substance's mass by its volume. Objects that have a density of less than 1 g/cm^3 will float, while those with a density of more than 1 g/cm^3 will sink because the density of pure water is 1 g/cm^3. For this reason, very large, heavy objects, such as cruise ships or aircraft carriers, will still float. They have enough volume to compensate for the large amount of mass.

CLASSROOM SAFETY

Students should handle the bowling ball carefully and immediately clean up any water spills.

ENGAGE

Place a soccer ball and a bowling ball side by side. Have the students compare their properties—size and weight. Even if a bowling ball is not available, many students will have lifted one at some time and can provide comparisons between the two balls. Soccer balls and bowling balls are close to the same size or volume, with the bowling ball being many times heavier. The bowling ball is obviously more dense.

Give each student group an assortment of balls: a golf ball, a ping-pong ball, a tennis ball, a large marble, a clay ball, a baseball, and a soccer ball. Have students compare the volume and mass of a tennis ball and a baseball without actually measuring them. Although their volumes are similar, the baseball is much heavier. The baseball, therefore is, more dense. Now raise the following question about the different balls: **How do mass and volume affect the density of a ball?** This is the question to be investigated.

EXPLORE

1. The balls in order of size or volume are as follows: marble, ping-pong ball, clay ball (may vary depending on its actual size), golf ball, tennis ball, baseball, soccer ball, and bowling ball.
2. The order of the balls from lightest to heaviest is as follows: ping-pong ball, marble, golf ball, clay ball (may vary), tennis ball, baseball, soccer ball, and bowling ball.
3. Students will now predict the density of each ball and order them from the least dense to the most dense.
4. Values will vary depending on the actual balls used, but sample values are included in Table 3.3.1 below. The bowling ball is too heavy to weigh on most school balances. You could use a bathroom scale, however, to estimate its weight in pounds. The mass of the bowling ball can be found as follows:

   Weight of ball in pounds ÷ 2.2 kilograms / pound × 1000 grams / kilogram = grams

   So, for a 10-pound ball we have: 10 lb ÷ 2.2 kg/lb × 1000 g/kg = 4545 g.

> **TEACHING FOCUS**
>
> ### Making Predictions
>
> The students must make predictions before conducting investigations. This ensures that they will access their own prior knowledge and become aware of their current thinking about a topic. After the investigation students should review their predictions and reflect on their learning by looking at how their thinking has changed. Help students understand that it does not matter whether their predictions were right or wrong. They won't be downgraded for inaccurate predictions. If the students' predictions are correct before a lesson, then one could argue that the lesson may not be needed.

Table 3.3.1

Type of Ball	Predicted Order of Density	Mass (g)	Volume (cm^3)	Calculated Density (g/cm^3)
Large marble		16.7	6.3	2.65
Clay ball		46.3	30.7	1.51
Golf ball		46.1	39.0	1.18
Ping-pong ball		2.5	28.5	0.09
Tennis ball		56.6	131.1	0.43
Baseball		133.1	194.9	0.68
Soccer ball		435	5311	0.08
Bowling ball (10 lb ball)		4545	5422	0.84

TEACHER: Grades 5–8

TEACHING FOCUS

Qualitative vs. Quantitative Understanding

The students have had two lessons to develop a qualitative understanding of density prior to calculating the numerical density of objects. For deep understanding, students must have many opportunities to develop conceptual understanding of a topic prior to mathematical computations. Otherwise, students may appear to understand the topic because they can accurately complete the calculations when in reality, they are only following an algorithm.

5. You have several options for helping students find the volume for each ball.
   - You can simply give students the sample information from the chart above.
   - Or, you could have them measure the circumference of each ball. The volume of a sphere can be calculated by the relationship $V = 4/3\ \pi r^3$. The radius r can be found by the relationship $C = 2\pi r$ or $r = C/2\pi$.
   - If combining these equations is too difficult for your students, a third option is to give them $V = c^3/59.2$ to calculate the volume.
6. Students will calculate the density for each ball (mass/volume). The students may be surprised to find that the soccer ball and the ping-pong ball have nearly the same density. They should find that the order of density of the balls is soccer ball, ping-pong ball, tennis ball, baseball, bowling ball, golf ball, clay ball, and marble. It is interesting to note that (in this case) the smallest ball is the most dense, while one of the largest balls is the least dense.

EXPLAIN

1. Students will compare their predictions of the order of density with the actual order.
2. The two balls are similar in volume but very different in mass. The clay ball has the higher density (is more dense).
3. The two balls are similar in mass, but very different in volume. The tennis ball has a much larger volume than the golf ball, but the golf ball is more dense.
4. The greater the mass of the ball compared to its volume, the higher the density of the ball. Balls with large volumes and small masses have low densities.

EXTEND

1. Students will use their prior knowledge from the previous lessons to make predictions about sinking and floating.
2. You will need deep containers such as 5-gallon buckets for testing these balls (especially the bowling ball). Students will probably be quite surprised to learn that the bowling ball will float. All 8 lb and 10 lb bowling balls will float, while only some 12 lb bowling balls will float (because bowling balls vary slightly in volume). No bowling balls heavier than 12 lb will float.
3. Students should notice a pattern: The balls that floated have densities of less than 1 g/cm^3 and those that sank have densities greater than 1 g/cm^3.
4. At this point students may not know that water has a density of 1 g/cm^3. Therefore, students should measure the mass and volume of four samples of water and calculate its density.

Teaching Tip

Addressing Alternate Conceptions

Students have misconceptions about many science topics, including sinking and floating. Common misconceptions are "big objects sink while small objects float" and "heavy objects sink while light objects float." You should choose learning activities that make students confront their own ideas and possible misconceptions and find out for themselves whether their ideas agree with how nature works. This enables students to construct ideas that are scientifically accurate.

Figure 3.3.1 Density of water

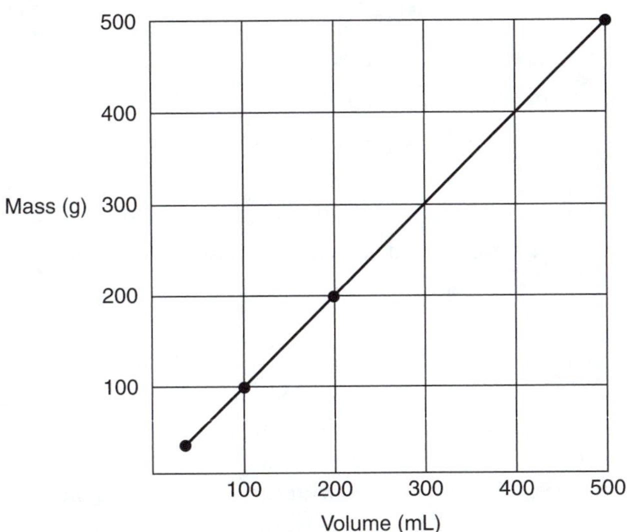

5. Have students plot the values of the mass and the volume of the four water samples. When the students connect the data points they will discover that the points form a straight line with a slope of 1 (Figure 3.3.1). Discuss with students the significance of this plot—no matter how large the water sample is, the density will be the same. That is, 100 mL of water has the same density as 1000 mL. Density is an intensive property—independent of quantity. Remember that many students hold the misconception that density increases with volume. They may believe, for example, that objects are more likely to float in a larger body of water than in a smaller one.
6. Students will now plot the mass and volume of each ball on the same graph as the water. They will find that the data points for the balls that sink are above the line because they have densities greater than 1 g/cm^3, and data points for the balls that float are below the line because they have densities less than 1 g/cm^3.

Teaching Tip

Graphing Concrete Relationships

It is helpful to make a visual representation of data when trying to make sense of it. Graphs are one type of representation that scientists often use when trying to understand their data. Graphs picture information in an organized manner. These pictures often show a relationship between the variables of interest that was not apparent before graphing.

APPLY

1. If you double the size of a glass marble, its mass will also double. The density of a substance is an intensive property and so is independent of the size of the sample.
2. The smaller marble will also sink for the same reason as above. The density of a substance is independent of the size of the sample.
3. The two authentic golf balls will be equal in mass. The fake ball may have either a smaller or larger mass. Students may suggest cutting the balls in half, looking inside them, and comparing what they are made of. This would work, but the emphasis here is on the relationship of mass and volume to density.

Teaching Focus Summary: Assessment

- Use pre-assessments to find out students' prior knowledge and possible misconceptions. Use this information to guide your teaching.
- Develop and use rubrics to score student assignments and focus on desired outcomes.
- Provide opportunities for student self-assessment, especially when students have made predictions prior to investigations.
- Drawings can be useful for assessing student understanding.
- Use performance assessments in addition to traditional assessments.

References

Ausubel, D. (1968). *Educational psychology: A cognitive view.* New York: Holt, Rinehart & Winston.

Carin, A., Bass, J., & Contant, T. (2005). *Teaching science as inquiry,* 10th ed. Columbus: Pearson Merrill Prentice Hall.

Katz, A., & Olson, J. (2006). Strategies for assessing science and language learning. In A. Fathman and D. Crowther (Eds.), *Science for English language learners* (pp. 61–77). Arlington, VA: NSTA Press.

Luft, J. (1997). Design your own rubric. *Science Scope, 20*(5), 25–27.

National Research Council. (1996). *National Science Education Standards*. Washington, DC: National Academy Press.

Tierney, R., & Simon, M. (2004). What's still wrong with rubrics: Focusing on the consistency of performance criteria across scale levels. *Practical Assessment, Research & Evaluation, 9*(2). Retrieved from http://PAREonline.net

Wiggins, G., & McTighe, J. (1998). *Understanding by design*. Alexandria, VA: Association for Supervision and Curriculum Development (ASCD).

INVESTIGATION

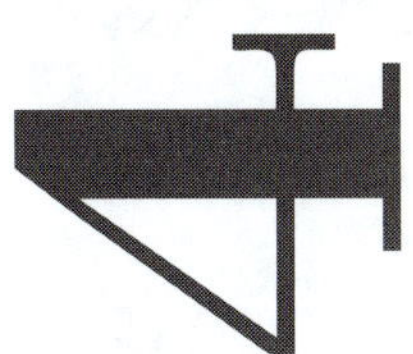

ENERGY

(5–8)

Teaching Focus: Integrating Mathematics in Science Learning

Lesson 4.1

How Far Can Your Bike Roll Uphill?

ENGAGE

Pretend you are riding your bike in a big park. Your bike chain comes off at the top of a hill. Your friends are waiting for you at the top of the next hill. If you coast down the hill, can you make it to where your friends are waiting? Show where your bike will end up on the picture below. How do the start and end points of the coasting bike compare? Explain your answer.

Use a model to explore the coasting bicycle problem. Make a track with two hills and a valley. The hills should be of the same height. Use a marble as a model for the bike. Let the marble start at different points on the hill. We will investigate: **How do the start and end points of the rolling marble compare?**

EXPLORE

1. Place the marble at the top of the first hill and mark it with a piece of tape. Use tape to mark where you predict the marble will stop rolling up the second hill. Release the marble and mark the spot where it stops rolling uphill. How did your prediction and the actual stopping place compare? Measure each height and record in the chart below. Repeat the procedure and compare results.

2. Start the marble halfway down the first hill. Use tape to mark where you predict the marble will stop rolling uphill. Mark where it stops. Measure and record. Was your prediction more accurate this time? Explain.

3. Start one-fourth of the way up the first hill and repeat the procedure. Are your predictions improving? Explain why.

4. Start the marble at the top of the first hill. Let it roll until it stops. Where does it finally stop?

Initial Starting Height	Prediction of Height of Marble on the Second Hill	Actual Height Reached on the Second Hill

EXPLAIN

1. From which starting point did the marble roll the greatest height up the hill? The lowest?

2. Where did the marble appear to have the most moving energy? The least amount of moving energy? How do you know? How would you explain moving energy to a friend? Moving energy is called kinetic energy. The word *kinetic* comes from the Greek word *kinetikos*, which means moving.

3. At which starting point does the marble have the most “stored” or “potential” energy before you let it go? The least stored or potential energy? What evidence do you have for these inferences? Graph your results. How would you explain stored or potential energy to a friend?

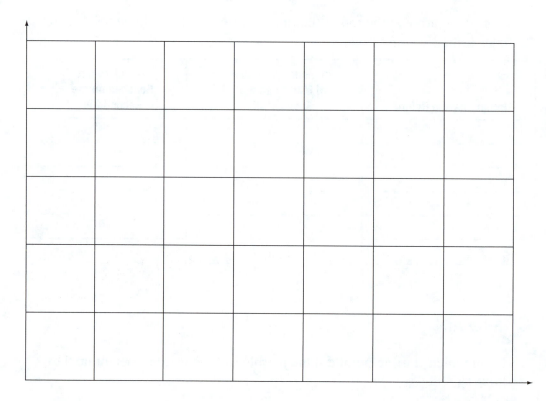

4. What happened when you let the marble continue to roll until it stopped? What happened to its moving energy? What happened to the amount of its stored or potential energy?

5. Is it possible for the marble to roll all of the way to the top of the second hill? Explain your answer.

6. Write a statement comparing the start height to the stop height of your rolling marble in this model.

EXTEND

1. What would happen if you used a larger marble? Could it reach the top of the second hill? Conduct an investigation to find out.

2. What other variables might affect how high the marble will roll? Describe how you could test each variable.

3. How might you change your model so that the marble would have enough moving energy to reach the top of a second hill? Try it and see what happens.

4. Explain what you think would happen if you let the marble roll back from the top of the second hill toward the first one. Try it and see.

APPLY

1. Go back to the problem with your bike and the hill. Use what you learned with the model. What would you need to know to predict whether or not you could coast to the top of the next hill?

2. Use the track and marble to make a roller coaster. Investigate to find out what conditions are necessary to have the marble do a loop-de-loop.

Lesson 4.1

How Far Can Your Bike Roll Uphill?

Teaching Focus: Integrating Mathematics in Science Learning

The need to understand and be able to use mathematics in everyday life and in the workplace has never been greater and will continue to increase.

National Council of Teachers of Mathematics (2000)

NSES CONTENT STANDARD, 5–8: MOTIONS AND FORCES

"The motion of an object can be described by its position, direction of motion, and speed" (National Research Council, 1996, p. 154). This investigation provides experiences that will enhance understanding of the relationship between potential and kinetic energy described in the 9–12 Standard: "Energy can be considered to be either kinetic energy, which is the energy of motion; or potential energy, which depends upon relative position" (National Research Council, 1996, p. 180).

DESCRIPTIVE OBJECTIVE

Students will conduct an investigation with rolling marbles to develop an operational definition of kinetic and potential energy.

MATERIALS

For each group of students, provide 6–8 feet of flexible Hot Wheels™ track, marbles of two different sizes, a meter stick, and masking tape. You can also make a flexible track by purchasing a 10-foot length of foam pipe insulation. Cut it in half laterally to end up with two 10-foot troughs or "tracks."

SCIENCE BACKGROUND

Energy is the ability to do work. There are many different forms of energy including thermal, mechanical, solar, nuclear, chemical, electrical, and so on. Energy is broadly classified as either kinetic or potential. The bicycle at the top of the hill has potential (or stored) energy as a result of gravity. This potential energy is a function of the position of the bicycle at the top of the hill. The higher the bicycle is on the hill, the greater its potential energy. As the bike begins to move down the hill, its potential energy changes into kinetic energy. Kinetic energy is energy of motion. When the bicycle reaches the bottom of the hill (lowest point), all of its energy is kinetic energy; it has no potential energy. As the bicycle continues up the second hill, its kinetic energy changes back into potential energy. When the bicycle stops on the second hill, all of its energy is now potential energy; it has no kinetic energy.

The students will discover that the marble does not reach its initial height on the second hill. This is because some of its energy is changed by friction into thermal energy. A small amount of the marble's energy is also changed into sound.

MISCONCEPTION INFORMATION

Students may find this topic difficult because the word *energy* is used in many different ways in everyday language and within textbooks (Taber, 1989, found over 80 different terms associated with energy). Some common misconceptions that you may find include:

- Force and energy are the same thing.
- Energy is a substantive entity, like a fluid moving from one place to another.
- If a body is not moving, no force is acting on it.
- Moving bodies always have a force acting on them in their direction of motion.

Stepans, J. (1996). *Targeting student's science misconceptions*. Riverview, FL: Idea Factory, Inc.

Taber, K. (1989). Energy—by many other names. *School Science Review, 70*, 57–62.

CLASSROOM SAFETY

There are no significant safety concerns with this exploration. Use normal classroom safety procedures. You may, however, want to make sure students do not trip on marbles.

ENGAGE

Ask questions to determine how much experience your students have with bicycles. Have they ever had the bike chain come off? Read and discuss the Engage problem. Have students indicate where they think the coasting bike will end up by placing a mark on the drawing. Focus their thinking on the question: **How do the start and end points of the coasting bike compare?** Have the students record their explanations in the space provided for later reference.

Set up the model using flexible track and a marble. Help the students compare it to the bicycle and hill problem. Emphasize the explorable question: **How do the start and end points of the rolling marble compare?**

EXPLORE

1. Securely tie or tape one end of the flexible track about 30 to 50 cm off the floor. Fasten the other end so that the track forms a U-shape. The bottom of the U should touch the floor. Use some double-sided tape to secure the track to the floor (Figure 4.1.1). Make sure to have both ends of the track at the same height above the floor. This ensures that the rolling marble will not reach the top of the track on the other side.

Figure 4.1.1

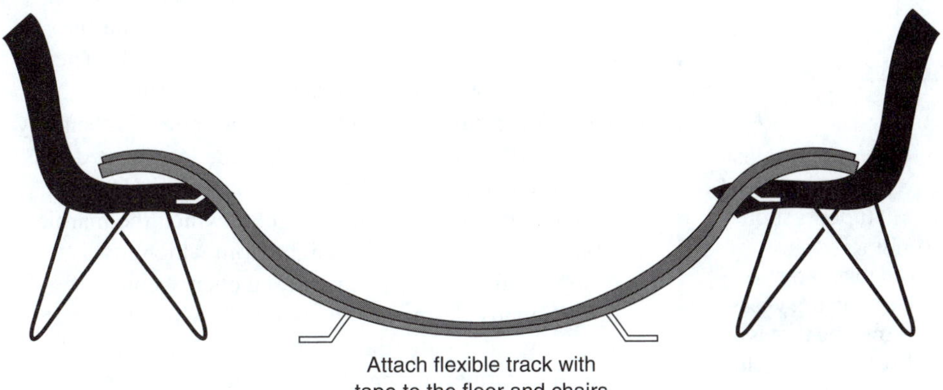

Attach flexible track with
tape to the floor and chairs

You may want to demonstrate the procedure for releasing and marking the marble before the students begin. Caution them to hold the marble still and to release it without pushing it. If students have trouble with the release, they can use a small piece of cardboard to hold the marble in place and then remove the cardboard to release the marble.

Student predictions will vary depending upon prior experiences. Students will measure the height of the starting points and ending points from the floor together with their predictions, and record them in the chart for comparison.

2. After the first experience, predictions usually become more accurate and precise. Move from group to group, asking the students what they are trying to find out. This helps them focus on the question: **How do the start and end points of the rolling marble compare?**
3. Student predictions should improve as they experience the relationship between start and stop heights.
4. The ball rolls back and forth until it stops at the bottom of the U.

> **TEACHING FOCUS**
>
> **Making Measurements**
>
> Students should practice measuring and collecting data in a variety of contexts to develop the ability to "understand, select, and use units of appropriate size and type to measure" (National Council of Teachers of Mathematics, 2000, p. 399). It is critical that the heights of the two sides of the U-shaped track be carefully measured. It is equally important that students collect accurate data on the drop points, and end points of the marble.

> **TEACHING FOCUS**
>
> **Accuracy and Precision**
>
> Accuracy refers to making measurements that are close to the actual or real measurement. Precision refers to making consistent measurements. In this case, an accurate measure of the ball's height is one that is close to where the marble actually stops moving. Students may measure inaccurately if they do not carefully place the tape on the track where the marble stops. Students introduce imprecision by sometimes measuring from the bottom of the masking tape, and sometimes from the top.

EXPLAIN

1. The marble rolled to the highest end point from the highest starting point and to the lowest end point from the lowest starting point. This is because the marble has more potential energy at a higher point and less at a lower point. In this case, the amount of potential energy is determined by the position of the marble above the floor.
2. The marble has the most kinetic energy when released from the highest point. When the marble is released from a higher position, gravity acts on the marble for a

greater period of time, causing it to roll faster. The marble has less kinetic energy when released from a lower point. Students should notice that the marble moves fastest when it is at the bottom of the U. Their explanation will likely focus around this point.

3. The marble has the most "stored" or "potential" energy at the highest starting point. It has the least stored or potential energy at the lowest starting point. Guide students to realize that the height at which the marble stops is a function of the height from which it was dropped. In other words, potential energy could be operationally defined as the height at which the marble stops—greater potential energy results in the marble traveling farther up the U. The students' graphs, therefore, should show initial position on the *x*-axis and stop height on the *y*-axis. Have the students save this graph for comparison to the graph of ball release and bounce height in the next lesson.
4. The marble eventually stops at the bottom of the U. Its kinetic energy is gone. Friction between the marble and the track (and the air) transforms the kinetic energy to heat energy in both the marble and the track. A small amount of the kinetic energy is transformed into sound as well. The stored energy becomes less and less until the ball stops.
5. The marble can never reach a point on the opposite hill equal to the height from which it started. Some of the marble's kinetic energy is lost through friction.
6. The stop height is always less than the start height. The amount of change is uniform and predictable.

TEACHING FOCUS

Review Components of Graphs

Review basic graphing components on a regular basis. All graphs should have a title to indicate what the graph is representing. Students should label each axis and indicate units for each, if appropriate. The dependent variable (the one that is measured) is usually placed on the *y*-axis, and the independent variable (the one that is manipulated) on the *x*-axis. Also, graphs should include a key or legend with the necessary information.

TEACHING FOCUS

Using Various Representations

The NCTM standards state that students should be able to "model and solve contextualized problems using various representations, such as graphs, tables, and equations" (National Council of Teachers of Mathematics, 2000, p. 395). You can help students learn to do this by enabling them to view the data they collect in different ways. In this lesson, students first represented the data in a qualitative manner by using tape to identify the starting and stopping points of the marbles. Then, students measured these points to obtain more quantitative data and recorded these data in a table format. Finally, students graphed the data to visualize relationships in the data.

EXTEND

1. Results obtained by using a larger marble should be consistent with those from a smaller one, although the larger marble probably will take longer to stop.
2. Students could generate several different ideas, such as a higher starting hill or a smoother track. Students should describe how they would test each idea.
3. If the starting hill is sufficiently higher than the second hill, the marble may roll all the way to the top of the second hill. If you push the marble, it may roll all the way to the top. Pushing gives additional kinetic energy to the marble.
4. Results should be consistent: The stop height should always be less than the start height. This question helps students develop flexible and reversible thinking.

Teaching Tip

Writing Statements of Conclusions

Inquiry-based science investigates questions to learn about the natural world. Students, therefore, must answer the explorable question based on the results they obtain. Effective science teaching is both hands-on and minds-on, so don't allow students to be merely physically active. Make sure they are mentally active as well.

APPLY

1. If the second hill is lower than the first, you could coast your bicycle all of the way.
2. The starting point of the marble must be higher than the top of the loop. The type of track and the amount of friction will determine how much higher the starting point should be. Have the students predict first and then try.

Creativity in Science

Teaching Tip

Many people believe that ideas in science are the result of the scientific method and logical thinking. Creativity, however, also plays a large role in the progress of scientific thought. As *Science for All Americans* states, "Inventing hypotheses or theories to imagine how the world works and then figuring out how they can be put to the test of reality is as creative as writing poetry, composing music, or designing skyscrapers" (American Association for the Advancement of Science, 1990, p. 5). Therefore, you should encourage students to find additional ways to affect how high the marble will roll. This will require them to use a blend of creativity and logical thinking.

Lesson 4.2
How High Will It Bounce?

ENGAGE

Stand next to a wall. Hold a tennis ball out level with the height of your shoulder. If you drop the ball, how high will it bounce? Place a sticky note on the wall to mark your shoulder height. Now mark how high you think the ball will bounce. How does your prediction compare to your classmates' predictions. Drop the ball and see what happens. How accurate was your prediction? Did the ball bounce back up to where you dropped it? Suppose you dropped the ball from waist height. How high will it bounce? We will investigate the following question: **How do the drop and bounce heights of a ball compare?**

EXPLORE

1. Tape a tall strip of craft paper to the wall so that it touches the floor. Next, prop a meter stick on the floor against the center of the paper strip. This will help you measure the drop and bounce heights.

2. Hold a tennis ball 100 cm above the floor. Drop the ball and have the observer mark the paper at the top of the bounce. Use the bottom of the ball for all your measurements. Do not push the ball as you release it! Do this three times and find the average bounce height. (**Hint:** Sit on the floor with your eyes at the level where you expect the ball to bounce.) Next, find and record the average bounce heights for balls dropped from 75 cm, 50 cm, and 25 cm. Record your measurements in the chart below.

Average Bounce Height (cm)

Drop Height (cm)	Trial #1	Trial #2	Trial #3	Average
100 cm				
75 cm				
50 cm				
25 cm				

3. Draw a graph using the averages that you calculated from your chart.

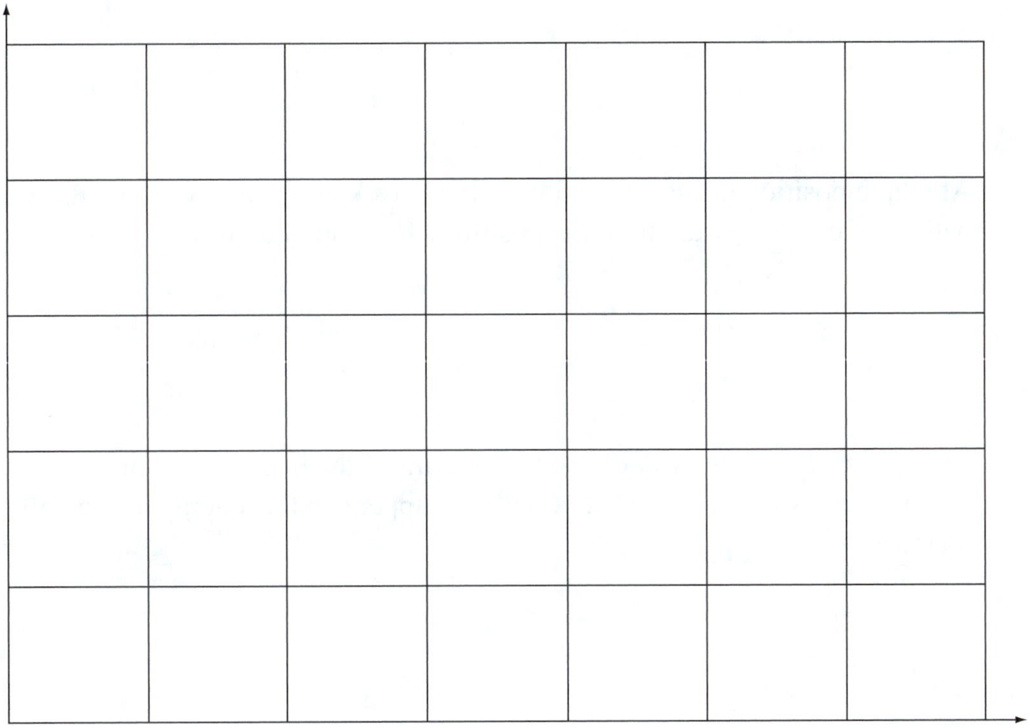

4. If a ball continues to bounce, what eventually happens? Why?

EXPLAIN

1. When did the ball have the greatest bounce height? The lowest?

2. From which drop height did the ball seem to have the most moving or kinetic energy? What evidence supports your answer?

3. At what point along its path does each ball have the greatest kinetic energy?

4. At which position does each ball have the least kinetic energy? Does the ball have any energy at all in this position? How do you know?

5. The bounce height is evidence of the amount of the ball's stored or potential energy. Explain what you think happens to this energy as the ball bounces.

6. Write a statement that describes how the drop and bounce heights compare for a tennis ball. Do the bounce heights show a pattern? Explain.

EXTEND

1. Use the pattern of measurements from your graph to make some predictions. How high would a ball dropped from 65 cm bounce? Try it and test your prediction.

2. Predict how high a ball dropped from 150 cm will bounce. Test your prediction.

3. Compare the graph you just made to the graph you made earlier on the starting and stopping points of the marble on the hill. How are they similar? How are they different?

APPLY

1. You now know a lot more about bouncing tennis balls. What about other kinds of balls? How do the bounce heights of volleyballs, golf balls, or super balls compare to those of tennis balls? What is your hypothesis? Design and conduct an investigation to test your hypothesis.

2. Which of the balls you used in your investigation loses the least energy each time it bounces? What evidence supports your answer?

3. Which ball loses the most energy each time it bounces? What evidence supports your answer?

Lesson 4.2
How High Will It Bounce?
Teaching Focus: Integrating Mathematics in Science Learning

NSES CONTENT STANDARD, 5–8: MOTIONS AND FORCES

"The motion of an object can be described by its position, direction of motion, and speed" (National Research Council, 1996, p. 154). This investigation provides experiences that will enhance understanding of the relationship between potential and kinetic energy described in the 9–12 Standard: "Energy can be considered to be either kinetic energy, which is the energy of motion; or potential energy, which depends upon relative position" (National Research Council, 1996, p. 180).

DESCRIPTIVE OBJECTIVE

Students will design and carry out investigations to determine the direct relationship between the drop height and the bounce height of balls. They will also be able to operationally define potential and kinetic energy as they relate to bouncing balls. In addition, students will be required to interpolate and extrapolate data.

MATERIALS

For each group of students provide a strip of craft paper 1 meter in length, a meter stick or measuring tape, masking tape, markers, tennis balls, and a variety of other balls such as golf balls, sponge balls, ping-pong balls, volley balls, hollow rubber balls, super balls, and so on. You may wish to obtain a set of so-called happy and sad balls. They appear identical, but one bounces like a normal rubber ball when dropped, while the other essentially splats with virtually no bounce at all. These are commercially available from science suppliers and novelty stores. For the Engage phase, students will need some sticky notes for predictions.

SCIENCE BACKGROUND

The content of this lesson is similar to that of Lesson 4.1. In this lesson, students will find that balls have their greatest potential energy just prior to being dropped. As balls fall, this potential energy is changed into energy of motion or kinetic energy. All of the potential energy is converted to kinetic energy in the instant before the ball strikes the floor. Thus, at this point the ball has its greatest velocity. As with the marble, the ball never bounces back to the original drop height because some of its kinetic energy is lost to the floor as heat (and a little sound). Further energy loss occurs as the ball pushes air out of its way (air resistance).

In the Extend phase, students will find that some balls bounce better than others. This is due to the differing elasticities of the collision of each of the balls with the floor. A perfectly elastic collision, while not possible, would cause the ball to bounce all the way back to its starting position.

CLASSROOM SAFETY

There are no significant safety concerns with this exploration. Use normal classroom safety procedures. You might want to make sure the students do not trip on the balls, however.

ENGAGE

Conduct the Engage phase as a teacher demonstration or a small group activity for students. Use the proposed questions to focus students' thinking. Students will use prior experience to predict the bounce height of a tennis ball. Ask them to explain how they estimated the bounce height. Discuss differences of opinion and ask for justification. You can substitute another type of ball if tennis balls are not available. Focus students' thinking on the following question: **How do the drop and bounce heights of a ball compare?**

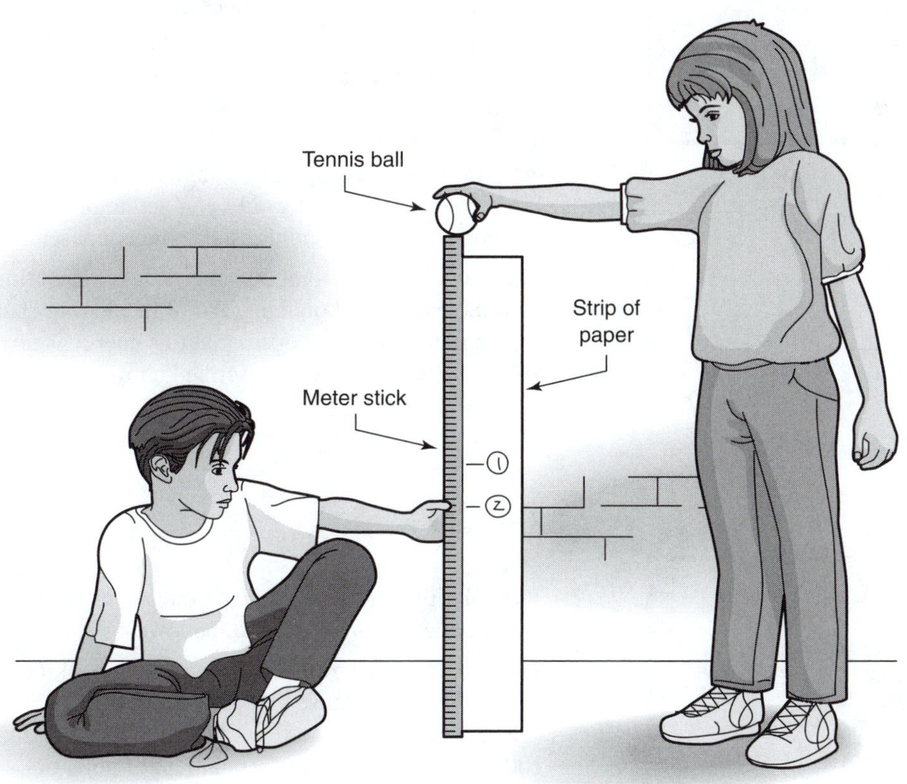

EXPLORE

1. Have each group construct a reference background for measuring. Tape a strip of craft paper, 1 meter in length, against the wall with one end touching the floor. Stand a meter stick on the floor in front of the paper. Tape the meter stick to keep it from falling over. Mark the paper every 5 centimeters along each side of the meter stick.
2. Remind the students to drop the ball, not push it, so that it falls freely. Observers should sit on the floor with their eyes at the predicted bounce height. Observers can use a marker to mark the paper at the highest point of the bounce. Mark both drop and bounce height at the bottom of the ball. If your students are using a meter stick without the grid, they can place their finger on the meter stick to mark the top of the bounce.

TEACHING FOCUS

Making Multiple Trials and Calculating Averages

To ensure reliability in an experiment, scientists perform multiple trials. Students should incorporate this practice into their investigations to gain more confidence in their data. Errors are more noticeable when several trials are made. For example, suppose that students collect the following data for a ball dropped from 50 cm: 24 cm, 26 cm, 26 cm, and 39 cm. The 39 cm data point is an example of what is called an *outlier*. It should immediately lead the investigator to ask, "Why is this data point so different from the others?" The most likely answer is that the outlier is an error—perhaps the ball was dropped from a greater height than the others, or perhaps it was inadvertently pushed, and so on.

Table 4.2.1 Sample Student Data

Drop Height	Bounce Height
100 cm	49 cm
75	38
65	33
50	25
25	12

Table 4.2.1 shows typical data on the bounce height for a tennis ball (not new). (**Note:** Data will vary depending on the condition of the tennis ball and the type of floor on which it bounces.)

3. Students should construct a graph that shows the bounce height for each of the four drop heights. Circulate among groups and ask students whether they observe a pattern developing on their graph. Ask them to refer to their graph to answer this question: From what drop height would you get no bounce? (A drop from 0 cm would result in no bounce.)
4. The ball's bounce height becomes smaller each time until the ball stops bouncing. All of its moving energy is then gone. Point out again that this energy is not lost; it is transformed, as described above.

TEACHING FOCUS

Review Types of Graphs

Review with students how to select an appropriate type of graph. Bar graphs are used with categorical data. This is data that can be grouped into categories such as color. Line graphs are used with continuous data such as time, height, or length. Students gain understanding from deciding what type of graph is appropriate for a particular set of data rather than obtaining it from the teacher each time. The NCTM standards state that students should be able to "select, create and use appropriate graphical representations of data, including histograms, box plots, and scatterplots" (National Council of Teachers of Mathematics, 2000, p. 401).

EXPLAIN

1. The ball dropped from 100 cm bounced highest. The ball dropped from 25 cm had the lowest bounce.
2. The ball dropped from 100 cm had the most kinetic energy. This is because that ball had the greatest velocity when it hit the floor. The ball dropped from 100 cm also had the greatest amount of potential energy because it bounced higher than the others.
3. The ball has the most kinetic energy just before it hits the floor. This is when the ball is moving fastest.
4. Each ball had the least amount of kinetic energy at the top of its bounce. (**Note:** Ask the students how much moving energy the ball had before it was dropped.) It has no energy of motion when held in place. Ask the following questions: Does the ball have potential or stored energy? What is the evidence that it does have stored energy? When the ball falls, the stored energy becomes moving energy. The higher the ball is held, the more stored or potential energy it has. It also has no kinetic energy when it is

compressed against the floor. It has stored or potential energy because it is compressed against the floor and can "bounce" back. The ball stores energy much like a spring. The greater the height from which it was dropped, the more the ball will compress when it hits the floor.

5. Before the ball is dropped, all of its energy is potential, changing to kinetic as the ball falls. The ball loses its moving energy when it hits the floor. Ask: Where does this energy go? Answer: Most of the ball's moving energy is stored when the ball compresses against the floor. Some of this energy is transferred to the floor and the ball as heat and some of it produces the sound heard as the ball hits the floor.
6. The patterns of drop and bounce heights are similar. For a tennis ball, the bounce height will be approximately half the drop height. The bounce height of a ball is always less than the drop height. The relationship between drop and bounce remains the same as the ball continues to bounce. (**Note:** Explain to the students that this consistent relationship allows them to predict how high a ball will bounce from any given drop height.)

EXTEND

1. Ask the students how they could use the pattern of bounce heights on their graphs to make predictions. For example, a tennis ball dropped from 65 cm should bounce about 33 cm depending upon its condition and the surface onto which it is dropped.
2. A tennis ball dropped from 150 cm should bounce about 75 cm high.
3. The two graphs will show similar patterns. The bounce height and stopping points for the ball are always less than the starting ones. This is because some of the ball's kinetic energy is transformed to heat and sound during the drop or bounce.

Teaching Focus

Interpolating and Extrapolating from Graphs

Ask students to use their data graphs to estimate values for points other than the collected data points. Students should be able to analyze the patterns within the graph and give a reasonable estimate that occurs within the total range (interpolation) or outside the total range (extrapolation). Students will interpolate the bounce height from 65 cm in question 1, and extrapolate the bounce height from 150 cm in question 2.

Teaching Focus

Comparing Data from Different Experiments

You can help students develop a deeper understanding of a concept by comparing results from one investigation to those from another. This allows students to look for similarities and differences between the two investigations. In this sense, mathematics is the study of patterns. Therefore, students should have opportunities to look for patterns. Seemingly unrelated events may actually be part of the predictability that can be found in nature.

The first two lessons of this investigation are a good illustration of this point. Each arrives at essentially the same conclusion—falling oscillating objects lose energy in a predictable way during each oscillation until all the kinetic energy has been converted to other forms of energy.

Planning Experiments

Inspect each group's procedures for the experiment. Question students about procedures, controls, variables, and the kind of evidence they need to arrive at a conclusion and answer their question. Have each group report its results using evidence to support conclusions.

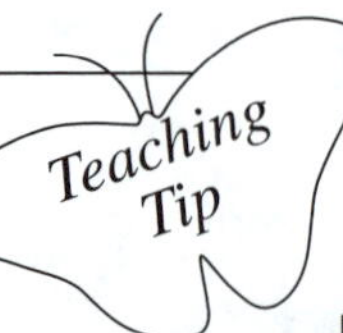

Experiments versus Investigations

Not all investigations are experiments. Experiments test the effect of some treatment on a given outcome under controlled conditions. The investigation suggested above is an experiment. It has a dependent variable (the bounce height of the balls) and at least one independent variable (the different kinds of balls). In this experiment, other possible variables, such as the temperature, are controlled (kept constant).

Some investigations involve inquiry but are not really experiments. Consider this example: Students investigate to test their prediction as to which ball is the most massive. Students could predict the order of the balls from least to most massive, based perhaps on a tactile observation, and then actually mass the balls to test their prediction. Although this activity certainly involves an element of inquiry, it doesn't qualify as an experiment. Thus, the students are not asked to frame a hypothesis about which ball is the least or the most massive. Instead, they are asked to make a prediction.

APPLY

1. Ask students to use their prior experience to place the balls (without actually dropping them) in order of their predicted bounce heights. Have students record their predictions for later reference.
2. Super balls usually bounce higher than other types of balls. Less of a super ball's moving or kinetic energy is changed to heat when it compresses against the floor at the bottom of its bounce. The evidence for this is the height of the super ball's bounce.
3. Balls with the lowest bounce lose the most moving or kinetic energy. The evidence for this is the height of the bounce.

Lesson 4.3
How Does the Kind of Floor Affect the Bounce?

ENGAGE

There are lots of different places to play basketball. What different kinds of floors or surfaces do basketball courts usually have? Does it make any difference what the floor is made of? Why?

Suppose you try to bounce a ball on concrete, tile, wood, and carpet. What happens? **How does the kind of floor affect the bounce of a ball?** We will conduct an investigation to answer this question.

EXPLORE

1. Stand a meter stick against a wall. Fasten it to the wall with tape. Record the kind of floor or surface at this spot. Hold the ball 100 cm above the floor and drop it. Have a partner observe the ball as it bounces in front of the meter stick. Have your partner mark the height the ball reaches at the top of its bounce with a sticky note. Repeat this procedure three times and record the average bounce height in the chart below.

Average Bounce Height (cm)

Type of Surface	Trial #1	Trial #2	Trial #3	Average
Carpet				
Tile				
Wood				
Concrete				

2. Go to a place that has a different kind of floor or surface. Repeat the procedure you performed in step 1. Record the average bounce height in the proper place in your chart. Repeat the same procedure on concrete, tile, wood, and carpet.

3. Draw a graph showing the average bounce height on each kind of floor.

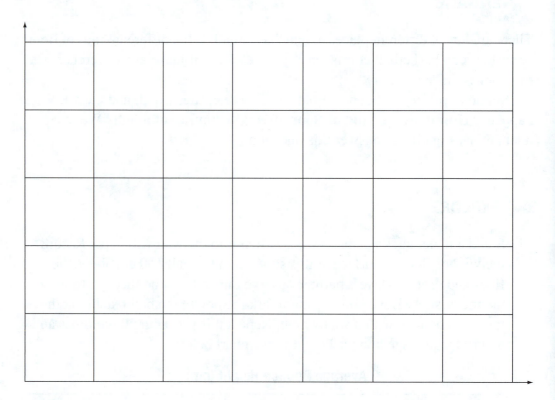

EXPLAIN

1. Which variables are the same for each test? Which have changed?

2. How did the potential energy of the ball compare on each test?

3. Which ball had the most kinetic energy after bouncing off which floor? The least? What evidence supports your answer?

4. Which surface absorbs the most kinetic energy from a bouncing ball? The least?

5. How does the kind of floor affect the bounce of the ball?

EXTEND

1. How could you get a ball to bounce the same height on a carpeted floor as it does on concrete? Test one of your ideas and explain the results.

2. Predict how high the same ball will bounce when dropped from the same height onto grass. Record your prediction. Test your prediction and explain the results.

APPLY

Tennis tournaments are played on different types of surfaces. Many are played on asphalt. Others are played on grass or clay courts. How do you think a tennis ball will bounce on these different types of courts? How could you test your predictions?

Lesson 4.3

How Does the Kind of Floor Affect the Bounce?

Teaching Focus: Integrating Mathematics in Science Learning

NSES CONTENT STANDARD, 5–8: MOTIONS AND FORCES

"The motion of an object can be described by its position, direction of motion, and speed" (National Research Council, 1996, p. 154). This investigation provides experiences that will enhance understanding of the relationship between potential and kinetic energy described in the 9–12 Standard: "Energy can be considered to be either kinetic energy, which is the energy of motion; or potential energy, which depends upon relative position" (National Research Council, 1996, p. 180).

DESCRIPTIVE OBJECTIVE

Students will conduct an investigation to determine that different types of floors affect the bounce height of a ball. They will also be able to compare the potential and kinetic energy of bouncing balls and describe the transfer of energy as a ball bounces.

MATERIALS

For each pair of students provide a meter stick, tape, sticky notes, and a ball (tennis ball, basketball, volleyball, rubber ball, etc.; the type doesn't matter as long as the ball has a reasonably high bounce).

SCIENCE BACKGROUND

Harder surfaces will compress the ball more and, therefore, absorb less of the ball's energy. Instead, much like a spring, more of the falling ball's kinetic energy is stored in the compressed ball. This results in a higher bounce. Softer surfaces, on the other hand, will themselves compress and thus absorb a greater amount of the falling ball's kinetic energy, resulting in a lower bounce height.

CLASSROOM SAFETY

There are no significant safety concerns with this exploration. Use normal classroom safety procedures. You might want to make sure that students do not trip on the balls.

ENGAGE

Talk with the students about their experiences playing basketball. Of what substances are basketball court floors made (wood, asphalt, concrete)? Pose the question: **How does the kind of floor** (concrete, wood, tile, carpet) **affect the bounce of a ball?** Have the students make predictions based on their prior experience.

EXPLORE

1. For each student group, stand a meter stick against the wall and fasten it with two strips of tape. Use a drop height of 100 cm. The observers should sit on the floor with their eyes at the bounce height. Help the students calculate the average bounce height from three bounces. Circulate among the groups and ask them what they are trying to find out. Focus the students' attention on the following question: **How does the kind of floor affect the bounce of a ball?**
2. Select areas with different kinds of floors (concrete, tile, wood, carpet) so that each group investigates at least three different kinds. It may be difficult to find an area in your school with different types of floors in close proximity. If your school has a gymnasium with a wood floor, then the locker rooms nearby may have a tile floor. You may even use large gymnastic floor mats for a type of floor, if these are available.
3. Students will make a bar graph of their data that shows the average bounce height of the ball on each type of floor.

Diversity—Gender Differences in Science

Teaching Tip

The topic of gender differences in science learning has received much attention in recent years. Many research studies have reported differences in attitude, achievement, and abilities; however, the studies often show mixed results (Dimitrov, 1999). Therefore, make sure your attitudes, expectations, and actions do not negatively influence your students. You might wish to videotape your interactions with students to analyze how you treat females versus males in areas such as:

- How often you call on students of each gender
- The type of feedback that you give to students
- What types of questions you ask

TEACHING FOCUS

Determining Appropriate Types of Graphs

Once again, instruct students how to select an appropriate type of graph. Bar graphs are used with categorical data. These are data that can be grouped into categories such as color. A bar graph is clearly needed in this investigation because the independent variable is categorical—type of floor. Students who attempt to construct a line graph will discover that they cannot determine an appropriate scale for the *x*-axis. Students may benefit from thinking this through for themselves.

EXPLAIN

1. The kind of ball and the drop height are held constant. The kind of floor varies with each test.
2. The drop height is the same (100 cm), so the potential energy is the same for each test.
3. The ball bouncing on concrete should bounce highest. The fact that it bounces the highest indicates that it has the most moving or kinetic energy. The ball bouncing off a carpet floor has the least kinetic energy and so has the lowest bounce.
4. The carpeted floor absorbs the most energy, causing the ball to have the lowest bounce. The floor that produces the highest bounce absorbs the least amount of energy from the ball as it bounces.

Review Independent and Dependent Variables

Teaching Tip

Most students of this age will have difficulties identifying variables in experiments. Therefore, students should practice identifying the independent and dependent variables in a variety of experiments and contexts. The independent variable is the variable that is changed or manipulated. The dependent variable is the variable that responds and is measured. In this investigation, the type of floor is the independent variable and the bounce height is the dependent variable.

Controlled Variables

In all experiments, some variables are purposely held constant. This assures that we are conducting a "fair" test. In this investigation, we are controlling the drop height, the type of release (no pushing), and the type of ball.

5. A ball will bounce higher or lower on different surfaces depending on how much of the ball's kinetic energy the floor absorbs. The more the floor compresses when hit by the ball, the more energy is transferred from the ball to the floor. Concrete compresses less than carpet, so less energy is transferred from the ball, causing the ball to bounce higher.

EXTEND

1. For a ball to bounce the same height from a carpeted floor as from concrete, the ball must either be dropped from a higher point or be thrown to the floor. The ball would need more kinetic energy to bounce the same height.
2. Have students refer to their data to make their prediction and explain it. If possible, have them test their predictions on the school lawn, a nearby park, or at home and then report their findings to the class.

APPLY

A tennis ball bounces higher on harder surfaces. Thus, it will bounce the least on a grass court. The students' tests should include the type of surface as the independent variable, and the bounce height of the ball as the dependent variable. They also should control for the type and brand of ball, drop height, release, and so on.

Teaching Focus Summary: Integrating Math and Science

- Students should practice making measurements in a variety of contexts to develop their ability to choose units appropriate for the task.
- Review basic graphing components and types of graphs on a regular basis. All graphs should include a title, labeled axes with units, and a key or legend.
- Students should be able to analyze the patterns within the graph and make a reasonable estimate that falls within the total range (interpolation) or outside the total range (extrapolation).
- Use various representations (qualitative, symbolic, pictorial) of the same data to help students view the data in different ways.
- Students, whenever possible, should perform multiple trials in their investigations to gain more confidence in their data and to detect possible errors.
- Have students compare data from different experiments, when appropriate, to look for patterns that may explain or connect different events.

References

American Association for the Advancement of Science. (1990). *Science for all Americans*. New York: Oxford University Press.

Dimitrov, D. (1999). Gender differences in science achievement: Differential effect of ability, response format, and strands of learning outcomes. *School Science and Mathematics, 99*(8), 445–450.

National Council of Teachers of Mathematics. (2000). *Principles and standards for school mathematics*. Reston, VA: NCTM.

National Research Council. (1996). *National Science Education Standards*. Washington, DC: National Academy Press.

UNIT II

Life Science

INVESTIGATION

LIFE CYCLE OF THE MEALWORM

(K–4)

Teaching Focus: Managing Inquiry Materials

Lesson 5.1
Moving Mealworms

ENGAGE

Take a look at the mealworm that your teacher is holding. Have you seen mealworms before? What do you notice about the mealworm? How does it remind you of other small animals such as a cat or a dog? How does a dog move around? What body parts does a dog use to move around?

You will watch the mealworm to learn more about how the mealworm moves around in its environment. Observe what mealworms do. See what body parts mealworms use to move and follow the path that mealworms take. Find out how mealworms interact with small objects in their environments. We will investigate the following question: **How does a mealworm move?**

EXPLORE

1. Watch three or four mealworms in a shallow container to observe how they move around.

2. What body parts does a mealworm use to move? Use a hand lens to look closer. Draw a picture of what you observe.

3. How do the mealworms move around objects in their environment? Place some small blocks in the container with the mealworms. Follow the path of a mealworm as it moves around. Draw a picture of the path the mealworm takes.

EXPLAIN

1. Use your observations and drawings to answer the following question: **How does a mealworm move?**

2. How does a mealworm use body parts on its head to move around?

3. What senses do you think a mealworm may be using to move?

EXTEND

1. Select one sense to investigate. How does a mealworm react or move to changes in ___________? Plan a way to test your ideas, remembering to be gentle to the mealworms so as not to hurt them. Outline your plan here:

2. Record your findings.

3. Share your findings with other student groups.

APPLY

1. Based on what you know about mealworms, build a simple maze for them. Make a plan for your maze using the materials provided by your teacher. Draw your plan for a mealworm maze below.

2. After your teacher approves your plan, build the maze and test it with the mealworms.

3. How did the mealworms move in the maze? Write a summary of your results with moving mealworms.

Lesson 5.1
Moving Mealworms
Teaching Focus: Managing Inquiry Materials

Studying animals in the classroom enables students to develop skills of observation and comparison, a sense of stewardship, and an appreciation for the unity, interrelationships, and complexity of life.

NSTA Position Statement

NSES CONTENT STANDARD, K–4: THE CHARACTERISTICS OF ORGANISMS

"The behavior of individual organisms is influenced by internal cues (such as hunger) and external cues (such as a change in the environment). Humans and other organisms have senses that help them detect internal and external cues" (National Research Council, 1996, p. 129).

NSES INQUIRY STANDARD, K–4

"Plan and conduct a simple investigation" (National Research Council, 1996, p. 122).

DESCRIPTIVE OBJECTIVE

Students will conduct investigations with mealworms to determine that mealworms use senses to detect cues from their environment.

MATERIALS

For each group of students, provide three or four mealworms in a shallow container such as a pie pan, hand lenses, and several small blocks. Students will need additional materials for exploring the mealworms' senses. These might include a flashlight or some other light source, vinegar on a cotton swab, or cotton balls. For maze building, provide small pieces of lightweight cardboard for a base, and additional building materials such as cardstock, craft sticks, clear plastic pieces, mirrors, and so on.

SCIENCE BACKGROUND: SETTING UP A MEALWORM HABITAT

Mealworms can be obtained from pet stores, bait shops, or biological supply houses. They are very inexpensive, usually 100 mealworms for about two dollars. Mealworms are not actually worms but the larval stage of the darkling beetle (*Tenebrio molitor*). (Pet stores may also have "super mealworms" (*Zophobas morio*) for sale. These are larger mealworms and may be a little more frightening to some students.) Keep the mealworms in a large, clear, flat container such as a plastic bin or an old aquarium. If the container has straight sides, it does not need a lid, thus allowing air circulation. Mealworms cannot crawl out of containers that have steeply angled sides with a slick surface, such as pie pans. They can, however, crawl out of containers such as paper plates or styrofoam meat trays. The mealworms will thrive in wheat bran, cornmeal or oatmeal. Keep the bran or meal about 4–5 centimeters deep in the container. Add a small piece of a potato or apple for moisture. Replace it when it dries out or becomes moldy. Do not add any water source to the habitat as mealworms can drown in very little water. Occasionally, you will need to make a fresh habitat, as molted skins and mealworm droppings (frass) will accumulate. The habitat should be kept in a warm, dry location, but out of direct sunlight.

MISCONCEPTION INFORMATION

Many young students have misconceptions as well as limited knowledge about insects. Some misconceptions that your students might have include:

- Insects are not animals.
- Insects are "bad," harmful, or scary.
- Larva die when they enter the pupa stage.

Some areas in which students may lack understanding or have questions include "baby insects," life cycles (including metamorphosis), and the classification of insects. For additional information, you may wish to refer to the following:

Barrow, L. H. (2002). What do elementary students know about insects? *Journal of Elementary Science Education*, *14*(2), 51–56.

Shepardson, D. (1997). Of butterflies and beetles: First graders' ways of seeing and talking about insect life cycles. *Journal of Research in Science Teaching, 34*, 873–890.

TEACHING FOCUS

Guidelines for Using Animals in Science Classrooms

The National Science Teachers Association (NSTA) has created a position statement called "Guidelines for Responsible Use of Animals in the Classroom." This statement is available for review at http://www.nsta.org/positionstatement&psid=44. This statement provides helpful information for working with live animals in a classroom. Teachers also need to be aware of local policies and guidelines for keeping classroom animals and for using animals in teaching activities.

TEACHING FOCUS

Ethical Treatment of Animals

Mealworms should always be treated with respect by the students. Have a discussion with students on guidelines to follow while handling mealworms. You can have this discussion during the Engage section of the lesson or as a separate mini-lesson. Develop a short list of general guidelines if your students have not worked with animals before, or remind them of guidelines if they have. These guidelines might include statements such as: (1) Be kind to the mealworms. (2) Touch the mealworms gently. (3) Don't hurt the mealworms. Post the guidelines in the classroom and refer to them during each lesson.

CLASSROOM SAFETY

Mealworms are clean and do not transmit disease, but children should wash their hands after handling them.

ENGAGE

Gather students around so that you can show them a mealworm that you are holding in your hand or in a clear container such as a petri dish. Ask the suggested questions to activate students' thinking and prior knowledge of other animals and how those animals make use of senses to move. Students may have noted that dogs smell many things as they walk. Have students record these ideas in the space provided, if desired. Discuss appropriate behavior by students toward the mealworms throughout the investigation. Focus the students' attention on the ways in which they will explore the following question: **How does a mealworm move?**

EXPLORE

1. Distribute the containers of mealworms and the hand lenses to each group of students. Encourage students to watch closely as the mealworms move around in the container. Mealworms are most active when they are at room temperature and are sluggish in cool environments.
2. The explorable question is split into two more specific questions to help students focus their explorations with the mealworms. The first question focuses on body parts that mealworms use to move, and the second one (#3) focuses on how mealworms interact with objects in their environment. Students should notice that mealworms have six legs near the front of the body, as well as two hind "legs" at the tail end. Students should also notice the antenna moving as the mealworm walks, the larval eye spots on the head, and the different segments of the abdomen. Students may say that the mealworm uses the antenna to feel its way around or the mealworm "sees" with its eyes. Help students with the names of body parts as needed (see Figure 5.1.1).
3. After the students have had a chance to observe and draw, give each group a few small blocks to place in the container. Encourage students to watch as the mealworms move around the straight-sided blocks hugging the walls or to observe whether they climb up and over shallow angled blocks. Move from group to group, asking students questions on how the mealworm moves in various situations. Students should follow the path of a mealworm as it moves around the container.

EXPLAIN

1. Students will have a variety of answers to the question "How does a mealworm move?" Accept all ideas at this point, noting in cases of disagreement that students will continue to observe mealworms in different situations in the Extend phase. Have all groups share at least one finding. Continue to give students the correct vocabulary for mealworm body parts as needed. Students may answer: *"The mealworm walks around and around the edge of the pan." "The mealworm tried to climb out of the pan but it was too slippery."* (This "slippery surfaces" answer can be saved and tested in Lesson 5.2.)

Figure 5.1.1

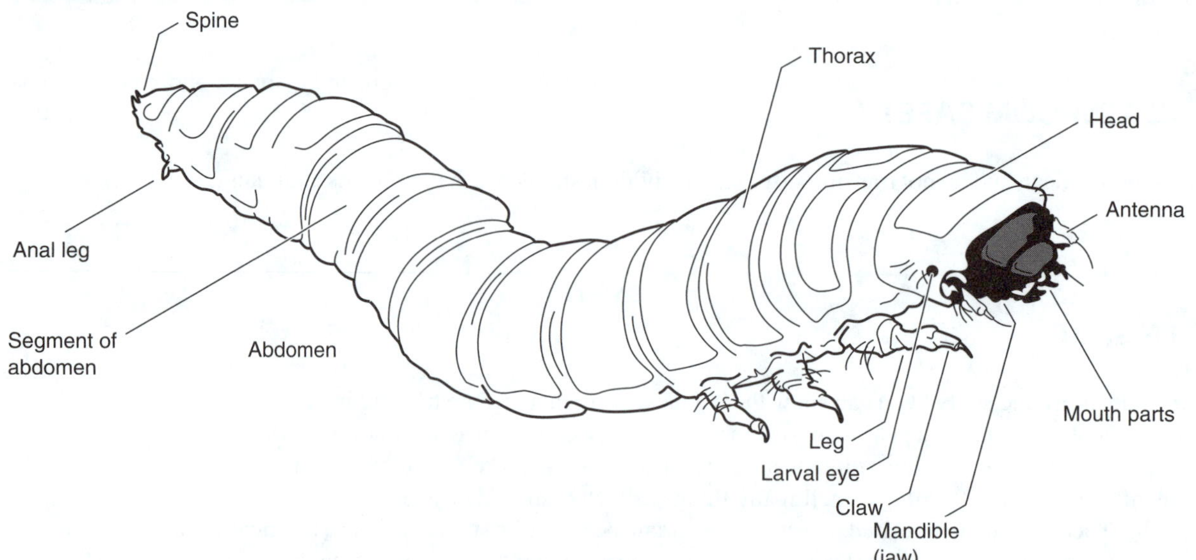

2. *"The mealworm feels its way around with its antenna."* (This idea can be saved and tested in the Extend phase.)
3. Student answers will vary but may include seeing, touching, and smelling.

   If you cannot complete the entire lesson in one day or one session, this is a good stopping point. When you are ready to begin again, do a quick review with the students and lead them into the Extend phase with a discussion of the following question: **What senses do mealworms use to move?**

> **Build Opportunities in Lessons for Sharing Ideas** *Teaching Tip*
>
> When students have completed an open-ended activity, they can benefit from sharing their findings with each other. Students will learn new information from each other and hear ideas different from their own. Students' ideas should be recorded when they will form the basis for another activity. Many teachers like to record these ideas on large chart paper to save them, especially when they won't be used immediately. This is in keeping with the Inquiry Standard: "Communicate investigations and explanations" (National Research Council, 1996, p. 122).

EXTEND

1. Students' answers will vary; for example, sight, touch (with antenna, the body, the legs, the tail, etc.), smell or taste (the mealworm may be searching for food and uses its antenna for smelling and tasting), hearing, and so on. Assist students with the names of the five senses as needed.
2. Students should select one idea to investigate. For example, "How does a mealworm react or move in response to changes in smell?" Have students make plans in small groups or brainstorm plans as a whole class before testing.

   Sample investigations can be conducted to test the mealworms' sense of smell. Students could dip one cotton swab into vinegar, and another into honey and then bran flakes. Students could watch how a mealworm reacts when each swab is held close to its head. Remind students to be gentle with the mealworms and to not touch them with the vinegar. Mealworms use their two antennae to smell, taste, and touch things in their environment. Mealworms will usually back up when they encounter undesirable circumstances.

   Students should record data and perform several trials with more than one mealworm. Not all mealworms will respond the same way, so students should test multiple times with multiple mealworms to look for trends.
3. Students should share their findings with the class. You probably should collect and save the data from the investigations on a large chart paper for future reference. You may want to use this Extend activity as an assessment exercise. Make sure the procedure that students followed and the data they collected align with the question. Students' answers will vary.

> **Allow Students to Investigate Their Own Ideas** *Teaching Tip*
>
> It is sometimes tempting to assign an idea to each small group, but students are usually much more motivated to work when they pursue their own ideas (Bransford, Brown, & Cocking, 1999, p. 90). Students will also gain experience in developing inquiry abilities (*National Research Council,* [1996]) that include asking a question, and planning and conducting a simple investigation.

APPLY

1. Students should have many ideas about mealworms' movements. The plan for a maze should demonstrate some of these ideas. Ask questions to promote students' thinking as well as to help them understand that the maze is for learning more about how a mealworm moves, not just for fun. Some possible questions might include the following: What will you find out about the mealworm from using these materials? How do you think the mealworm will react to clear plastic? Why do you want to include a mirror in your maze? Simple mazes with clear goals are more helpful for

Teaching Focus

Use Commonplace Materials to Improve Accessibility to Science

For many science inquiry investigations, students should use commonplace materials. A teacher can become frustrated by constantly searching for materials that students request. Designate a location in the classroom where you collect and keep "good junk" materials handy for students to find and use whenever needed. This area could include scrap pieces of cardboard, yogurt or margarine containers, tin cans, craft sticks, cotton swabs, wax paper, aluminum pie pans, and so on. Decide on and post guidelines for access to the materials as well as their neat storage and use.

student learning. Complex mazes may be too confusing to allow students to draw conclusions.

2. Review and approve students' maze building plans. Students should draw a diagram of the maze. The drawings will help students to design the maze and later will be used as a plan to follow in building the maze. Younger students usually can convey more information in a drawing than in a written description. If students do not have a clear plan to follow with the study of mealworm movement as its goal, then the building of the maze may turn into a craft type activity rather than a science investigation.
3. Student summaries should describe new information that they learned from observing the mealworms moving through the mazes. For example, students may observe that mealworms walk along walls or barriers and even turn corners, use their antenna to touch objects as they walk, and do not need food as a reward to go through a maze. Look for students' descriptions that show an understanding that external changes in the environment influence the mealworms' behavior.

Lesson 5.2
Where Do Mealworms Go?

ENGAGE

Take a look at our mealworm habitat. What do you notice? Where are the mealworms? What are possible reasons for where the mealworms are? Write your ideas below.

Now we have lots of great ideas to try with the mealworms. To test some of our ideas, we will start by investigating the following: **Do mealworms go to light or dark places?**

You will need to conduct a fair test with the mealworms to answer that question. To make the test fair, you must treat all the mealworms in the same way. Only one thing at a time is changed in a fair test. You will change the amount of light in the test by having both a light place and a dark place for mealworms to go. Count the number of mealworms in each place to answer the following question: **Do mealworms go to light or dark places?**

EXPLORE

1. Make a test habitat for the mealworms. Lay a sheet of dark colored construction paper in a small tray to cover approximately half of the surface.

2. Place several mealworms in the tray near the edge of the paper (see Figure 5.2.1). Observe the mealworms for 3 minutes. Count how many mealworms are underneath the paper (dark place). Count how many mealworms are in the tray or on top of the paper (light places). Record your data.

Figure 5.2.1

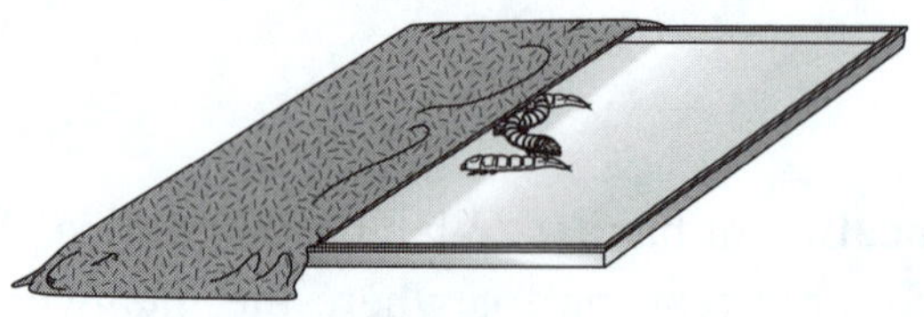

Trial #1	Light Places	Dark Places
____________	____________	____________

3. Repeat the test two more times. Record the data for each test.

Trial #2	Light Places	Dark Places
____________	____________	____________

Trial #3	Light Places	Dark Places
____________	____________	____________

4. Graph the results of all three tests.

EXPLAIN

1. How many times did mealworms go to dark places?

2. How many times did mealworms go to light places?

3. Do mealworms tend to go to light or dark places?

4. What are some possible reasons that not all of the mealworms go to the same place?

EXTEND

1. Review your ideas on why the mealworms were under the cereal. Select one of your ideas from the Engage phase for further testing to find out what other kinds of places mealworms go to in their environment. For example, **do mealworms go to ___________or ___________ places?**

2. Create a test habitat for the mealworms. After your teacher approves your test habitat, try it out with the mealworms. Observe the mealworms for 3 minutes. Count the mealworms and record your data.

Trial #1	**Places**	**Places**
____________	____________	____________

3. Repeat the test two more times. Record your data for each test.

Trial #2	**Places**	**Places**
____________	____________	____________

Trial #3	**Places**	**Places**
____________	____________	____________

4. Add up the numbers of mealworms for all three trials for each place that you tested. To which place did the mealworms tend to go more often?___________ Write a summary to answer your question.

5. Share your findings with other student groups.

APPLY

Now you know a lot more about where mealworms tend to go. Design a habitat for mealworms for your classroom. Draw a picture of the habitat. Write a summary that answers the following question: Where do mealworms go?

Lesson 5.2

Where Do Mealworms Go?

Teaching Focus: Managing Inquiry Materials

NSES CONTENT STANDARD, K–4: THE CHARACTERISTICS OF ORGANISMS

"Organisms have basic needs. . . . Organisms can survive only in environments in which their needs can be met. The world has many different environments and distinct environments that support the life of different types of organisms" (National Research Council, 1996, p. 129).

NSES INQUIRY STANDARD, K–4

"Ask a question about objects, organisms, and events in the environment" (National Research Council, 1996, p. 122).

DESCRIPTIVE OBJECTIVE

Students will conduct investigations with mealworms to determine that mealworms prefer a very dry, warm, and dark environment with plenty of meal to eat.

MATERIALS

For each group of students, provide a small, flat tray such as a pie pan or cookie sheet, dark-colored construction paper, and a timing device such as an egg timer. For investigations in the Extend phase, students will request a variety of things such as different types of mealworm food (apple slices, peanut butter, cereal, carrots, etc.); different materials for habitats such as leaves, shredded newspaper, and small pieces of clear cellophane; and different surface materials such as foil, terrycloth, and sandpaper.

SCIENCE BACKGROUND

Mealworms live in dry, dark, warm environments. They tend to crawl under things to find dark locations. Mealworms will usually avoid wet or cold locations by backing up or wandering around until they find a "better" location. Mealworms also tend to avoid slick or smooth surfaces, such as aluminum foil, in favor of a rough surface, such as a paper towel. Sometimes mealworms use their mouth parts to hang onto surfaces if they are moved quickly. Mealworms will even hang onto the skin of a student's or teacher's hand. Mealworms, however, do not hurt or injure students.

> **TEACHING FOCUS**
>
> **Manage Science Materials by Creating Group Tubs or Boxes**
>
> For science activities that require many materials for each group, students need an efficient, convenient system to get materials and to clean up afterward. For group work, teachers can put all basic materials for each group in a tub or on a tray such as a dishpan, a cafeteria tray, or a cookie sheet. Assemble tubs ahead of time so that students can pick up tubs immediately after the Engage phase, clean up after the activities, and return the tubs. Having a routine and set expectations with your students makes managing materials less stressful!

TEACHING FOCUS

Ethical Treatment of Animals

Students should always treat mealworms with respect and not harm them in the investigations. Remind students of the class's guidelines.

CLASSROOM SAFETY

Mealworms are clean and do not transmit disease, but children should wash their hands after handling them.

ENGAGE

Gather students around and show them the mealworm habitat. If you need to pick the habitat up or move it, try not to disturb the mealworms. Most of the mealworms in the habitat will be hidden from view until they are disturbed. Ask the suggested questions to activate students' thinking and previous learning from Lesson 5.1. Have students record these ideas in the space provided, if desired, or record them as a group on the chalkboard. Because young elementary students have difficulty controlling variables in an experiment, this lesson focuses on students conducting a "fair test." Students will follow a suggested format for testing in the Explore phase that they will use again with their own ideas in the Extend phase. Focus the students' attention on the following question: **Do mealworms go to light or dark places?**

Teaching Tip

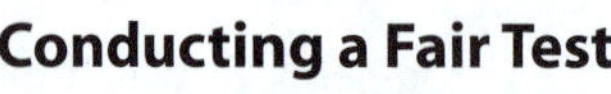

Conducting a Fair Test

In a science experiment, typically only one factor or variable is changed at a time to determine what effect it might have in the experiment. This is a complex type of thinking that is very difficult for young children. It is easier for young children to think about conducting a fair test. Students should try to keep everything the same in their tests except for the one variable that changes. Throughout the lesson, ask students questions such as "Is it fair to put some mealworms here and some mealworms there or should they all be started in the same place? Is it fair to give some mealworms more time to move?"

EXPLORE

1. In this lesson, the format of the Explore activity will enable students to gain experience in testing their own ideas later in the Extend phase. The explorable question is narrowed here to help students control variables and test one factor at a time: **Do mealworms go to light or dark places?**
2. Help students realize that conducting a fair test means that they will change only the amount of light with the construction paper. Students should carefully put several (three to five) mealworms near the paper in the tray at the same time. Students should watch the mealworms for 3 minutes without touching them or moving the tray. After 3 minutes, students should count how many mealworms are underneath the paper in a dark place and how many are in the light. (If the mealworms are sluggish, you might put the habitat in a warmer spot). Students will probably wonder what to do with a mealworm that is partially under the paper. A general rule is that if the mealworm is halfway on each side, then count the side that the head is on. If the mealworm is more than halfway on one side, then count it as being on that side.
3. Students will repeat the test two more times, recording the number of mealworms. Not all mealworms will do the same thing each time.
4. Students should make a bar graph (histogram) for their totals.

TEACHING FOCUS

Addressing Students' Fear of Working with Small Animals Like Mealworms or Insects

Many students, at first, may be afraid of the mealworms or of any insects and may refuse to pick up the mealworms with their hands. Show students how to move the mealworms by having them crawl onto a small artist's paintbrush or by gently scooping them up with a plastic spoon.

Developing Bar Graphs or Histograms

Teaching Tip

Bar graphs or histograms are an appropriate type of graph to represent categorical data. The students will be comparing two types of places, light and dark, so they will have two categories of data. They will place these categories on the horizontal *x*-axis of the graph. The data that was measured or counted (the number of mealworms) will go on the vertical *y*-axis. (See Figure 5.2.2.) Students should always label the axes and title the graph.

Figure 5.2.2 Sample student data

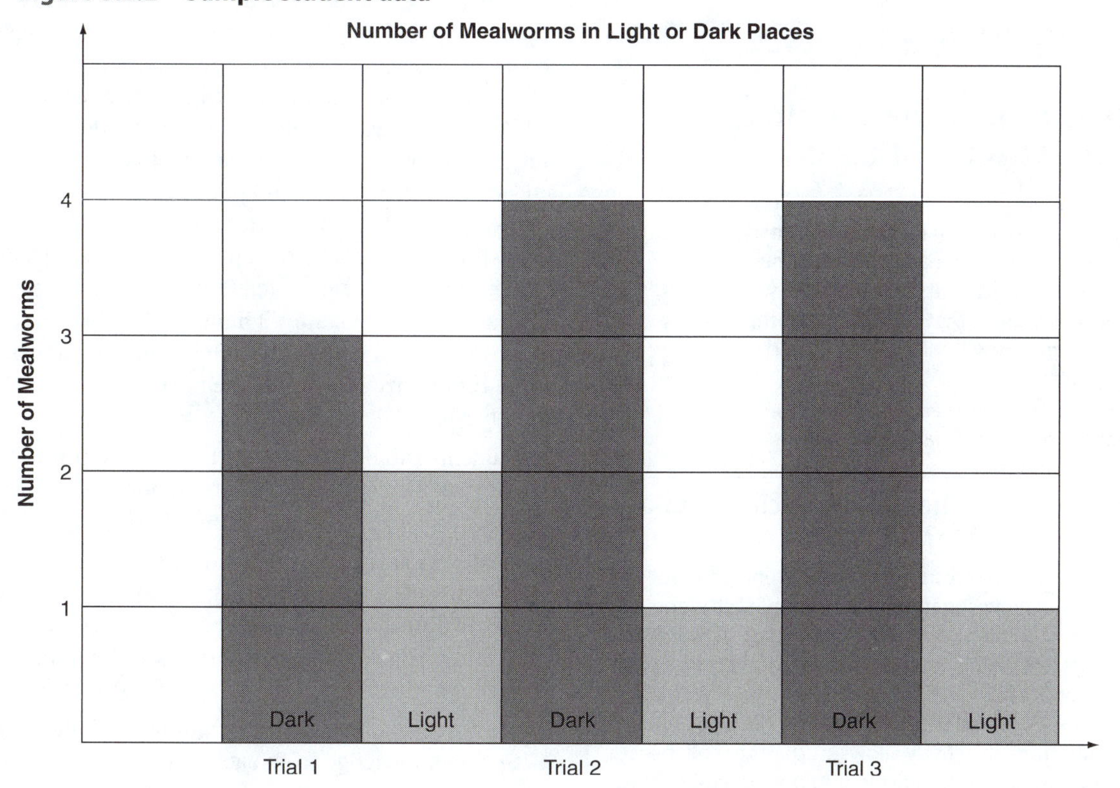

EXPLAIN

1. Discuss what the students found out from the fair test. Student answers will vary.
2. Student answers will vary. See sample data.
3. Mealworms tend to go to dark places, but not all mealworms will go to darker places each time. In this case, with the data of an entire class from three trials, the mealworms should clearly prefer a dark place. If appropriate, you may want your students to add up class totals and make another bar graph from the class data. Help students understand that a mealworm habitat should have some dark places for the mealworms. Assist students with the vocabulary word *habitat*, the place where an animal or plant lives.
4. Mealworms, as well as other organisms, are affected by other factors such as hunger, temperature, molting, and so on.

EXTEND

1. Students should have generated several possible reasons in the Engage activity for why the mealworms tend to stay underneath the bran. Now they will conduct another fair test to find out other places that mealworms will go to. Some ideas might be places

with mealworm food such as bran versus some other type of food, warm versus cold places, wet versus dry places, smooth versus rough surfaces, leaves versus clear cellophane pieces, and so on. (**Caution:** Make sure that wet paper towels do not have any puddles of water if students test for wet versus dry places. Mealworms will drown in very little water!)

2. Check each group's plan prior to students conducting the test to ensure that only one variable is tested and that the students have determined an appropriate way to accomplish this. Assist students in using the term *fair test* in an appropriate way. A sample investigation might be to test warm versus cold places. Students could choose two ceramic tiles, putting one tile in the refrigerator or cold water and the other in warm water or in their hands for a few minutes. Students would then place the two tiles upside down and side by side in a tray and put the mealworms in the middle, where the tiles meet. (Because the surface of the tiles is very slippery to mealworms, place the unglazed side up for this test.) Students will watch the reactions of the mealworms and count them after 3 minutes. Mealworms usually back away from undesirable environments such as the cold tile. Emphasize respect for the mealworms so that they are not harmed.
3. Students should perform multiple trials, if time permits. Three trials may not provide conclusive data.
4. Students should analyze the data to draw a conclusion. Sometimes the data may show that the mealworms have no preference for one place over another. You can help students think about this in their own lives.
5. Students should share their findings with the class to gain knowledge from each test that was conducted. Afterward, help students summarize their learning about mealworm environments. Groups may have conflicting results.

TEACHING FOCUS

Discuss Appropriate Animal Investigations with Students

You should always know what tests students are planning to perform with live animals. Most children are not intentionally cruel, but they may not foresee harmful results. For example, some students may believe that if you cut a worm into halves, both halves will still live. You would never want students to do this!

Teaching Tip

What Would Scientists Do?

The results from the Extend phase of this investigation may enable students to think about how scientists deal with conflicting results. The *NSES* Inquiry Standards state that "Scientists review and ask questions about the results of other scientists' work" (National Research Council, 1996, p. 123). Discussing results from an activity allows students to collaborate on their findings, as scientists do, to find possible reasons for different results. Young children might find out that they performed tests differently, collected data differently, or changed more than one variable at a time. The discussions can point out the need for repeating an experiment, for making accurate measurements, and for recording data.

APPLY

Students will now have much more knowledge about what types of places mealworms prefer. Encourage students to apply that knowledge (dry, dark, warm environments with "hiding places" and plenty of food) to the habitats they design. Decide whether you want students to actually use these ideas to build individual habitats for Lesson 5.3. Use the rubric in Table 5.2.1 to assess students' habitat designs.

Table 5.2.1 Rubric for Habitats for Mealworms

Criteria	1 point	3 points	5 points
Container	Students use a container but mealworms will likely escape from it.	Students use a steep-sided container that prohibits mealworms from crawling out, but is too large or too small.	Students select an appropriate-sized container with steep sides that prohibits mealworms from crawling out.
Environment	Students consider the environmental conditions, but select an inappropriate area such as a sunny window.	Students select a warm place to store the habitat.	Students select a warm place to store the habitat with little disturbance. Students consider a way to provide darkness for the mealworms.
Food	Students consider food, but have not learned what mealworms eat.	Students include a small portion of meal for food.	Students include a large quantity of grain for food and an appropriate source of moisture (not water).

Lesson 5.3

What Do Mealworms Look Like As They Grow?

ENGAGE

Look at two of your friends in class. Describe what they look like. How are they alike? How are they different? What do you think they will look like as they grow up?

Now look at the two mealworms that your teacher is holding. Describe what mealworms look like. **How are the mealworms alike? How are they different? What will the mealworms look like as they grow?**

EXPLORE

1. Observe two mealworms in a shallow container. Look for ways in which the mealworms are the same. Look for ways in which the mealworms are different. You may want to use a hand lens and a ruler. Record your observations.

Same	**Different**

2. Draw each mealworm and show how they are different.

EXPLAIN

1. Why do you think that not all mealworms look exactly the same?

2. Label all of the parts of the mealworm that you know on your drawings. Add additional labels that your teacher provides.

3. How do you think the mealworm will change as it grows? Write down your ideas. Make another drawing that shows how you think the mealworm may change.

EXTEND

To find out how mealworms change, you will observe mealworms for several weeks. Make a record of your observations. **What do mealworms look like as they grow?**

Date	Drawing	Observations

After several weeks, you should see the mealworms undergo some exciting changes. How did the mealworms change?

APPLY

What other living creatures do you know that make similar changes as they grow?

Lesson 5.3

What Do Mealworms Look Like As They Grow?

Teaching Focus: Managing Inquiry Materials

NSES CONTENT STANDARD, K–4: LIFE CYCLES OF ORGANISMS

"Plants and animals have life cycles that include being born, developing into adults, reproducing, and eventually dying. The details of this life cycle are different for different organisms" (National Research Council, 1996, p. 129).

DESCRIPTIVE OBJECTIVE

Students will observe and describe the changes that a mealworm goes through in its life cycle including the larval stage, the pupa, and the adult.

MATERIALS

For each group of students, provide two mealworms of different sizes or colors (mealworms are much paler in color immediately after molting), a hand lens, and a ruler, if appropriate. For the Extend phase, students will need to observe the mealworms regularly. The students should use a small container of their own such as a baby food jar or small plastic margarine container for this activity.

SCIENCE BACKGROUND

Mealworms undergo a complete metamorphosis during their life cycle: egg, larva, pupa, and adult (see Figure 5.3.1). Other organisms that undergo complete metamorphosis include butterflies, moths, bees, and frogs. Some organisms go through an incomplete or simple metamorphosis of three stages: egg, nymph, and adult. The nymph usually looks similar to the adult but may be missing some parts that will slowly appear as the nymph grows. Grasshoppers are a common example of organisms that undergo incomplete metamorphosis.

> **TEACHING FOCUS**
>
> **Ethical Treatment of Animals**
>
> Students should always treat mealworms with respect and not harm them in the investigations. Remind students of the class guidelines.

CLASSROOM SAFETY

Mealworms are clean and do not transmit disease, but children should wash their hands after handling them. For this extended activity, you may continue to use the habitat you used in the first lesson. Mealworms will go through their entire life cycle within the habitat if provided enough food and moisture. You will probably need to clean the habitat once during this period to remove molted skins and droppings.

Figure 5.3.1 Changes of a mealworm throughout its life cycle

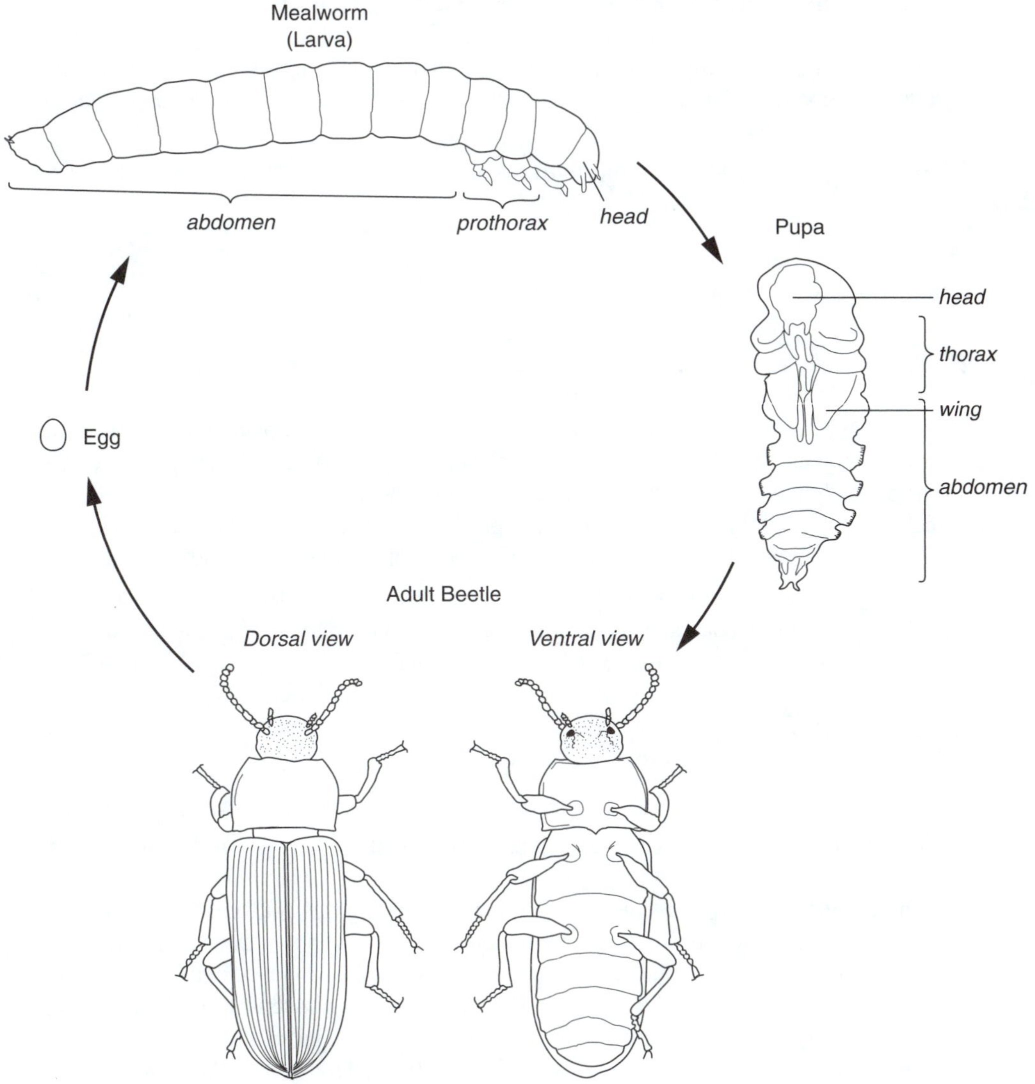

ENGAGE

Ask two students to stand together. Ask the class to describe the two students and describe similarities and differences. Students of the same age often share many characteristics, but they are not identical. (Even twins have slight differences.) Have students predict what the students will look like as they grow. Then, gather students around to observe two mealworms that you are holding in your hand or in a clear container such as a petri dish. Ask students to describe the mealworms. Students should be able to give many details now that they haved participated in the first two lessons. Ask students how they could find more similarities and differences in the mealworms. Focus students' attention on the following questions: **How are mealworms alike? How are they different? How will they change as they grow?**

EXPLORE

1. Distribute the materials to each group of students. Encourage students to look closely and use the hand lens and ruler, if appropriate. Moving mealworms are difficult to measure, so you may just want students to compare mealworms rather than try to

measure their length or width. Students should find that the mealworms have many of the same characteristics such as number of legs (six), number of segments (13), two antennae, and so on. Differences may include length, width, or color. Mealworms grow in length and girth each time they shed their skins or exoskeletons. The color of a mealworm varies with the age of its exoskeleton, from pale white immediately after molting to dark golden yellow.

2. Students' drawings should indicate that while mealworms are very similar, they are not identical.

EXPLAIN

1. Students will have various answers to the question because it asks "Why do you think. . . ." Mealworms vary in appearance, as all organisms do, but mainly because they vary in age and in the amount of time since their last molting. Explain the process of molting to students. Mealworms and similar organisms have a hard exoskeleton that protects the animal but does not grow or expand. Therefore, the animal must cast off or *molt* its exoskeleton several times during its juvenile period of growth. The hard exoskeleton splits and is cast off, and the animal emerges with a new soft exoskeleton, which will harden.
2. Students should label the parts of the mealworm so that they can discuss similarities and differences. Give students the appropriate names as needed after they have completed as much on their own as possible. You may want to make a transparency of Figure 5.3.2.

EXTEND

1. Student answers will vary for changes to the mealworm (e.g., it gets bigger, gets older, changes in color, etc.). Some students may know about the life cycle of a butterfly and relate that to mealworms. Accept their ideas, but don't tell students about the metamorphosis. Allow students the excitement of finding this out for themselves. You can speed up the mealworms' life cycle by providing them with ample food and moisture from a slice of apple or potato and by keeping them in a warm place in the classroom. You could also start a colony a few weeks before teaching these lessons; thus, the mealworms will be older and closer to undergoing metamorphosis. The larval stage may last for approximately 2 months, depending on food supply and temperature. You should provide students with the appropriate vocabulary as needed throughout the Extend phase of the

Figure 5.3.2

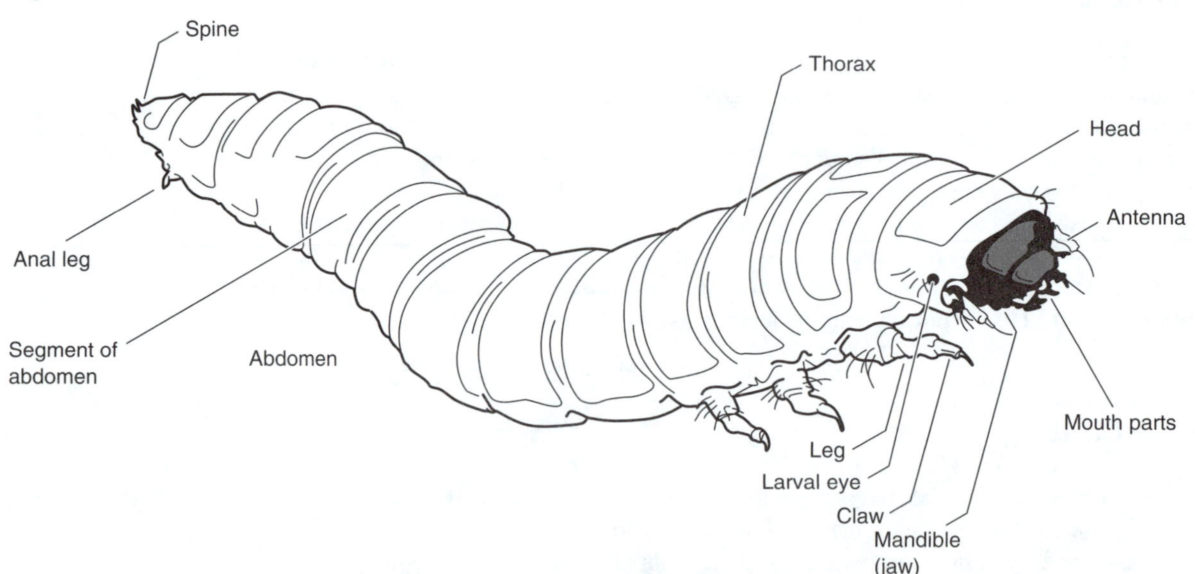

lesson (e.g., when students find that mealworms have entered the *pupa* stage).

2. Students should regularly observe the mealworms and make drawings and written observations. It is helpful and exciting for students to keep their own small container of three or four mealworms to watch. These containers can be stored in their desks or in a small basket when students aren't observing them.
3. Students may be surprised when mealworms move into the pupa stage and may think they have died. Most pupae will twitch if lightly touched, so you can do this to show that they are alive during this stage. The pupal stage generally lasts 1 to 2 weeks depending on temperature. The adult beetle will emerge and will darken in color as the exoskeleton hardens. The adults will lay eggs and soon die. After the students have observed the beetles, explain the process of metamorphosis. (See details in the Science Background section.)

APPLY

Students can document and apply their learning by creating classroom books. The students can experience an authentic science writing assignment by generating a portion of a book on metamorphosis or on the life cycles of insects. Most insect species such as butterflies, moths, beetles, and flies undergo complete metamorphosis. A few insects such as grasshoppers and cockroaches undergo incomplete metamorphosis. For a book on metamorphosis, you could also include the metamorphosis of amphibians such as frogs, toads, salamanders, and newts. Because students may find it difficult to gather enough suitable information to write individual reports, they might prefer to write and illustrate short reports in pairs or small groups. Each group then could focus on the life cycle of a different animal. These reports can be organized into a class book.

TEACHING FOCUS

Managing Regular Observations

For ease in management, you should develop a routine for completing observations over a period of time. Decide whether you will have one large habitat for all the students to watch for changes, or one small habitat for each student. Students enjoy having their own habitats to observe and will generally watch them more closely if they have easy access to them. In addition, biological processes cannot be scheduled, thus the class will miss many exciting changes if students have only one habitat to watch.

TEACHING FOCUS

Disposing of Animals Used for Experimentation

Decide what you will do with the mealworms once the students have finished observing the life cycle. NEVER RELEASE ANY PURCHASED ORGANISM INTO THE LOCAL ENVIRONMENT. Many invasive and undesirable species are accidentally spread through such careless practices. Even though mealworms are quite common, you should plan other ways to dispose of the mealworms. For example, you could simply keep the mealworms in the classroom, give them to another teacher to use, give them to someone as food for pet reptiles, or, as a last resort, put them into a freezer to kill them very quickly and humanely.

Teaching Focus Summary: Managing Inquiry Materials

- Follow local policies and the NSTA guidelines for live animals in the classroom.
- Closely supervise all student activities with animals.
- Model appropriate care, handling, and respect for the animals with students.
- Develop a system for distribution and cleanup of materials.
- Do not release purchased organisms into the local environment.

References

Bransford, J. D., Brown, A., & Cocking, R. (Eds.). (1999). *How people learn: Brain, mind, experience, and school*. Washington, DC: National Academy Press.

Mason, A. (1998). *Mealworms: Raise them, watch them, see them change*. Tonawanda, NY: Kids Can Press.

National Research Council. (1996). *National Science Education Standards*. Washington, DC: National Academy Press.

National Science Teachers Association. (1991). *Guidelines for responsible use of animals in the classroom*. Retrieved September 28, 2004, from http://www.nsta.org/positionstatement&psid=2

INVESTIGATION 6

FLOWERING PLANTS (5–8)

Teaching Focus: Integrating Reading in Science Instruction

Lesson 6.1

Flower Power

ENGAGE

Based on your past experiences, draw a quick sketch of a flower. Now take a look at the flower that your teacher is holding. What do you notice about the flower? How is it similar to other flowers that you have seen? How is it different? How does it compare to your sketch? What are the different parts of a flower? What is inside a flower? How can you classify what you find in a flower?

We will investigate the following question: **What parts make up a flower and how might these parts be classified?**

EXPLORE

1. Examine your flower closely with a hand lens to see the different parts. Use a toothpick to carefully remove the different pieces of the flower. As you remove the parts, classify them into groups. Explain why you made the different groups.

2. Compare your classification system of the flower parts with those of other students. How is yours the same? Different?

3. Examine the different parts of the flower. Sketch what you observe.

4. Obtain a different type of flower from your teacher. Do you think it will have the same types of parts as the first flower? Repeat steps 1–3 above.

EXPLAIN

1. How do the parts of the two different flowers compare? How are they alike? Different? Compare your findings with those of your classmates.

2. Your teacher has a diagram of the parts of a flower. How does your classification of the parts compare to the flower parts in the diagram? Use the diagram to label the parts of your two flowers.

3. How does the flower you drew at the beginning of the lesson compare to the diagram?

EXTEND

1. You probably observed a great deal of variation among the flowers. Scientists classify some of these variations in the ways that are described below. Read each passage and determine how the characteristics of your flowers compare.

SCIENCE READING

MONOCOTS AND DICOTS

The major way scientists classify flowering plants is by counting the number of petals, sepals, or stamens that a flower has. Petals, stamens, and sepals are always found in groups either of 3, or of 4 or 5. For example, six petals in a flower would be a multiple of 3, but not a multiple of 4 or 5.

Flowering plants are classified into two large groups. Monocots have petals, sepals, and stamens that occur in groups of 3. For example, a flower that has six petals must be a monocot because 6 is a multiple of 3. Dicots have petals, sepals, and stamens that occur in groups of either 4 or 5. So, if you count four sepals, the flower must be a dicot because 4 is a multiple of 4 ($4 \times 1 = 4$). Monocots and dicots have other characteristics that are used for classification. These characteristics are shown in Table 6.1.1.

Table 6.1.1

Characteristic	Dicotyledons	Monocotyledons
Arrangement of petals, sepals, and stamens	4 or 5, or multiples of 4 or 5	3, or multiples of 3
Number of seed leaves (cotyledons)	2	1
Usual pattern of the veins in the leaf	Network of veins in many arrangements	Veins are parallel

Figure 6.1.1 A dandelion

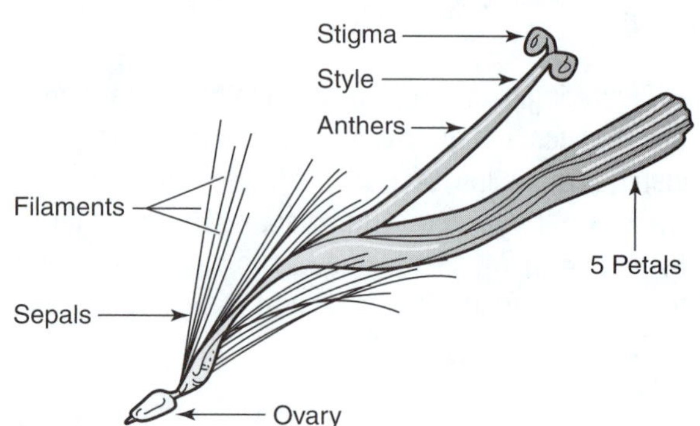

COMPOSITE FLOWERS

Some flowers are actually made up of many tiny flowers. Each of these tiny flowers is a complete flower with all of the parts noted before. These flowers are known as *composite* flowers (rather than a single flower). In some composite flowers, all of the tiny flowers are the same. The dandelion (Figure 6.1.1) is a common example of a composite flower. Unless you looked closely, however, you would not notice that each is actually made up of dozens of tiny flowers. Other composite flowers, such as sunflowers, have two types of tiny flowers: one type around the edge of the composite flower, and the other in the center.

MALE AND FEMALE FLOWERS

Most of the flowers that we see every day contain both male and female parts. Some flowers, however, contain the male parts (the stamens) but not the female part (the pistil). Other flowers may contain a pistil, but not the stamens. You can recognize a female flower by finding the pistil and looking for the ovary, which often looks like a tiny fruit. If you look at a male flower, you will find the stamens easily and see that the pistil is missing. Sometimes both male and female flowers are found on the same plant. A pumpkin plant, for example, has both male and female flowers (Figure 6.1.2). Sometimes, however, a plant has only male flowers or only female flowers. The holly is an example of this type of plant.

Figure 6.1.2 Pumpkin flowers

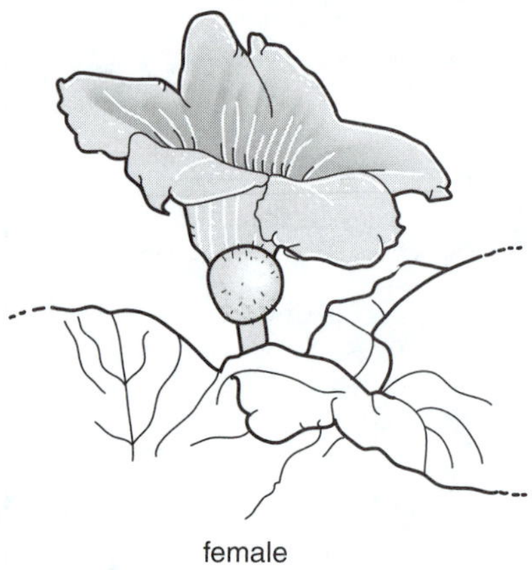

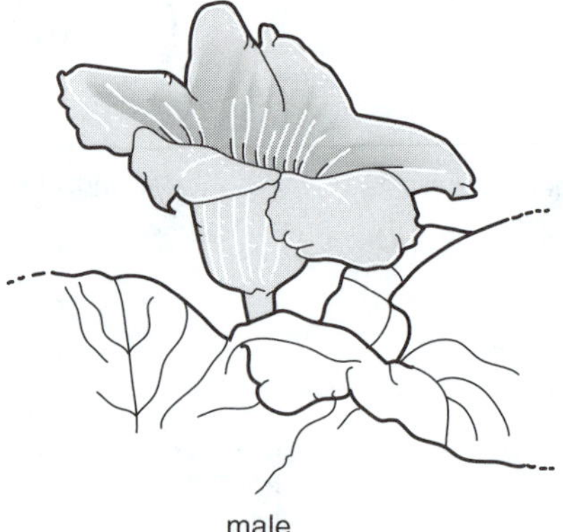

2. Keeping the above reading in mind, observe your flowers again. Which description fits your flower best? Explain. Observe your classmates' flowers to determine what type they are.

3. Pretend you are an inspector at an artificial flower factory. Examine the artificial flower that your teacher provides. Did the person that designed the flower understand flower parts as well as you? Explain why or why not.

APPLY

1. Now that you know some of the classifications of flowers, let's look at another pattern that you might find in your flowers. Mathematicians find patterns in nature and express those patterns with numerical relationships. You may be familiar with the Fibonacci sequence (0, 1, 1, 2, 3, 5, 8, 13, 21, . . .). In this sequence of numbers, each new term is the sum of the two previous terms. This pattern is often found in nature, and often the numbers of petals on flowers are Fibonacci numbers. Count the number of petals on your flower from the previous activity. Is it a Fibonacci number? Compare your results to those of your classmates.

2. Now count the number of petals on an artificial flower provided by your teacher. Is it a Fibonacci number? Compare your results to those of your classmates. Do you have more Fibonacci numbers from the real flowers or the artificial flowers?

Lesson 6.1
Flower Power
Teaching Focus: Integrating Reading in Science Instruction

A seed hidden in the heart of an apple is an orchard invisible.

An Old Welsh Proverb

NSES CONTENT STANDARD, 5–8: DIVERSITY AND ADAPTATIONS OF ORGANISMS

"Although different species might look dissimilar, the unity among organisms becomes apparent from an analysis of internal structures" (National Research Council, 1996, p. 158).

DESCRIPTIVE OBJECTIVE

Students will investigate flower structure to determine the basic structures common to most flowers as well as some of the differences among flower types.

MATERIALS

For each group of students, provide two or three different kinds of flowers (see the description below for help in selecting flowers), hand lenses, and small tools such as toothpicks, tweezers (or forceps), and small cuticle scissors (often available at "dollar" stores), for taking the flowers apart. During the Explain phase of the lesson, students may find it helpful to tape their flower parts to a sheet of heavyweight paper. You will also need either an overhead transparency or photocopies of the flower diagram (p. 151). Finally, you need artificial flowers (most are usually missing some of their parts) for the application portion of the lesson. Either silk or plastic flowers should work.

SCIENCE BACKGROUND

Ideally, these lessons on flowers should be taught within a larger unit on plants. Although students can learn a great deal about flowers and fruit separately, the experience of observing fruit grow from flowers on plants is very valuable and exciting. Flowers are the reproductive organs of the large group of plants known as the *angiosperms*, or flowering plants. The flower's function is to produce seeds through sexual reproduction by the process of pollination. After fertilization, the flower develops into a fruit that is the container for the seed(s).

The structures of flowers vary widely, but most flowers have the same basic parts: sepals, the outside whorl of petal-like structures that are often green; petals, the thin, often colored structures that surround the center of the flower; the androecium, the male structures (including the stamens with the pollen); and the gynoecium, the female structures (including the pistil where seeds are produced).

Flowers can be classified into two major subclasses, monocotyledons and dicotyledons, based on the variation in their structures. See the student readings for additional information on classification.

MISCONCEPTION INFORMATION

Although much research exists on students' ideas about plants, little research focuses on flowers and fruits. You may, however, encounter misconceptions such as the following:

- All fruits taste sweet.
- Some vegetables have seeds.
- A sunflower or a dandelion is a single flower.

For information on plant misconceptions, you may wish to refer to the following:

Bianchi, L. (2000). So what do you think a plant is? *Primary Science Review, 61*, 15–17.

Ozay, E., & Oztas, H. (2003). Secondary students' interpretations of photosynthesis and plant nutrition. *Journal of Biological Education, 37*(2), 68–70.

CLASSROOM SAFETY

Check on students' allergies before bringing flowers into the classroom. Children should wash their hands after handling the flowers. Although many flowers are edible, caution students not to ingest any flowers because some flowers are poisonous.

ENGAGE

Have students, based on their prior knowledge, make a sketch of a flower. Display a flower and initiate a discussion about students' experiences with flowers. Encourage students to consider how flowers can be compared. Focus students on the following explorable question: What parts make up a flower and how might these parts be classified?

EXPLORE

1. Initially, students find it easier to observe larger flowers whose individual parts are readily visible such as tulips, daffodils, or lilies. Depending on the flower, a magnifying lens is a necessary tool for examining the parts. The toothpick is useful for splitting open the

TEACHING FOCUS

Introducing Vocabulary

Avoid naming the parts at this time as this will divert students' attention from the conceptual question. Students can easily become bogged down with vocabulary, especially new, unfamiliar terms. Generally, you should introduce vocabulary during the Explain phase of a learning cycle lesson. As a rule of thumb, you should not introduce vocabulary until it is inconvenient not to have it. This usually occurs at some point in the lesson—usually during discussion in the Explain phase.

Teaching Tip

Developing the Process of Classifying

It is tempting to simply tell students the names of the four major flower parts (stamen, pistil, sepal, and petal). But doing so merely leads to students following directions and not to an understanding of classification. Classification is an important skill for students to develop. Because classification requires higher order thinking it takes time and practice to develop. Therefore, a better strategy is to have students focus on the actual sorting, reflect on the specific observations they made, and then use them to develop their classification scheme.

pistil of many flowers. In addition, your students, depending on their maturity, can use inexpensive cuticle scissors and tweezers for dissection, which are often available at "dollar" stores. Alternatively, you could borrow dissection equipment from a secondary school science teacher. Encourage students to devise their own categories for classification of the flower parts. As noted above, students do not have to use the proper terminology for naming their groups.

2. Student classifications are likely to be incomplete. They may show knowledge of some rudimentary flower parts, but probably not of all of them (particularly the internal parts).

   Encourage students to critically compare their classification of plant parts with those of their classmates. This exposes them to alternative ways of thinking about flowers and the classification of flowers.

3. After discussing their classification systems with classmates, students should be prepared to make a sketch of the critical parts of their flower.

4. In this part of the investigation, the students are trying to determine whether any two different flowers have the same basic parts. Their work will be easier if the two flowers have significant differences, such as size, the type of flower, or the number of each flower part. You may wish to review the readings related to flower variation in the student pages. Flowers to consider include roses, carnations, daisies, and so on.

TEACHING FOCUS

Diversity—Provide a Language-Rich Environment

Provide many opportunities for students to learn the language of science as they experience science. All students will find this helpful, but especially English language learners. You may want to have a word wall that focuses on the science unit. Many teachers use index cards for important vocabulary. A picture or diagram on each card may help support student learning. You can reorganize these cards to include new words throughout a unit. You could also arrange the cards into large concept maps on the classroom wall, connecting them with pieces of yarn.

TEACHING FOCUS

Vocabulary Development

Although scientists have names for numerous parts besides the four basic parts, students should not be overloaded with vocabulary. For example, a pistil can be divided up into several parts including the stigma, style, and ovary. Use the vocabulary you need to communicate at the desired level of detail with your students.

EXPLAIN

1. Students should find similarities, such as the categories of parts, but should also see variations. For example, they may find a flower with only five petals, or with dozens of petals. They may find that some stamens are tall and others quite small. The amount of pollen may vary as well. In addition, they may discover that some flowers are missing some of the reproductive parts. They will likely also discover that some flowers are made up of hundreds of tiny but complete flowers. Help students to understand the *NSES* Content Standard: Even though the flowers do not all look alike, they are similar based on the internal structures.

2. After this discussion, you should give students the names of the different flower parts to allow for easier communication (see Figure 6.1.3). You could make an overhead transparency of a basic flower or photocopies for each student. Students should probably take the time to label their own flower parts because the size and shape of the actual flower parts can vary from the diagram.

   Students may notice the "plant juice" inside the pistil. This is likely to be nectar, the primary reason that insects are attracted to flowers. Insects depend on flowers for nectar, and many flowers, in turn, depend

Figure 6.1.3 Parts of a flower

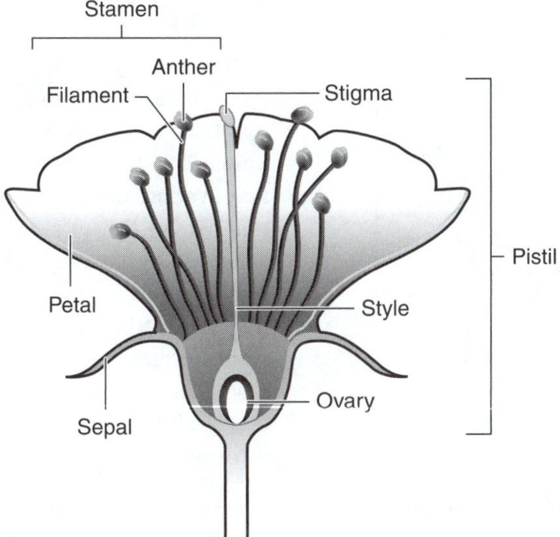

on insects for pollination. Point out the powdery material on the stamens and tell the students that it is pollen. If the students carefully open the pistil, they may find tiny ovules that may develop into seeds after being fertilized by pollen. Some flowers pollinate themselves, and others are pollinated primarily by insects. Note that pollination is the focus of Lesson 6.2 (see page 153).

3. Students should be able to recognize growth in their understanding of the structure of a flower.

EXTEND

1. It is appropriate to have students read at this point in the lesson cycle. This is because the exploration experiences have provided a concrete foundation on which the students can build an understanding of the more abstract content in the readings. Refer to diagrams and readings in the student readings.
2. Students may encounter difficulty observing all the flower parts for several reasons. First, flowers vary widely in size and so some parts may be very small. Some flowers have parts that are fused together, or may develop specialized parts. Furthermore, the individual flowers in composite flowers are extremely small. Therefore, the individual parts are proportionately even smaller and difficult to observe. If you do not have access to all of the above types of flowers, you can find excellent photographs of various flowers on numerous Web sites or in botanical books.
3. You may wish to use this activity as an assessment item. When selecting artificial flowers, make sure that some are incomplete.

TEACHING FOCUS

English Language Learners

After students have manipulated the parts of the flower and thought about the characteristics used for its classification, they are prepared to learn appropriate vocabulary. Not only is this practice a good one for all students, it is a particularly effective one for ELL children because it enables them to connect new English words to concrete objects. You may want ELL students to label flower parts in their native language as well if they are familiar with the terminology.

TEACHING FOCUS

Help Students Use Effective Reading Strategies in Science

As students read nonfiction text after conducting explorations, use those opportunities to teach effective reading strategies or to remind students of the strategies from their reading lessons. Some strategies that are especially important for reading science content information include: previewing the text and headings to become aware of what is included in the reading; using the visuals for cues such as photographs, diagrams, and graphs; and focusing on the first sentence in a paragraph to identify the main idea. Provide additional support for using these strategies with ELL students as necessary.

Teaching Tip

Integrating Math and Science

It is often noted that mathematics is the language of science. But sometimes students fail to see the purpose of learning mathematics. One of the Mathematics Standards (National Council of Teachers of Mathematics, 2000, p. 394) states that all students need to "understand patterns, relations, and functions." Furthermore, the *Science for All Americans* report (American Association for the Advancement of Science, 1990) also lists patterns of change as one of the themes for studying science. When appropriate, emphasize that many patterns found in nature can be expressed mathematically (Maatta, Dobb, & Ostlund, 2006).

APPLY

1. In this activity, students will look at another pattern that occurs in nature: Fibonacci numbers. This number sequence has been known for hundreds of years and occurs over and over again in nature. Examples are the numbers of flower petals, the spirals of the scales of a pinecone, or the spirals in a seashell. For further information on Fibonacci numbers and examples of flowers, you may want to refer to http://britton.disted.camosun.bc.ca/fibslide/jbfibslide.htm or search for other Web sites with Fibonacci information.

2. Many artificial flowers do not follow the Fibonacci sequence. As a class, students should see this pattern more frequently in flowers from nature than in artificial flowers.

Lesson 6.2
Flower Pollination

ENGAGE

You have already examined the parts of a flower. In this investigation you will try to determine the function of some of those parts. In addition, you will look at the role of certain insects in the life cycle of flowering plants. You have probably observed bees and butterflies as they go from flower to flower, landing on one after another. You also learned in the last lesson that this is how flowers are pollinated.

As insects move from one flower to another, they collect and transfer pollen. How can you design an insect to be the best possible pollen collector?

Discuss possible characteristics with your partners. Use one of these characteristics to build a model of an insect. Then build another model without that characteristic. You can then compare the models to see which insect will collect more pollen from an actual flower.

We will explore the following question: **How can you design an insect that is the best possible pollen collector?**

EXPLORE

1. Discuss possible characteristics with your partner.

2. Select one characteristic and develop a plan for building your model insect. Make a list of the materials that you will need and present it to your teacher for approval.

3. Build the two models using the materials provided by your teacher.

4. Determine which model collects more pollen from an actual flower. Record your results.

EXPLAIN

1. Explain why you think one model is a better pollen collector than the other.

2. Share your models and your findings with your classmates by taking a Wisdom Walk among the other groups.

3. What characteristics lead to effective pollen collecting?

4. Read to learn more about different ways in which plants can be pollinated besides insects.

EXTEND

1. Review how pollen travels from the stamens to the pistil. How could this happen without an insect? Based on your reading, discuss with your partners how to design a flower that could pollinate itself.

2. Make a sketch of your idea.

3. Report your idea to the class. Discuss the strengths and weaknesses of each design. Develop a list of questions that you have about the designs.

APPLY

Your teacher will provide you with an artificial flower. Use it to devise at least one method of pollination. Include drawings in your answer to explain your idea.

Lesson 6.2

Flower Pollination

Teaching Focus: Integrating Reading in Science Instruction

NSES CONTENT STANDARD, 5–8: REPRODUCTION AND HEREDITY

"In many species, including humans, females produce eggs and males produce sperm. Plants also reproduce sexually—the egg and sperm are produced in the flowers of flowering plants" (National Research Council, 1996, p. 157).

DESCRIPTIVE OBJECTIVE

Students will build models of insects to discover important characteristics necessary for pollination.

MATERIALS

For each pair of student partners, provide materials for building insects (and insect parts) such as pipe cleaners, wire, toothpicks, modeling clay, different types of tape, and other sticky materials. The students may need wire cutters to cut the pipe cleaners and wire because these are difficult to cut with scissors. In addition, you will need to supply hand lenses and, for the Apply phase, artificial flowers.

SCIENCE BACKGROUND

Pollination is the process of uniting the male and female gametes to bring about fertilization and seed production in flowers. A pollen grain lands on the tip of the pistil and begins to grow a tube, which goes down through the pistil to reach the ovary. The sperm then travels down the pollen tube to fertilize the egg.

Pollination can happen in several different ways. Wind pollination is a common method in which pollen travels through the air and lands on the tip of the pistil of the flower. Other flowers are pollinated by animals or insects that move pollen from one flower to another. Still other flowers undergo self-fertilization in which the pollen and ovules can come from the same flower.

CLASSROOM SAFETY

Check on students' allergies before bringing flowers into the classroom. Children should wash their hands after handling the flowers. Although many flowers are edible, caution students not to ingest any flowers because some are poisonous.

ENGAGE

Initiate a discussion with students to bring out their prior knowledge and experiences with insects, flowers, and pollination. Show a photograph of a bee or butterfly on a flower to provide a concrete visual during this discussion. Focus students on the question for the investigation: How can you design an insect to be the best possible pollen collector?

Figure 6.2.1 Insect models

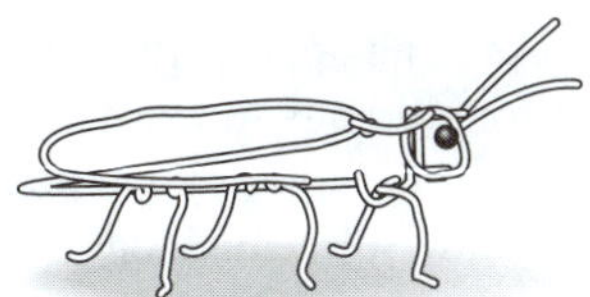

EXPLORE

1. Students must have time to think and plan their models before building them. They will need to figure out how to change only one characteristic rather than several. For instance, students might say that insects with hairy bristles will collect more pollen on themselves than will insects that do not have bristles. Students could make an insect from a pipe cleaner to simulate lots of bristles and make another insect from plain wire (Figure 6.2.1). To control the variables in this case, both models would have to have the same body shape.
2. When you review the students' plans, make sure that they are changing only one characteristic at a time. Depending on your students' experience in conducting controlled experiments or fair tests, you may need to scaffold this activity closely. See the Teaching Tip on conducting fair tests (p. 132) for additional information.
3. Look over the students' plans for the model insects before sharing with them the types of materials that are available for them to use. This may allow the students to express their own creative ideas.
4. After flowers have been opened for a while, not very much pollen is left on the stamens. For this reason, use fresh flowers for this activity if at all possible. Flowers cut from the outdoors may have no pollen because they usually have been subjected to the wind and numerous insects. This is less of a problem with purchased flowers. Flowers with tall stamens and large anthers such as lilies will be the easiest for students to test.

EXPLAIN

1. Students should draw a conclusion from the results of their test. Then, they should try to draw inferences to explain this conclusion. For example, the pipe cleaner insects with their hairy bristles should collect more pollen than will the smooth-legged wire insects. This is because the pipe cleaner bristles are stickier (more adhesive) and have a greater surface area than the smooth wires.

Teaching Tip

Wisdom Walk

In a Wisdom Walk, students circulate around the room to view and learn from the work of others (thus gaining wisdom). This type of practice can lead to a community of learners in which students learn from not only their own work but the work of their classmates as well. While you don't want this activity to turn into a competition, much learning can occur by analyzing one's own mistakes. For more information, see the Inquiry Standards (National Research Council, 2000, pp. 121–124).

The Wisdom Walk can also help keep students on task because they are likely to take more pride in their work knowing others will be reviewing it.

Teaching Focus

Selecting Reading Materials

If you use a science text, have students read the appropriate pages. Students should also read from other sources such as nonfiction trade books, magazines such as *National Geographic Explorer,* or Web sites.

Reading is most appropriate during this stage of the Learning Cycle. As noted by Barman, during this phase, "the teacher assumes a more traditional role [and] . . . may use a textbook, audiovisual aids, or other teaching materials to facilitate concept introduction" (Barman, 1992, p. 59).

2. When students conduct a variety of tests, they always benefit from hearing and seeing others' results. Because the insect models are difficult to show from the front of a classroom, you can have students take a Wisdom Walk around the room to see all the other models.
3. Have a class discussion to determine the characteristics of effective pollen collectors. Help students understand that very few insects collect pollen intentionally; rather, pollen clings to them as they seek nectar for food.
4. The Explain phase is an appropriate time in the Learning Cycle for students to learn additional information about pollination by reading. If possible, find some selections that describe wind pollination, animal pollination, or plants that self-pollinate.

Teaching Focus

Finding Quality Trade Books

Numerous science books are published each year, so it can be time consuming to find and select high-quality children's books appropriate for your class. Each year the National Science Teachers Association publishes a set of lists called *Outstanding Science Trade Books for Students K–12* that contains books selected by a panel of experts from NSTA and the Children's Book Council. These lists can be accessed at the NSTA Web site: http://www.nsta.org/ostbc

TEACHER: Grades 5–8

EXTEND

1. Many flowers do not require insects or wind for pollination. They are self-pollinated, meaning that the pistil is fertilized by pollen from the stamens of the same flower. The advantage of this method is that the flower is more likely to be pollinated and thus produce more seeds. The disadvantage of self-pollination is the lack of variation that occurs when plants cross-pollinate. Self-pollinated flowers have several adaptations that enable this process to occur. First, the pistil and stamens must mature at the same time. The height relationship between the pistil and stamens must be such that the pollen can fall from the stamens and land on the pistil. Furthermore, some flowers, such as those on common bean or pea plants, do not open until after self-pollination has taken place.
2. Have students draw their ideas for a flower that could pollinate itself. (You might have students build models of their flowers if they need more experiences with pollination.)
3. Have students share ideas for possible pollination. Encourage students to discuss strengths and weaknesses in each of the designs. This discussion, based on the questions that students generate, will help them to understand the pollination process more fully as well as appreciate some of the diversity found in flowers.

Teaching Tip

Science as Inquiry

As noted in the *National Science Education Standards* (National Research Council, 1996, p. 148): "Students should develop the ability to listen to and respect the explanations proposed by other students. They should remain open to and acknowledge different ideas and explanations, be able to accept the skepticism of others, and consider alternative explanations."

APPLY

Once again, artificial flowers can be used as a performance assessment item. Students must develop a plausible method of pollination based on the characteristics of the flower. They should look for the presence or absence of the pistil and stamens and the size and relative positions of these parts.

Lesson 6.3
Fruits and Vegetables

ENGAGE

Think about how foods are classified at grocery stores—dairy, meats, produce, frozen foods, canned goods, and others. In the produce section you can find foods that are referred to as either fruits or vegetables. In the canned foods section, however, you find one section for fruits and another for vegetables. This raises the question of how fruits are different from vegetables. In this exploration you will try to classify each food your teacher provides as either a fruit or a vegetable.

We will explore the following question: **What are the characteristics of fruits and vegetables?**

EXPLORE

1. Examine the foods that your teacher provides. Look for characteristics of each and then use these characteristics to classify the foods as either fruits or vegetables. After you have divided them into two groups, make a chart such as the one below to record your ideas.

Fruit		Vegetables	
Name of Fruit	Characteristics	Name of Vegetable	Characteristics

2. What are some characteristics that are typical of all fruits?

3. What are some characteristics that are typical of all vegetables?

EXPLAIN

1. Compare your classification scheme to those of your classmates. How is it similar? How is it different?

2. Find a food that you classified as a fruit but someone else classified as a vegetable. How is your classmate's classification system different from yours?

3. Read to learn more about how scientists classify fruits and vegetables.

4. How does a scientist's classification of fruit compare with your scheme? If necessary, revise your fruit and vegetable classification chart.

Fruit		Vegetables	
Name of Fruit	Characteristics	Name of Vegetable	Characteristics

EXTEND

1. Now that you know more about fruit, plan an investigation to find out about fruit and seeds. Brainstorm some possible questions with your class. For example, one question might be the following: Do larger fruits have larger seeds? Make a list of several questions.

2. Select one question for your investigation. Write a plan to conduct your procedure. Make a list of materials that you will need. Submit your plan to your teacher for approval.

3. Conduct your investigation. Record your data in a chart to share it with your classmates. Draw a conclusion based on your results to answer your question.

4. Share your investigation with your classmates.

APPLY

Look at the food that your teacher has provided. Decide whether it is a fruit or a vegetable based upon what you have learned. Give reasons for your answer.

Lesson 6.3

Fruits and Vegetables

Teaching Focus: Integrating Reading in Science Instruction

NSES CONTENT STANDARD, 5–8: REPRODUCTION AND HEREDITY

"Reproduction is a characteristic of all living systems; because no living organism lives forever, reproduction is essential to the continuation of every species" (National Research Council, 1996, p. 157).

DESCRIPTIVE OBJECTIVE

Students will examine fruits and vegetables to determine that the fruits are the container for seeds that form in the flowers.

MATERIALS

For each group of students, provide several different fruits and vegetables. Be sure to include some items that are commonly referred to as vegetables but are technically fruits, such as tomatoes, squash, pea pods, green peppers, and so on. Try to avoid hybrids such as navel oranges or seedless watermelons that do not have seeds. You may want to ask students ahead of time to bring in a fruit or vegetable from home. Student groups will also need some newspaper to protect their desks or some flat container such as a cookie sheet or tray on which to open up the fruits and vegetables. If you want the students to cut open the foods, provide a knife. Students may also need hand lenses to view very small seeds such as those on strawberries.

SCIENCE BACKGROUND

In flowering plants, fruit are the containers for the seeds of the next generation. Fruit are the mature ovaries that develop within the flower and aid in the dispersal of the seeds. Fruits are classified by the arrangement of the female parts of the flower. The most diverse group of fruits are known as simple fruits and can be soft and fleshy, dry and woody, or papery. This scientific definition of a fruit is contradictory to the common definition of fruit as an edible part of the plant that is soft, fleshy, and sweet. Therefore, many common "vegetables" such as beans, peas, and green peppers are actually fruits. In addition, nuts and other seeds, such as the winged seeds of maple trees and dandelions, are all fruits!

CLASSROOM SAFETY

Check on students' allergies before bringing fruits and vegetables into the classroom. Some children are strongly allergic to strawberries or peanuts. Children should wash their hands after handling fruits or vegetables. Caution students not to eat the food that they are working with because handling has made it unsanitary. If you wish, have some fruit on reserve that students can taste after the lesson is completed.

ENGAGE

Converse with students to elicit their prior knowledge about fruits and vegetables. Many students will have the misconception that all fruits are sweet. Do not tell students the scientific definition of a fruit at this point. Rather, encourage them to express their ideas, allowing them to undergo conceptual change during the investigations and reading. Focus the conversation on the explorable question: **What are the characteristics of fruits and vegetables?**

EXPLORE

1. Provide each group with several different kinds of fruits and vegetables. Include at least one of the fruits that are commonly called vegetables. Encourage students to observe the characteristics of each food item. Have students record their ideas in a chart from which they will draw inferences.
2. Students will need to examine their classification schemes for patterns of common characteristics. Some common characteristics such as "fruits taste sweet" may appear (although, in fact, not all fruits taste sweet), but students may also have noticed that every fruit has seeds in it.
3. Some characteristics that students might include are the following: "foods from a plant that we eat," "can be different colors," and "they are from different parts of a plant." Vegetables can be leaves (e.g., lettuce), roots or tubers (e.g., potatoes), stems (e.g., asparagus), or flowers (e.g., broccoli).

> **TEACHING FOCUS**
>
> **Reading Charts and Tables**
>
> Many students will need much practice to develop the cognitive ability to construct and read data tables easily. Encourage students to make a chart when they are collecting data. Constructing charts will help students develop the ability to understand information that is presented in an abstract format. You may wish to compile the data from each group on a large chart at the front of the room.

EXPLAIN

1. Have students share their classification schemes and compare them to look for similarities and differences. This type of activity helps students see a variety of ways of thinking and encourages them to be open to new ideas.
2. A green pepper might be a typical example. Students are likely to classify it as a vegetable, ignoring the fact that it is filled

> Teaching Tip
>
> **Creating Cognitive Dissonance**
>
> For conceptual change to occur (see the Introduction), students must experience dissatisfaction with their ideas. This mental conflict is called *cognitive dissonance*. Having students share their preliminary conclusions can often result in cognitive dissonance as students hear conflicting ideas and therefore question their own. This is the first step in constructing new concepts that address the shortcomings of their earlier ideas.

with seeds. Because of the seeds, others will classify it as a fruit. This can become a point of discussion that helps the class develop understanding.

3. Select some reading material for students on fruit and vegetable classification. You might choose some pages from a text series, some nonfiction trade books, or an appropriate Web site. You should look for information that discusses the scientific definition of fruit, the different types of fruit (dry vs. fleshy fruits), and the development of fruits from the flowers.
4. Following the reading, have students compare their classification scheme to a scientist's classification of fruit and revise as necessary.

TEACHING FOCUS

Using Science Materials to Teach Reading

Because it can be difficult to allocate time in elementary schools, you may want to use your science textbook or other nonfiction materials rather than a basal reading series to actually teach reading. Research has shown that this can be an effective strategy because the hands-on science gives the readers prior experience with the content and creates a purpose for reading (Romance & Vitale, 1992).

EXTEND

1. In this lesson, students gained firsthand experience with fruit before generating their own ideas for the exploration. Now, help the students brainstorm some possible questions about fruits and seeds. Some examples might include the following: Do larger fruits have larger seeds? Do all pumpkins have the same number of seeds? Where are seeds located in fruit? Does the size of the seed relate to the number of seeds in a fruit?
2. Students should select one question for investigation and write a procedure. When reviewing the plans, make sure that students' plans help them answer the question. If the materials that students request are not available, help them find an appropriate, affordable substitute.
3. Once again, have students record data in a chart, if possible, to gain experience in making and reading data tables.
4. Have students share the results of their investigations with their classmates. This way, everyone gains the knowledge from the numerous questions that were investigated.

Teaching Tip

Metacognition

Have students compare their new understandings to their initial knowledge of fruits and vegetables. The goal of this comparison is for students to reflect on the development of their own knowledge. Learning about your own understanding is referred to as *metacognition*. Bransford, Brown, and Cocking, in *How People Learn* (1999, p. 35), note that "The ability to recognize the limits of one's current knowledge, then take steps to remedy the situation, is extremely important for learners at all ages."

APPLY

Select a fruit that was not used in the classification activity or the investigations to determine whether students can overcome their earlier misconceptions and incorporate a new definition of a fruit. Select something that the students have not seen yet, such as a peanut in a shell.

Diversity—Include Examples of Scientists from Many Cultures

Whenever possible, integrate examples of scientists, inventors, and researchers from many different cultures. As an example, rather than conducting a special unit of African-American scientists during February, which is designated as Black History Month, integrate information about George Washington Carver and his voluminous work with soybeans and peanuts during a plant unit.

Teaching Focus Summary: Integrating Reading in Science Instruction

- Introduce new vocabulary to students after the exploration in the Explain phase of the Learning Cycle.
- Choose an appropriate level of detail for new vocabulary so that your students are not overwhelmed with new words.
- Have students read nonfiction texts after the exploration phase. Choose from a variety of types of reading materials such as textbooks, children's trade books, magazines, and so on.
- Students need much practice at making and reading data tables and charts.

References

American Association for the Advancement of Science. (1990). *Science for all Americans*. New York: Oxford University Press.

Barman, C. (1992). An evaluation of the use of a technique designed to assist prospective elementary teachers' using the learning cycle with science textbooks. *School Science and Mathematics, 92*(2), 59–63.

Bransford, J. D., Brown, A. L., & Cocking, R. (Eds.). (1999). *How people learn: Brain, mind, experience, and school.* Washington, DC: National Academy Press.

Maatta, D., Dobb, F., & Ostlund, K. (2006). Strategies for teaching science to English language learners. In A. Fathman and D. Crowther (Eds.), *Science for English language learners* (pp. 37–59). Arlington, VA: NSTA Press.

National Council of Teachers of Mathematics. (2000). *Principles and standards for school mathematics*. Reston, VA: Author.

National Research Council. (1996). *National Science Education Standards*. Washington, DC: National Academy Press.

National Research Council. (2000). *Inquiry and the National Science Education Standards*. Washington, DC: National Academy Press.

Romance, N., & Vitale, M. (1992). A curriculum strategy that expands time for in-depth elementary science instruction by using science-based reading strategies: Effects of a year-long study in grade four. *Journal of Research in Science Teaching, 29*(6), 545–554.

INVESTIGATION 7

BONES

(5–8)

Teaching Focus: Using Questioning Strategies

Lesson 7.1

How Many Do You Have?

ENGAGE

Hold out your hand and flex all of your fingers. Your hand has many bones that allow your fingers to move. How many bones do you think are in your hand? Predict and record the number. Now try to count the number of bones in your hand. How do you know where two bones come together? How many bones did you count?

Now, let's try to count the number of bones in other sections of your body. We will investigate the following question: **How many bones do you have in your body?**

EXPLORE

1. First, try to figure out how many bones are in your arm. Add in the number of bones you counted in your hand. Record your findings in the chart below.

2. Now count the number of bones in your leg, ankle, and foot. Record your findings in the chart below.

3. Repeat the process to figure out how many bones are in your torso and your head.

Section of Body	Number of Bones
Left arm with hand	
Right arm with hand	
Left leg with foot	
Right leg with foot	
Torso (neck, chest, hips)	
Head	
Total	

4. How many total bones did you count in your body?

EXPLAIN

1. Share your findings with your classmates. Record the data for the class averages in the chart below.

Section of Body	Class Average
Left arm with hand	
Right arm with hand	
Left leg with foot	
Right leg with foot	
Torso (neck, chest, hips)	
Head	
Total	

2. How do your numbers compare with the class average?

3. What is the average total number of bones in the human body?

4. What could you do to make a more accurate count of the bones in your entire body?

EXTEND

1. Your teacher will provide you with skeleton pictures. Closely examine them to refine your investigation.

2. Record your new information in the chart below.

Section of Body	Revised Totals
Arm with hand	
Leg with foot	
Torso (neck, chest, hips)	
Head	

3. How many bones do you have in your body, based on the visuals?

4. How do these revised totals compare to your previous findings?

APPLY

Look at the sample model of a skeleton that your teacher provides. How is it similar to a real human skeleton? How is it different? Does it accurately portray the number of bones in a human body? Explain.

Lesson 7.1

How Many Do You Have?

Teaching Focus: Using Questioning Strategies

Unless we know what children think and why they think that way, we have little chance of making any impact with our teaching no matter how skillfully we proceed.

Osborne and Freyberg (1985, p. 13)

NSES CONTENT STANDARD, 5–8: STRUCTURE AND FUNCTION IN LIVING SYSTEMS

"Living systems at all levels of organization demonstrate the complementary nature of structure and function" (National Research Council, 1996, p. 156).

DESCRIPTIVE OBJECTIVE

Students will investigate to determine the number of bones in the human body.

MATERIALS

No materials are needed for the Explore phase. Students will use their bodies to count the number of bones. For the Extend phase, provide each pair of students with a detailed diagram of the human skeleton such as an enlarged photocopy of the diagram below, a picture from a textbook or reference book, or x-rays. For the Apply phase, you will need to provide one or more sample models of skeletons for students to critique. It would be interesting to choose some inaccurate skeleton models such as holiday decorations, key chains, and so on.

SCIENCE BACKGROUND

Bones are living tissues in the body that provide shape and support, protect organs, allow movement, and manufacture blood cells. The bones in an animal are organized into a system known as a *skeleton.* The adult human skeleton (see Figure 7.1.1) has approximately 206 bones, which may be referred to by either their common or scientific names. Infants have approximately 90 more bones than do adults. Many of these bones fuse together as the child grows. Although it is sometimes a common practice to have students memorize all 206 names, this is not recommended. It is not inappropriate, however, for students to learn the names of the major bones to communicate effectively with each other.

Figure 7.1.1 Human skeleton

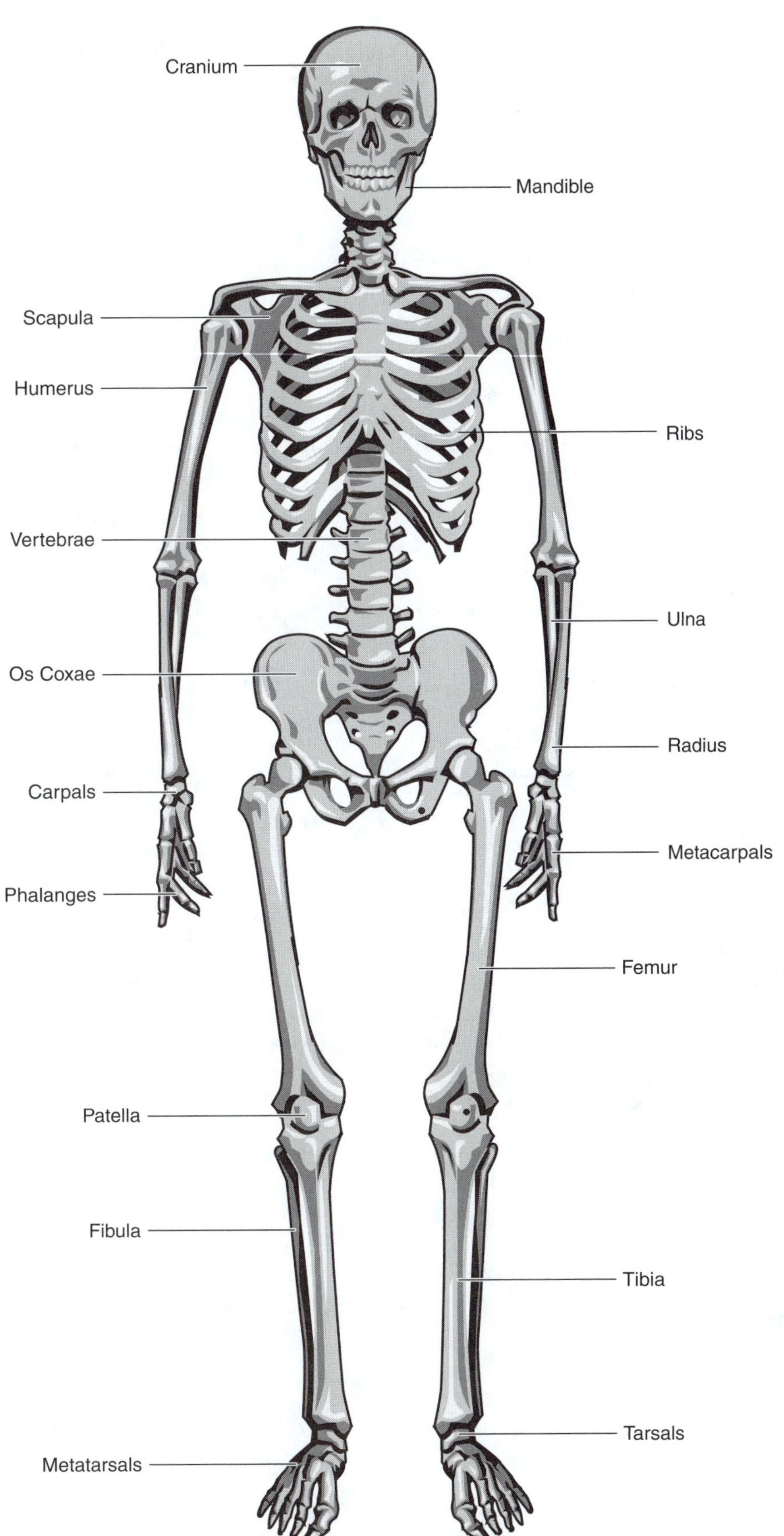

MISCONCEPTION INFORMATION

Much research has been conducted on children's misconceptions regarding the differences among what is living, once living, and nonliving as well as how animals are classified, including what an animal is. Much less is known, however, about misconceptions related to skeletal structures. Some student misconceptions include:

- Birds with larger bones fly slower.
- Birds with fewer bones fly faster.
- Bones are round because they contain marrow.

For additional information, you may wish to refer to the following:

Cox-Petersen, A., Marsh, D., Kisiel, J., & Melber, L. (2003). Investigation of guided school tours, student learning, and science reform recommendations at a museum of natural history. *Journal of Research in Science Teaching, 40*(2), 200–218.

Reiss, M., & Tunnicliffe, S. (1999). Children's knowledge of the human skeleton. *Primary Science Review, 60*, 7–10.

Tunnicliffe, S., & Reiss, M. (1999). Students' understanding about animal skeletons. *International Journal of Science Education, 21*, 1187–1200.

CLASSROOM SAFETY

There are no special safety concerns. Because students will be investigating their skeletons tactilely, however, they should be paired according to gender and be respectful of one other.

TEACHING FOCUS

Uncovering Students' Thoughts and Ideas

During the Engage phase, ask questions that focus on helping students express their own ideas about a topic. Some sample questions for the above Engage activity include: What do you notice about your hand? What do your fingers look like when you bend them? How could you try to count your bones? How does moving help you to count bones? What is your plan for keeping track of the number of bones?

Try to avoid questions that ask for content answers in the Engage phase. The Engage phase of the lesson is not intended to teach the concept, but rather to focus students on an explorable question. For example, you want to avoid questions such as "What are the names of the bones in the arm?" or "Of what are bones made?"

ENGAGE

Begin the lesson by capturing students' interest in their bones. Have them observe their hand as they move their fingers. Encourage students to share observations and then predict the number of bones in one of their hands. If students have trouble keeping count, have them sketch their hand to record the number of bones in each of their fingers and wrist. Also check during this time that students are feeling for bones, can identify where two bones meet, and can make a reasonable count so that they can repeat the process for other sections of the body in the Explore phase. Then, focus students' attention on the explorable question: **How many bones do you have in your body?**

EXPLORE

1. Students will follow the same procedure as in the Engage phase to find out how many bones are in their bodies. Students should record the data in the chart.
2. To help students determine the number of bones in their wrists, suggest that they analyze the different ways in which they can move their wrist and fingers. Then make a sketch showing the bones that this requires.
3. Students will repeat the process to figure out how many bones are in the torso and the head. Answers might vary widely from group to group. It is more difficult to count bones in some sections of the body than in others. This is especially true of the skull. In fact, there is really no way to count the six bones in the ears. Many of the cranium bones are fused together and therefore also are difficult to count.
4. Have students share their findings. The students' totals will probably be less than 206.

EXPLAIN

1. Refrain from telling students the correct answer at this point so that they can revise their own work. Record each group's data in a large chart so that students will be able to compute averages for each section. (You many want to save this chart for use in the Extend phase.)
2. Answers will vary depending on how thorough the students' estimates were.
3. The class average will probably not be 206 bones. The process of getting a closer approximation is more important than the specific answer at this time.
4. Encourage students to brainstorm strategies to more accurately count the bones in the body. They will probably suggest using different types of reference materials.

TEACHING FOCUS

Interacting with Student Groups

Inquiry-based teaching enables you to meet with each group of students and discuss their work. Move from group to group to observe the students, making sure they know what question they are trying to answer, to check their ideas for finding the answer to the question, and to assist with materials, if necessary. As you interact with the groups be sure to regularly scan the classroom to monitor all of the students.

Teaching Tip

Integrating Math by Computing Averages

When people think of an average usually they are talking about the mathematical mean—the sum of the total divided by the number of events. The mean is easily computed and usually provides a good value for the average (known to statisticians as *central tendency*). The mean, however, is not the best description of the average for sets of data that include extreme values (known as *outliers*). For example, consider the following data for the number of head bones for seven student groups: 2, 2, 3, 11, 11, 12, and 14. The mean is 7.7 bones. Let's consider another measure of average, or central tendency, called the *median*. To determine the median you order the data from smallest to largest and find the data point in the middle. This technique gives less importance to the outliers. For example, consider the above data again. We can easily see that the median is 11 bones, a value closer to being correct and less influenced by the extreme low values.

Table 7.1.1 Number of Bones in the Human Body

Section of Body	Revised Totals
Arms with hands	60
Legs with feet	60
Torso (neck, chest, hips)	60
Head	26
Total	206

EXTEND

1. Now provide each group with visuals such as diagrams, pictures from reference books or encyclopedias, Web sites, x-rays, models, and so on. Try to have several different visuals available so that groups may check more than one source while counting.
2. Students will give totals for each section. Student counts will still vary depending on the information used. This is because many bones (such as the three bones in the middle ear) are not shown on skeleton diagrams. Other bones that are fused together such as in the skull are also quite difficult to count. Table 7.1.1 gives the correct number of bones for each section of the body.
3. Student answers will vary. You may want to add a column to the previous class chart to enable students to compare groups once again.
4. Students should realize that while their totals may still not be entirely accurate, they are probably more realistic than the previous counts. You may provide the students with the scientifically accepted answers for each section of the body at this point, if you wish.

TEACHING FOCUS

Brainstorming

Brainstorming is a strategy for collecting many ideas from students very quickly. Brainstorming begins with a very general open-ended question. You should accept all ideas generated by the brainstorming process without stopping to reflect on each one. After you have collected and recorded many ideas, you can sort through them and select select some that may be more fruitful for answering the question.

TEACHER: Grades 5–8

Teaching Tip

Performance Assessment

Performance assessment enables students to demonstrate their understanding by applying their knowledge to a novel situation. Please see page 80 for more information.

APPLY

Provide an inaccurate model of a skeleton, such as a holiday decoration, so that students can compare it to their new understandings. You may want to use this activity as a performance assessment.

Lesson 7.2
Comparing Skeletons

ENGAGE

Look at the bone that your teacher is holding. What do you notice about the bone? Where have you seen bones before? What were they like? Have you ever seen an entire skeleton from an animal before?

To investigate an animal skeleton, we will use the bones of small animals found in an owl pellet. The owl pellet may contain the bones of several different animals. You should be able to arrange them into groups. We will investigate the following question: **How can you put a skeleton back together?**

EXPLORE

1. Unwrap the foil and observe the owl pellet. Describe the pellet.

2. Gently pull apart the pellet into two pieces. **Very carefully** separate the bones from the fur using your fingers or toothpicks.

3. Use the hand lens to observe the bones. Sort the bones into several categories. Label your categories and record a name for each category.

4. Arrange the bones into a skeleton. You may have extra bones if the owl ate more than one animal, or you may be missing some bones.

5. When you finish arranging the skeleton, obtain a diagram from your teacher and compare it with your skeleton. Reposition the bones of your skeleton, if necessary.

6. Glue the skeleton onto a sheet of cardboard or stiff paper. Label the categories of bones that you identified earlier.

EXPLAIN

1. Make a prediction about the type of animal that you have. What evidence did you use from the skeleton to make the prediction?

2. Take a Wisdom Walk to view your classmates' skeletons.

3. How do your classmates' skeletons compare with yours? How do they compare with each other?

4. How does the rodent's skeleton compare with a human skeleton?

EXTEND

1. Observe the skeletons of the different animals in the pictures that your teacher provides.

2. How are the skeletons similar?

3. How are the skeletons different?

4. How do these skeletons compare with a human skeleton?

5. How do the bones determine the shape of the animal?

APPLY

Examine the picture of a mystery skeleton. Describe and identify the major body parts of the skeleton. To which type of animal do you think it belongs? Explain.

Lesson 7.2

Comparing Skeletons

Teaching Focus: Using Questioning Strategies

NSES CONTENT STANDARD, 5–8: STRUCTURE AND FUNCTION IN LIVING SYSTEMS

"Living systems at all levels of organization demonstrate the complementary nature of structure and function" (National Research Council, 1996, p. 156).

DESCRIPTIVE OBJECTIVE

Students will dissect an owl pellet to reconstruct the skeleton of a rodent (or bird) to compare and contrast it with the bones of humans and of other animals.

MATERIALS

For each pair of students provide one owl pellet and two paper plates, a hand lens, tweezers, and toothpicks. You may wish to mist water from a spray bottle on the pellets as students pull them apart. This prevents the fur from dispersing into the air. After students assemble the skeleton, provide each pair of students a photocopy of skeletons of small rodents, glue, and a piece of cardboard or stiff paper. For the Extend phase you will need pictures of skeletons from various animals. These may be found in textbooks, reference materials, or Web sites. Save one of these pictures for use in the Apply phase. Having a bone to display is helpful to stimulate students' thinking in the Engage phase. If you cannot get bones from a science lab, then use a cooked chicken or beef bone that has the meat removed. Wash the bone in warm soapy water to remove grease, if necessary.

SCIENCE BACKGROUND

Owl pellets are an ideal way for students to investigate bones and can be purchased readily from science supply stores. Owls (and other birds of prey) swallow small rodents or birds whole rather than chewing them. Therefore, the bones are not crushed. Because the owl cannot digest the bones or fur, the owl coughs up, or regurgitates, the remains in the form of a pellet. Each pellet contains the skeleton of one or more small animals. The bones can be assembled to reconstruct the skeleton and determine the type of animal that the owl consumed. Because owls eat several rodents and regurgitate several pellets a day your students probably will not find a complete skeleton. We recommend the use of sterilized owl pellets. These should not be difficult to obtain, as owl pellets are usually sterilized before they are sold.

CLASSROOM SAFETY

Check for student allergies to animal fur prior to conducting the activity. Students should wash their hands with soap after handling the owl pellets.

ENGAGE

Obtain a real bone, such as a chicken or beef bone, to show to students. Use the suggested questions in the student lesson to bring out students' prior knowledge. If students are not familiar with owl pellets, you will need to explain them. Some students may have the mistaken idea that owl pellets are animal feces. Lead the discussion to the explorable question: **How can you put a skeleton back together?**

EXPLORE

1. The purchased owl pellets usually come wrapped in foil. Students should make their observations before they take the pellet apart because it will be destroyed in the process.
2. If students are working in pairs, have them gently pull apart the pellet into two pieces to enable each student to retrieve some of the bones. If students are working in larger groups, provide a portion of the pellet to each student. Students should use care to avoid breaking too many bones as they pull the owl pellets apart. Students can usually pick out the bones with just their fingers, but some may prefer to use a tool such as a toothpick or tweezers. Toothpicks can help scrape fur off the bones.
3. Many of the bones will be extremely small, so encourage students to use the hand lens to observe them. Students should sort the bones into several categories before trying to assemble a skeleton. Some students will sort the bones by major body sections, such as those used in the previous lesson. Other students may sort them according to major bone groups such as ribs, backbones, and so on.
4. After the students have removed all of the bones from the fur and other material, they will attempt to arrange the bones into a skeleton. They may have extra bones if the owl ate more than one animal, or they may be missing some bones. The students may throw the fur away after they check it completely for tiny bones.
5. Provide a copy of the diagram (Figure 7.2.1) to help the students arrange the bones. The pelvis is often difficult for students to place, but they may be able to see how the femur and pelvis fit together in the ball and socket joint.
6. Have students preserve their work by gluing their skeletons onto sheets of cardboard or stiff paper and labeling them. You may wish to display these on a bulletin board or chalk ledge after they have dried.

TEACHING FOCUS

Explorable Questions

Science is a way to investigate the natural world, so the explorations in this text center on answering a question to learn about natural phenomena. Some characteristics of effective explorable questions include the following: they are broad, open-ended questions; they generally focus on what happens rather than why something happens; and they allow students to try out their own ideas and collect evidence to answer the question. Try to avoid explorable questions that require only memorized answers by students or emphasize only why something happens rather than what or how.

Diversity—Using Inquiry Science to Assist English Language Learners

Teaching Tip

"Learning science and learning a second language are cognitive processes that support each other" (Baumgarten & Bacher, 2006, p. 26). In science, students observe, predict, classify, infer, and communicate findings, among other process skills. These skills are very similar to the processes used in learning a second language. In language learning, students use the following processes: "explain, infer, analyze, draw conclusions, synthesize, compare/contrast (and) persuade" (Baumgarten & Bacher, 2006, p. 33). Encouraging English language learners to use these processes makes them confident in their ability to learn new science content as they are learning a new language.

Incorporating Classification

Teaching Tip

Classification is a type of logical thinking that scientists frequently use to organize information about the natural world. Classification is always based on observations. Students require much practice to develop advanced classifying abilities.

Figure 7.2.1 Comparison of bird and rodent bones

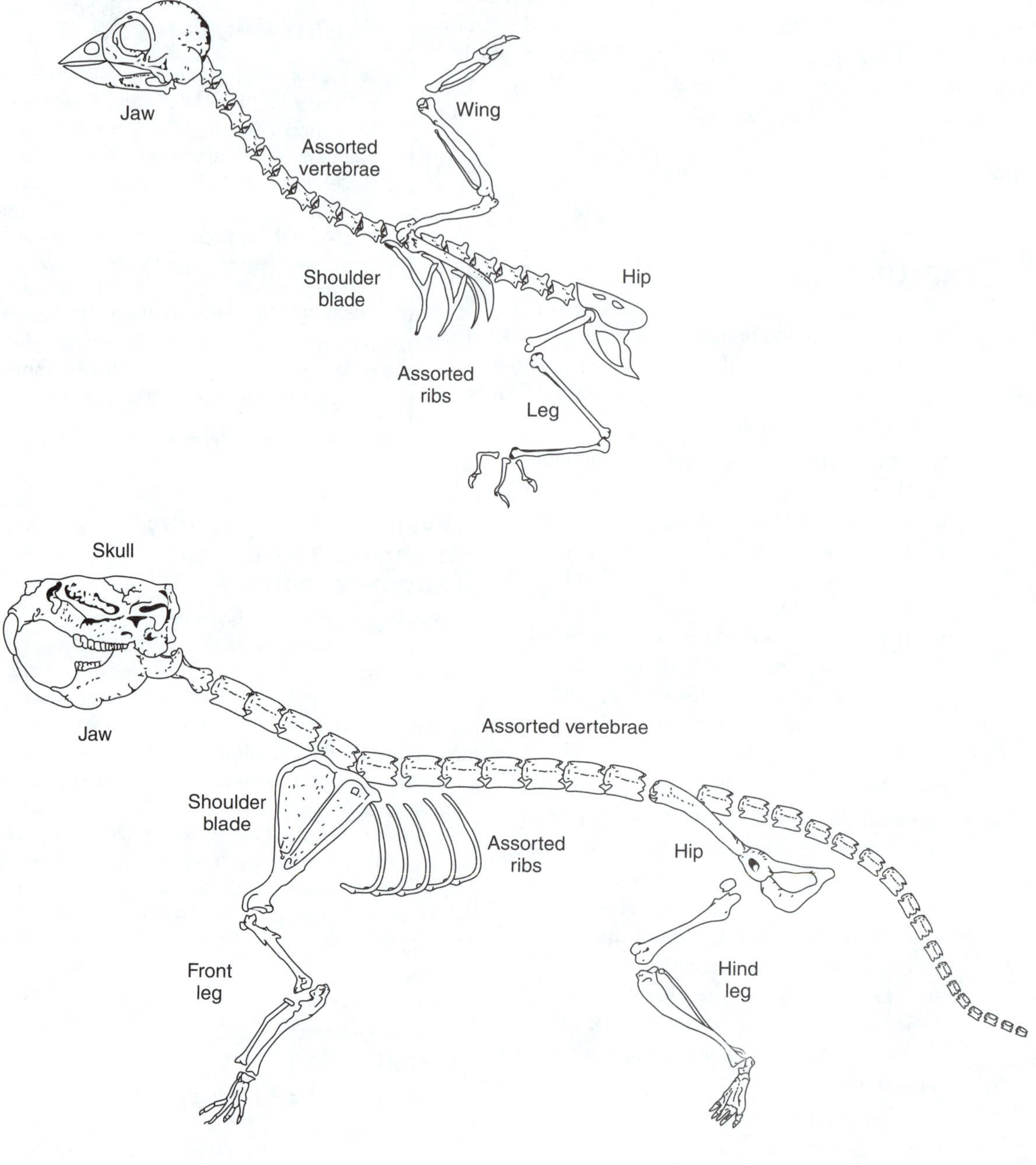

EXPLAIN

1. Students are usually very interested in identifying their skeleton. Encourage them to use evidence from the skeletons rather than simply guess. Students may be able to distinguish birds by their beaks or feather remnants and rodents by their characteristic gnawing teeth.
2. Because students will want to see other skeletons, have them take a Wisdom Walk (see Investigation 6, page 157) around the room to observe their classmates' skeletons.
3. Students should record their observations of their classmates' skeletons. This will enable them to discover possible shortcomings in their representations of the

skeletons. Making comparisons also helps students notice important details. Students may make observations about the sizes of the skeletons, the differences between the skull of a rodent and the skull of a bird, or the differences between other bones. Besides noticing differences students should also look for similarities.

4. Students should observe many similarities between the skeletons of a rodent and a human. Both skeletons have vertebrae, a rib cage, and four limbs in the same relative positions. Other similarities include the structure of the legs, with one long bone for the thigh and two bones for the calf of both rodents and humans. Students might also observe differences such as the relative size of the skeletons, the greater length of the front teeth of rodents, or the dissimilar shape of the skulls.

TEACHING FOCUS

Wait Time

Effective questioning strategies result in students using higher order thinking. Therefore students should have sufficient time to think before answering a question. Waiting up to 3 seconds after asking a question, gives students more time to think about the answer and give a thoughtful response. Mary Budd Rowe's research indicates that giving students more wait time enables them to suggest increasingly complex ideas in their responses. It also results in a greater number of students responding (Rowe, 1973, 1996).

EXTEND

1. Provide some pictures, diagrams, or photos of skeletons of different animals. You also could borrow some actual skeletons from a local high school science teacher. A veterinarian may be able to provide x-rays of small animals for students to compare.
2. Once again, students should make observations to compare the skeletons. Answers will vary depending on the animals provided, but will probably include some of the ideas listed above in the Explain phase.
3. Students' answers will vary depending on the skeletons provided.
4. See #4 above in the Explain phase, as the answers should be similar.
5. Students should begin to realize that the bones determine the shape or structure of the animal.

APPLY

Provide a picture of the skeleton of a mystery animal that is familiar to students. (You could use the image option of your favorite Web search engine to obtain a wide selection of skeleton images.) Students should now be able to describe and identify the major body parts of the skeleton and make a reasonable prediction. If you use this activity as a performance assessment, remember that the evidence and explanations provided by the student are more important than naming the animal correctly.

Lesson 7.3

How Strong Are Your Bones?

ENGAGE

Look at the bones in a human skeleton. What do you notice about the shape of the bones? Imagine cutting across one of the bones and then looking at the end. What shape would it be? Do this for several different bones. What shapes did you find? Because one of the functions of bones is to provide support, bones must be strong enough to hold up the animal. What shape of bone is the strongest? How could you design a test to find out? List your ideas.

Now we will investigate the following question: **What shape of bone is strongest?**

EXPLORE

1. Your teacher will provide you with some paper to make model bones for your investigation of the above question.
   - What factor will you test in your investigation of the model bones?
   - What factors will you need to keep the same in each of your model bones as you build them?
   - What observations and measurements will you need as evidence to answer the explorable question?

2. Record your data in the chart below.

Shape of Model Bone	Evidence of Strength

EXPLAIN

1. Which shape was the strongest?

2. Find out the results of your classmate's investigations.

3. Did you see any patterns in the strengths of different shapes?

EXTEND

1. Now, let's look at the shape of natural objects that require a lot of strength. Examine the pictures that your teacher provides.

2. What about engineered structures?

3. What do you notice about the shapes of all these structures?

4. Why do you think this shape is found in natural and engineered structures?

APPLY

Think about what you have found out about bone shape and strength. Why do you think bones have different shapes?

Lesson 7.3

How Strong Are Your Bones?

Teaching Focus: Using Questioning Strategies

NSES CONTENT STANDARD, 5–8: STRUCTURE AND FUNCTION IN LIVING SYSTEMS

"Living systems at all levels of organization demonstrate the complementary nature of structure and function" (National Research Council, 1996, p. 156).

DESCRIPTIVE OBJECTIVE

Students will investigate to determine that cylindrical bones are stronger than bones of other shapes such as square, triangular, or rectangular polyhedrons.

MATERIALS

For each pair of students provide several sheets of heavy paper, scissors, rulers, and several books to use as weights to test the strength of the model bones. If you don't have enough copies of the same book for testing, then have students weigh the books on a bathroom scale to determine the amount that each model bone can support. For the Engage phase, you will need a model or picture of a human skeleton. (A model is preferred.) For the Extend phase you will need pictures of natural and engineered cylindrical objects such as trees, plant stems, utility poles, water towers, silos, building columns, table or chair legs, and so on.

SCIENCE BACKGROUND

Bones are cylindrical in part because the cylinder is the strongest shape for a hollow column. Students should notice that noncylindrical columns fail at the corners. This is because the corners are the greatest distance from the center of the column (see Figure 7.3.1). If we think of this distance as a lever, we see that a greater force is therefore applied at these corners. A cylinder minimizes this distance. All other factors being equal, the more sides a column has, the stronger it is, with the cylindrical column having an infinite number of "sides."

CLASSROOM SAFETY

Normal classroom safety procedures are needed for building and testing the model bones.

Figure 7.3.1 Strength of square and cylindrical columns

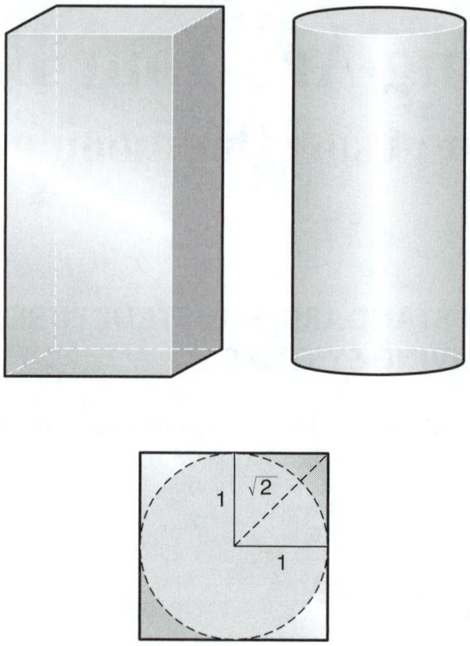

ENGAGE

Obtain a model skeleton to generate interest and focus the students' attention on the shape of the bones. Have students record their ideas individually or as a class. Ask students why they think bones are of different shapes. Pick up on the idea that bones provide support and ask whether bone shape is related to strength. Focus the discussion on the explorable question: **What shape of bone is strongest?**

Teaching Focus

Convergent and Divergent Questions

We can classify questions broadly into two categories: convergent and divergent. Generally, convergent questions have only one answer, typically either yes or no. They tend to discourage speculative or creative thinking on the part of the students. We are all familiar with teachers who play the "guess what's in my head game" as they "shop" for the "right" answer in their questioning. Convergent questions can be used to focus an exploration or investigation on a specific area of inquiry. For example, in the Engage phase above, the explorable question "What shape of bone is strongest?" is a relatively convergent question.

Divergent questions have multiple appropriate answers. They do encourage creative and speculative thinking on the part of the students. They are useful for generating ideas that may lead to additional questions for investigation. In the Engage phase above the question "Why do you think bones have different shapes?" is an example of a divergent question.

EXPLORE

1. Before students begin to build and test their models, they should demonstrate their understanding of the experimental design. Shape is the factor that students are testing as the independent variable. They may test model bones with round, triangular, and square cross sections. They will need to keep several factors constant, such as the length of the bones, the approximate diameter of the bones, and the

method of taping the paper into the shape. Students will record the number of books, or the actual weight of the books as evidence to determine the strength of each shape of bone. Some students may wish to try polygons of other shapes, including hexagons and octagons.

TEACHING FOCUS

Questioning Guidelines

In *Primary science: Taking the plunge* (Harlan, 1985) Jos Elstgeest provides the following guidelines for "productive" and "how and why" questions in science teaching. Productive questions encourage students to focus on what they are doing and what they are trying to find out. Questions of this type may lead students to broaden the scope of their investigation. How and why questions help students think of explanations for their results. Elstgeest's guidelines are listed below.

Guidelines for "productive" questions

1. Study the effect on children of asking different kinds of questions so that you can distinguish the "productive" from the "unproductive."
2. Use the simplest form of productive question (attention focusing) during initial exploration to help children take note of details that they might overlook.
3. Use measuring and counting questions to nudge children from purely qualitative observation toward quantitative observation.
4. Use comparison questions to help students order their observations and data.
5. Use action questions to encourage experimentation and the investigation of relationships.
6. Use problem posing questions when children are capable of setting up for themselves hypotheses and situations to test them.
7. Choose the type of question to suit the children's experience in relation to the particular subject of enquiry.

Guidelines for "why" and "how" questions

1. When asking questions to stimulate children's reasoning, make sure they include "what do you think about" or "why do you think."
2. Don't ask questions of this type until children have had the necessary experience they need so they can reason from evidence.
3. When children ask "why" questions consider whether they have the experience to understand the answer.
4. Don't be afraid to say you don't know an answer, or that no one knows (if it is a philosophical question).
5. Break up questions whose answers would be too complex into ones that concern relationships that children can find out about and understand.
6. Take children's questions seriously, as an expression of what interests them; even if the questions cannot be answered, don't discourage the asking.

Reprinted by permission from *Primary Science: Taking the Plunge* by Wynne Harlen.

Table 7.3.1 Sample Student Data

Cross-Sectional Shape of Model Bone	Evidence of Strength
Round	Five books
Square	Two books
Triangle	Two books

2. Table 7.3.1 shows sample data for bones made from heavy tablet paper. Answers will vary widely depending on paper, size, books, and so on.

EXPLAIN

1. Cylindrical bones can support more weight than can other shapes of bones.
2. Although the data may vary widely, students should agree that cylindrical bones can carry the most weight.
3. If students are careful in collecting their data and controlling variables they should see that as the number of sides of a column increases, its strength increases as well.

EXTEND

1. Have students observe pictures of natural objects such as trees, plant stems, other skeletons, and so on.
2. Give the students an assortment of pictures of common objects such as utility poles, silos, chair legs, and so on.
3. Students should see that many natural and engineered supporting columns are indeed cylindrical.
4. Cylindrical columns are the strongest shape using the least amount of material. Therefore, institutional furniture, such as the tables and chairs found in most classrooms, has round legs. Students are likely to question why all columns are not cylindrical. This would be a good question for further study. To that end it may be interesting for students to interview local builders or architects. Some reasons may include ease of assembly, cost, and so on.

Teaching Focus

Reflecting on Your Questioning Skills

It is a good practice to tape yourself as you teach science and interact with your students in discussions as well as while they are investigating. This enables you to reflect on aspects of your questioning technique, including the following:

1. Divergent versus convergent questions
2. Wait time
   a. Do you wait at least 3 seconds?
   b. Do you answer your own questions?
3. Gender and ethnic equity
   a. Do you call on all students equally?
   b. Do you ask all students the same types of questions?
   c. Do you provide all students the same type of responses?
4. Do you call on students from all parts of the classroom (rather than those in the front or in a specific area)?
5. Do you call on volunteers as well as nonvolunteers?
6. Do you project a friendly and nurturing image so students feel comfortable and secure in responding?
7. Pattern of discourse. Most classroom discussions follow the pattern shown in "a" with the teacher dominating the discussion. You can increase the involvement of your students by working toward the pattern shown in "b."
   a. teacher—student—teacher—student—teacher—student or
   b. teacher—student—student—student—student—teacher

APPLY

Bones have many functions. One is strength and support. Those bones are primarily cylindrical. Another function is protecting critical organs of the body such as the brain, heart, and lungs. These bones are not cylindrical. Ribs, for example, are flatter and therefore cover a greater area with less material. The pelvis has a rather unique design and is critical for walking. You may wish to have students compare the pelvises of different animals. That of the penguin is particularly interesting.

Teaching Focus Summary: Questioning Strategies

- During the Engage phase, ask questions that help students express their own ideas about a topic rather than asking for science content answers.
- Interact with student groups while they are conducting the explorations. Ask students questions to ensure that they know what they are trying to find out and how they will find it out.
- Use open-ended explorable questions that focus on what happens rather than why something happens. Allow students to try out their own ideas and collect evidence to answer the question.
- Use wait time to give students a few seconds to respond to a question. This results in more complex responses, increases the number of student responses, and increases students' speculative thinking.
- Follow the guidelines for asking productive questions of students.
- Reflect on your questioning skills to improve your teaching practice.

References

Baumgarten, A., & Bacher, M. (2006). Planning science and English instruction: One teacher's experience. In A. Fathman and D. Crowther (Eds.), *Science for English language learners* (pp. 25–36). Arlington, VA: NSTA Press.

Elstgeest, J. (1985). The right question at the right time. In W. Harlen (Ed.), *Primary science: Taking the plunge*. Oxford: Heinemann.

National Research Council. (1996). *National Science Education Standards*. Washington, DC: National Academy Press.

Osborne, R., & Freyberg, P. (1985). *Learning in science: The implications of children's science*. Hong Kong: Heinemann.

Rowe, M. B. (1973). *Teaching science as continuous inquiry*. New York: McGraw-Hill.

Rowe, M. B. (1996). Science, silence, and sanctions. *Science and Children, 34*(1), 35–37.

INVESTIGATION 8

HEREDITY

(5–8)

Teaching Focus: Using Educational Technology in Classroom Practice

Lesson 8.1

Examining Our Traits

ENGAGE

Look at the picture of the two siblings that your teacher is holding. How are the two people similar? How are they different?

Now look at two students in your class. What are some physical characteristics that are similar between the two students? How are you similar to them?

Study the pictures of the two ears in Figure 8.1.1. Look at the ear lobes. How are they different?

The two different kinds of ear lobes are an example of a physical characteristic. We can compare ourselves to each other to see how many characteristics we share. We will investigate the following question: **What physical characteristics do you have in common with your classmates?**

Figure 8.1.1

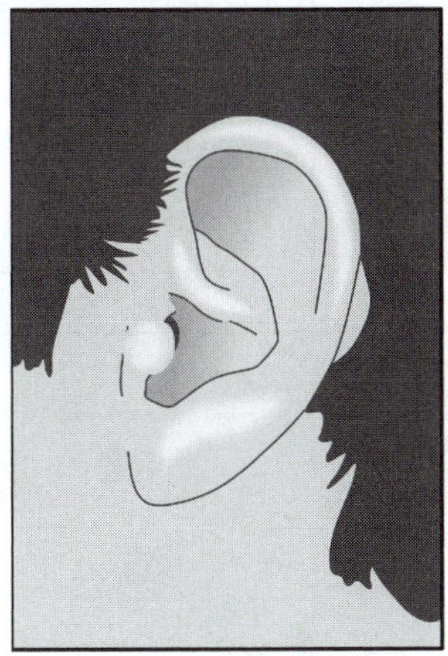

Detached ear lobe

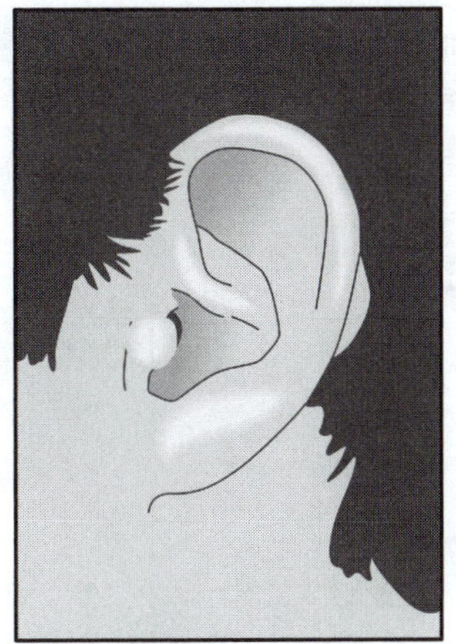

Attached ear lobe

EXPLORE

1. Work with a partner to determine if you possess the following traits. Record your responses in the following chart.

Physical Characteristics	Yes, I Have This Trait	No, I Do Not Have This Trait
Detached earlobes 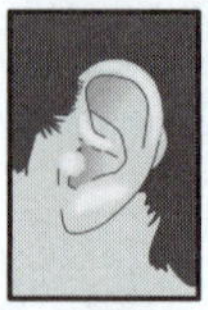		
Hitchhiker's thumb 		
Naturally curly hair 		
Dimples 		
Cleft chin 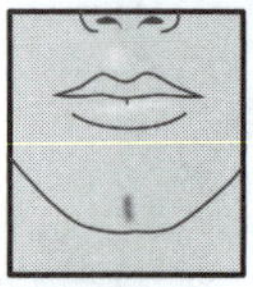		
Freckles 		
Right-handed 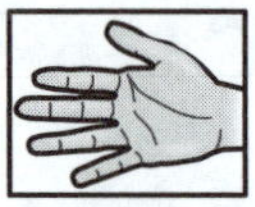		
Widow's peak 		

Physical Characteristics	Yes, I Have This Trait	No, I Do Not Have This Trait
Can roll tongue		
Can see the colors red and green red green		

2. How many traits do you share with your partner?

3. Work with another pair of students to compare the number of traits that you share with each of them.

EXPLAIN

1. First, tally the number of students in your group that possess a trait. Then, as a class, tally the number of students that possess each of the traits. Record the information in the chart below.

Physical Characteristics	Number of Students in Group with the Trait	Number of Students in Class with the Trait
Detached earlobes		
Hitchhiker's thumb		
Naturally curly hair		
Dimples		
Cleft chin		

(continued)

Physical Characteristics	Number of Students in Group with the Trait	Number of Students in Class with the Trait
Freckles		
Right-handed		
Widow's peak		
Can roll tongue		
Can see the colors red and green		

2. Graph the results from your class for the number of students that possess each trait.

3. What is the most common trait in your class? The least common trait in your class?

EXTEND

1. Although you and your classmates share many traits, each of you is unique because you have a certain combination of traits that is different from that of others. How many different traits would you have to look at to identify a classmate as a unique individual?

2. Have the entire class stand and select one student to begin. That classmate will say whether he or she has detached earlobes. Everyone with the same trait remains standing, and students without that trait must sit down. For all students still standing, continue with the next trait, a hitchhiker's thumb.

Students with both traits remain standing. Continue until only the first student is standing. Is that student unique? Play the game again with another student.

3. How many traits were needed to identify your classmate as a unique individual?

APPLY

How do you think your class compares with a larger population for these traits?

Calculate the frequency of each of the following traits.

$$\frac{\text{Number of students with the trait}}{\text{Number of students in the class}} \times 100 = \_\_\_\_\_\_\_\%$$

Trait	Frequency in Our Class	Frequency in the General Population
Hitchhiker's thumb		25%
Tongue rolling		70%
Right-handed		93%
Color-blind		8% males, <1% females

How does your class compare with the general population?

Lesson 8.1
Examining Our Traits
Teaching Focus: Using Educational Technology in Classroom Practice

Education is that which remains, if one has forgotten everything he learned in school.

Albert Einstein (1950)

NSES CONTENT STANDARD, 5–8: REPRODUCTION AND HEREDITY

"Every organism requires a set of instructions for specifying its traits. Heredity is the passage of these instructions from one generation to the other. The characteristics of an organism can be described in terms of a combination of traits" (National Research Council, 1996, p. 157).

DESCRIPTIVE OBJECTIVE

Students will determine some of their physical characteristics or traits that make them unique individuals and compare these to those of their class and the general population.

MATERIALS

For the Engage phase, the teacher will need a picture of two siblings who resemble each other. Students will work in pairs to look for the traits, but each pair of students should have a small mirror to confirm that each student possesses each of the traits.

SCIENCE BACKGROUND

As humans we share many characteristics with others, but we are all unique individuals. This is because the traits that we possess are based on the genetic information that our parents provide. This information is located in the 23 chromosome pairs that are present in each of our cells. Each parent contributes half of the genetic information, or one set of 23 chromosomes, to each offspring, resulting in new combinations of genetic information. These 23 pairs of chromosomes contain more than 60,000 genes. Some genes determine one specific trait, while other traits are the result of many genes interacting.

Each gene consists of two parts, one located on each of the chromosomes in the pair (one from the mother and one from the father). Therefore, a trait controlled by one gene can have the same information, or different information, from each parent. The different forms of a gene are referred to as *alleles* and are represented by capital and lowercase letters. For instance, one trait that is examined in the survey is earlobe attachment. One form of earlobe attachment is unattached or free earlobes, designated by "E," and another form is attached earlobes, designated by "e." If both alleles are the same, the gene is referred to as *homozygous* (EE or ee). If the two alleles are different, Ee, the gene is called *heterozygous*. If EE and Ee result in the same physical characteristic, the allele "E" is called the *dominant* allele and is always designated by a capital letter. The other allele, e, is referred to as the *recessive* allele. Recessive alleles are always indicated with a lowercase letter. In some traits, the heterozygous form, Ee, results in a different physical characteristic than does either of the homozygous forms, EE or ee. In that case, the variation is referred to as *codominant*. Sometimes, students think that the dominant allele is the most common, but this is not always the case. Also, some may think that the dominant allele is "better" or is the most desired, which also is not always the case. The dominant traits in this lesson are detached earlobes, hitchiker's thumb, tongue rolling, dimples, right-handedness, freckles, curly hair, cleft chin, widow's peak, and normal color vision.

In this lesson, students will look for a variety of traits that are considered to be determined by a single gene. New research indicates that this might not necessarily be true for all of the traits in the survey. That is, some of the traits explored here may be controlled by more than one gene.

Note: Students will determine the presence or absence of several physical characteristics in themselves and compare these traits to those of their classmates. They will not collect the data from their family members because some students may not have access to their biological parents or may not know that one or both of their parents is not a biological parent.

MISCONCEPTION INFORMATION

Many students find the study of genetics difficult because the abstract nature of the concepts does not allow them to directly observe the processes. Some misconceptions that you may find include:

- Offspring inherit genes only from the parent of the same gender.
- Acquired characteristics in parents can be inherited by the offspring.
- Genetic ratios of Punnett squares are fixed numbers rather than probabilities.

For additional information, you may wish to refer to the following:

Cavallo, A. (1996). Meaningful learning, reasoning ability and students' understanding and problem solving of topics in genetics. *Journal of Research in Science Teaching, 33*, 625–656.

Clough, E., & Wood-Robinson, C. (1985). Children's understanding of inheritance. *Journal of Biological Education, 19*(4), 304–310.

TEACHING FOCUS

ISTE *National Educational Technology Standards*

The International Society for Technology in Education (ISTE) has developed educational technology standards for students, teachers, and administrators. These standards focus on six areas for students: (1) basic operations and concepts, (2) social, ethical, and human issues, (3) technology productivity tools, (4) technology communications tools, (5) technology research tools, and (6) technology problem-solving and decision-making tools. More information on the technology standards can be found at http://cnets.iste.org.

CLASSROOM SAFETY

There are no special safety concerns.

ENGAGE

Show the students a picture of two siblings to begin the discussion on similar and different traits. Then, select two students from the class to observe similar and different traits. Point out the difference between attached and detached ear lobes as shown in the picture. Focus the discussion on the following question: **What physical characteristics do you have in common with your classmates?**

EXPLORE

1. Students should work in pairs to determine whether they possess each of the traits. You will probably have to help students understand each of the traits. Refer them to the pictures as examples.
2. Students will total the number of traits that they share with their partner to look for commonalities.
3. Have two pairs of students work together as a group to compare traits and to tally data for use in the Explain phase.

> Teaching Tip
>
> **Compiling Data**
>
> Because compiling data from 25 or more students can be time consuming, use ways to speed up the process. In this lesson, we have students work in small groups to tally their data as a group. As groups finish the process, they can transfer their findings quickly on a large chart for the class to use. You could also use a blank transparency on an overhead.

> **TEACHING FOCUS**
>
> **Using a Graphing Program**
>
> Students may practice making this graph using a computer program such as Microsoft Excel®. Many programs of this type are very user friendly, and after students have learned how to use the features, they will be able to make graphs easily and efficiently.
>
> As an alternative, you could make an electronic graph, projecting it for the class to view and discussing it after they have completed a graph on paper.

> Teaching Tip
>
> **Use Many Modalities of Learning**
>
> It is helpful to use many different modalities of learning, especially with an abstract topic such as inheritance. In this activity, we use several different ways to demonstrate the concept of uniqueness in humans: examining visual physical characteristics, graphing the results, and using a kinesthetic activity.

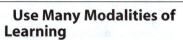

EXPLAIN

1. Students will work in groups first to tally the data for their group and then contribute their group's information to the class totals. Put a large chart on the board or on a large sheet of paper.
2. Students will make a bar graph for the data, putting the different traits on the x-axis and the number of students who possess each trait on the y-axis.
3. Students will analyze the graph to determine the most common trait and the least common trait. These will vary from class to class depending on the sample of students.

EXTEND

1. Help students understand that although we are all similar, much variation exists in the distribution of the traits that each of us possesses.
2. This activity helps make the above statement very concrete. Usually, the chosen student discovers that she or he possesses a unique set of these characteristics after four to six rounds of the game. Because we are looking at 10 traits, theoretically 2^{10} (or 1024) different combinations are possible.

APPLY

Students will calculate the frequency of each of the following traits for their class data, then compare their results with the frequency in the general population.

$$\frac{\text{Number of students with the trait}}{\text{Number of students in the class}} \times 100 = \underline{\hspace{2cm}}\%$$

Trait	Frequency in Our Class	Frequency in the General Population
Hitchhiker's thumb		25%
Tongue rolling		70%
Right-handed		93%
Color-blind		8% males, <1% females

The frequencies for one class may be different from those of the general population due to the small sample size.

Lesson 8.2
A Litter of Puppies*

ENGAGE

Look at the picture of a litter of puppies. Have you seen newborn puppies before? What did they look like? How were they similar? How were they different?

How were the puppies like their parents? How were they different from their parents?

Your teacher has two paper dogs that will represent the parents of puppies. Look at the traits of the parent dogs. What do you think the puppies will look like? What traits do you think the puppies will have? How will they be similar to their parents? How will they be different?

We will investigate the following question: **What traits will the puppies have from their parents?**

EXPLORE

1. Your teacher will provide you with the traits of the two parent dogs. You will work with a partner to sort the strips of paper with the mother's information into pairs of strips of the same length. Turn the strips face down to conceal the writing. Now select one strip from each pair. Put these strips in the "puppy pile." Put the unused strips back into the mother envelope.

2. Repeat the process with the father's information. Add the selected strips to the "puppy pile." Put the unused strips back into the father envelope.

*This lesson was adapted from Judy M. Nesmith's *Plantbop Lesson.* Used with permission.

3. Now you will determine the traits that your puppy will have by decoding the information. Pair up the paper strips according to length. Record the information for each pair in the chart below.

Pairs of Strips for Trait	Mother's Information	Father's Information
Tail		
Nose		
Eye color		
Fur color		
Face markings		
Gender		

4. Build your puppy based on the traits. Your teacher will give you a key you can use to decode the traits.

5. Place your completed puppy in the "nursery" in your classroom.

EXPLAIN

1. Compare the puppy you built to the parents. What traits does it share with the mother? How is it different from the mother?

2. What traits does it share with the father? How is it different from the father?

3. Examine the other puppies. How are they all alike? How are they different?

4. Tally the puppies that possess each of the traits and record the numbers in the chart below. Calculate the frequencies of the traits and record them in the chart below.

Trait	Number of Puppies with the Trait	Frequency of the Trait in the Entire Litter of Puppies
Straight tail		
Curly tail		
Triangle nose		
Round nose		
Brown eyes		
Blue eyes		
Yellow fur		
Orange fur		
Red fur		
Face markings		
No face markings		
Female		
Male		

5. How could you get so many variations if the puppies all had the same parents?

EXTEND

1. One way to predict the probability of the various forms of a trait is to make a tool known as a *Punnett square*. The Punnett square shows the alleles from each parent and all of their possible combinations. Each parent can pass either of the two alleles for a gene to the offspring, resulting in four possible combinations. See the example for tails for your puppies in Table 8.2.1.

Table 8.2.1 Sample Punnett Square for Tails

Mother/Father	t	t
T	Tt	Tt
t	tt	tt

As you can see, of the four possible combinations of the alleles two different forms occur that are called *genotypes* (namely, Tt and tt). In this case, T is the dominant allele and, if present, will always result in a *phenotype* (how the trait shows up in physical appearance) of straight tails, and t is the recessive allele resulting in the phenotype of curly tails. What is the probability that a puppy from these parents will have a straight tail? A curly tail?

2. Use the information in Table 8.2.2 to make a Punnett square for each of the two traits. Refer to the key provided by your teacher for decoding the traits to determine the probabilities of what these puppies will look like.

Table 8.2.2 Data for Punnett Squares

Trait	Mother	Father
Fur color	Ff	Ff
Eye color	Ee	Ee

3. What is the probability that a puppy will have yellow fur? Red fur? Orange fur?

4. What is the probability that a puppy will have brown eyes? Blue eyes?

5. Consider two different parent dogs. Suppose the mother had EE for eye color (brown) and the father had ee for eye color (blue). Make a Punnett square to determine the probabilities for the puppy's eye color.

Another tool used to study inheritance patterns is a *pedigree*, a family tree chart that tracks a particular trait through several generations. See the example provided by your teacher that shows the occurrence of curly tails through three generations of dogs.

Imagine you are a dog breeder looking for a mate for your puppy that has grown up to be a champion dog. Decide whether or not you want the offspring of your dog to have curly tails. From the last generation of dogs, select which dog you want to breed with your champion. Make a Punnett square to determine the probability of producing a puppy with a curly or a straight tail.

Lesson 8.2

A Litter of Puppies

Teaching Focus: Using Educational Technology in Classroom Practice

NSES CONTENT STANDARD, 5–8: REPRODUCTION AND HEREDITY

"In many species, including humans, females produce eggs and males produce sperm. An egg and sperm unite to begin development of a new individual. That new individual receives genetic information from its mother (via the egg) and its father (via the sperm). Sexually produced offspring never are identical to either of their parents. Every organism requires a set of instructions for specifying its traits. Heredity is the passage of these instructions from one generation to another" (National Research Council, 1996, p. 157).

DESCRIPTIVE OBJECTIVE

Students will simulate the processes of meiosis and fertilization and construct a "baby" from the genetic information to predict the probabilities for dominant, recessive, and codominant patterns of inheritance.

MATERIALS

For the Engage phase, the teacher will need a picture of a litter of puppies with a parent dog, if available, and two paper parent dogs prepared ahead of time (see Figure 8.2.1). Note that the mother dog will have a straight tail, round nose, brown eyes, orange fur, and white face markings, with a pink collar to indicate she is female. The father dog will have a curly tail, triangle nose, brown eyes, orange fur, and white face markings, with a blue collar indicating he is a male.

Figure 8.2.1 Mother and father dogs

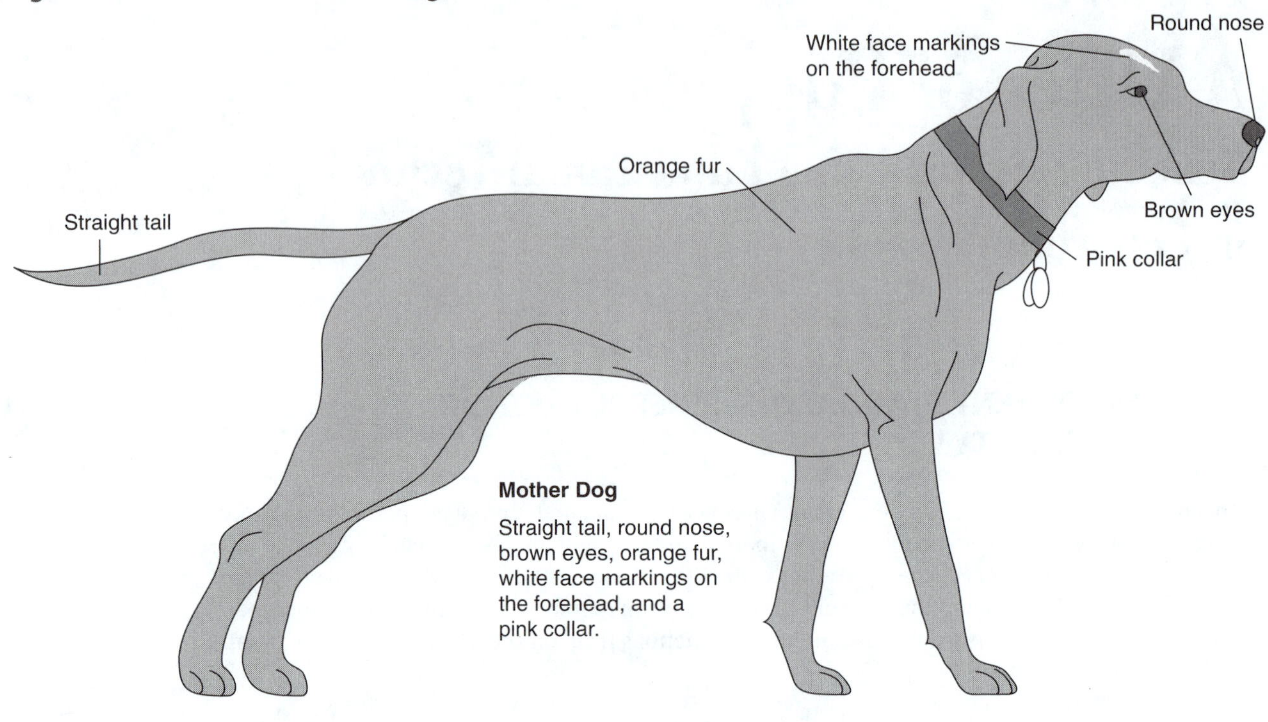
White face markings on the forehead
Round nose
Orange fur
Straight tail
Brown eyes
Pink collar
Mother Dog
Straight tail, round nose, brown eyes, orange fur, white face markings on the forehead, and a pink collar.

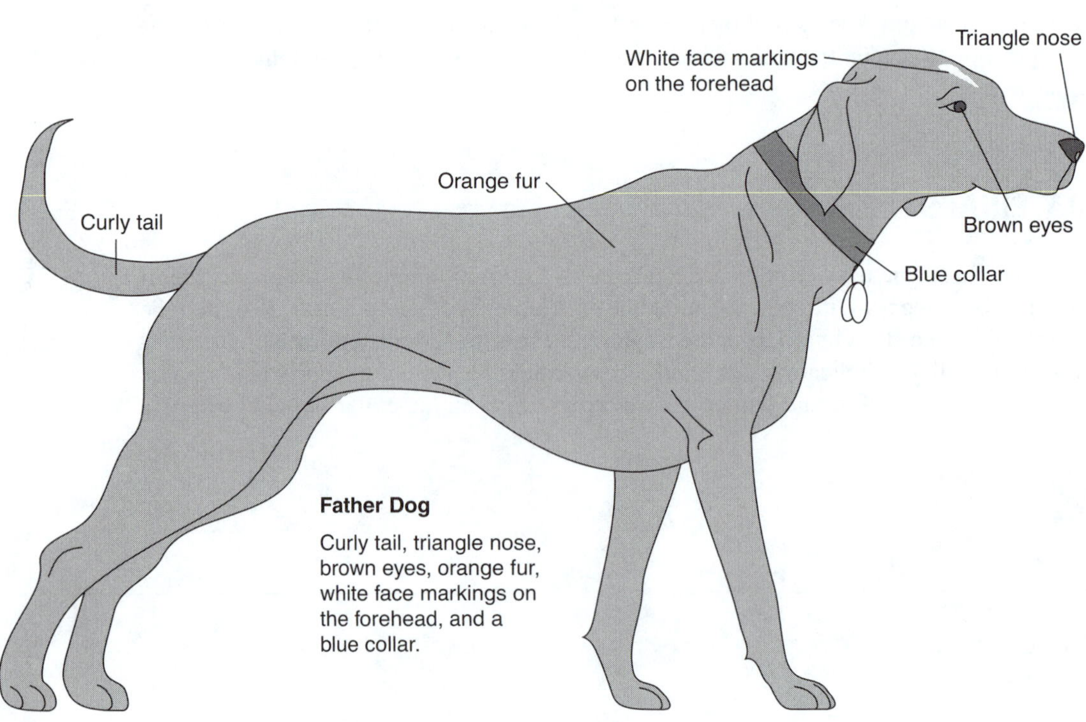
White face markings on the forehead
Triangle nose
Orange fur
Curly tail
Brown eyes
Blue collar
Father Dog
Curly tail, triangle nose, brown eyes, orange fur, white face markings on the forehead, and a blue collar.

For each pair of students, provide a stiff paper copy of the puppy, crayons or markers for adding the traits, scissors, tape, and a set of prepared chromosomes from each parent in separate envelopes. Each of the six pairs of chromosomes from both the mother and father should be the same length (e.g., 2, 3, 4, 5, 6, and 7 cm). Make the mother's chromosomes from pink paper and the father's from blue paper. Label each with the letter for the allele and the name of the trait (see Figure 8.2.2). The same information is also summarized in Table 8.2.3.

Table 8.2.3 Parent Dogs' Traits and Chromosomes

Trait	Mother's Chromosomes	Father's Chromosomes
Tail	Tt	tt
Nose	nn	Nn
Eye color	Ee	Ee
Fur color	Ff	Ff
White markings on face	Mm	Mm
Gender	XX	XY

Figure 8.2.2 Mother and father chromosomes

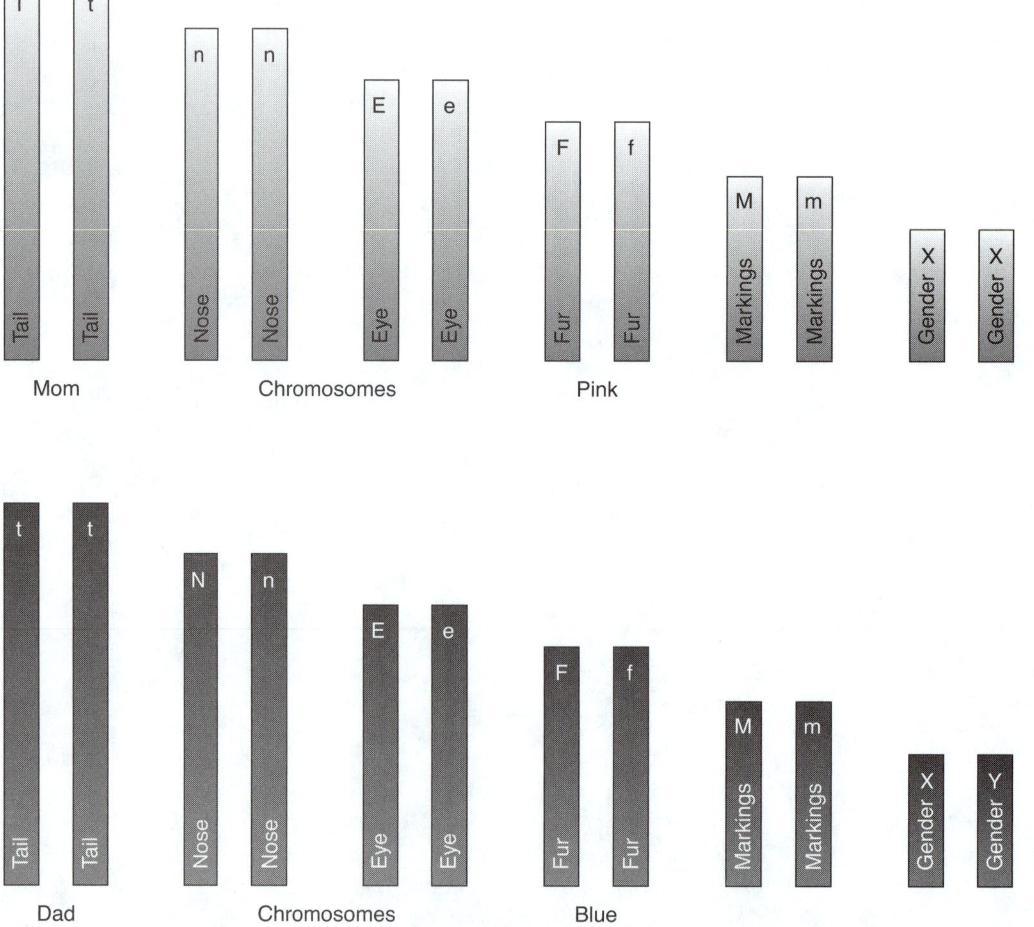

You will also need to provide the students with a key they can use to decode the alleles after they have created the puppies. You could also put the key on an overhead transparency for the entire class to refer to when creating the puppies.

Key to Puppy Traits

Straight tail = TT or Tt
Curly tail = tt

Triangle nose = NN or Nn
Round nose = nn

Brown eyes = EE or Ee
Blue eyes = ee

Yellow fur = FF
Orange fur = Ff
Red fur = ff

White markings on face = MM or Mm
No markings on face = mm

Female puppy = XX
Male puppy = XY

SCIENCE BACKGROUND

For the discussion on dominant, recessive, and codominant patterns of inheritance, see the Science Background section of the previous lesson.

The process of meiosis leads to the new combinations of genetic information from a set of parents in the offspring of the next generation. The two sex cells combine to give the resulting offspring a full set of chromosomes, half from the mother and half from the father.

The results of meiosis can be symbolized with a *Punnett square*, a tool that identifies the genotypes (the allele combinations) resulting from the union of a set of parent cells. A Punnett square shows all possible genotypic combinations from each parent for a particular trait. (Punnett squares are used in the Extend phase of this lesson and in the next lesson.)

Another tool used to study inheritance is the *pedigree* or *family tree*. (A pedigree is used in the Apply phase of this lesson.) This chart allows geneticists to follow a trait as it passes from one generation to another. A pedigree uses circles to represent females and squares to represent males. Circles and squares filled in with a color mean that a trait is present in that individual, and those half-filled with color mean that the person is a carrier (the person does not display the trait). A carrier is a person with one dominant and one recessive allele. Some recessive traits may not show up in the phenotypes in one generation, that is, they seem to "skip" a generation.

CLASSROOM SAFETY

There are no special safety concerns here.

ENGAGE

Show students a picture of a litter of puppies and at least one parent to begin the discussion of inheritance of traits. Then, show the two prepared paper parent dogs for the investigation. Encourage students to predict what the puppies will look like. Focus students' attention on the explorable question: **What traits will the puppies have from their parents?**

EXPLORE

1. Students will work in pairs to create a puppy based on the parents. As a result, the class will have a large sample of offspring to enable them to see variation of the traits. Provide students with the envelopes containing the father's and mother's chromosomes. Students will simulate the process of meiosis by selecting one chromosome of each pair from the mother's envelope to pass onto the puppy. Unused chromosomes will be put back into the envelope and not used.
2. Repeat the process for the father's chromosomes.
3. Students will record the alleles for each strip. This will enable them to identify the genotypes of each trait later in the lesson.
4. Provide students access to the key to decode the phenotypes at this point, and no sooner. This prevents students from manipulating the traits that their puppies will have.
5. Students should display the puppies so that everyone can view the offspring and the parents.

TEACHING FOCUS

Using a Digital Camera

You could take a digital photograph of each puppy. Then, you could paste all of the pictures onto one or two pages for printing to enable each group to examine the puppies' characteristics easily. You could also put the digital photographs into a class album or post them on a class Web site.

Teaching Tip

Communicating Learning

This lesson enables students to communicate their work to others. You could have students document their work with the digital pictures suggested above. The puppies and their parents could also be displayed in a hallway, on a bulletin board, in a media center, and so on to share with the entire school. Students could also communicate their learning electronically through a class Web site to those outside the classroom.

EXPLAIN

1. Students will notice that the puppies have some, but probably not all of their mother's characteristics (it is mathematically possible, however).
2. The puppies will also have some of the father's traits, but will not be identical to the father. Students may also notice that some of the puppies have a trait that neither of the parents possesses, such as red or yellow fur.
3. Because there are 2^6 (or 64) possible combinations of the six traits, the students should notice that the puppies are not all alike, but rather share some traits and not others. Students will also notice that some puppies look very similar, while others look very different. They may also relate this observation to themselves or to other families that they know. Some siblings within a family will look very similar and others quite different.
4. Students will examine the puppies and calculate the frequency of each trait. The numbers shown in the chart below are calculated using Punnett squares and are the percentages expected for a sufficiently large population of offspring. Repeating the combination of the parent dogs eventually would yield results that approach these percentages.

Trait	Number of Puppies with the Trait	Frequency of the Trait in the Entire Litter of Puppies
Straight tail		50%
Curly tail		50%
Triangle nose		50%

Trait	Number of Puppies with the Trait	Frequency of the Trait in the Entire Litter of Puppies
Round nose		50%
Brown eyes		75%
Blue eyes		25%
Yellow fur		25%
Orange fur		50%
Red fur		25%
Face markings		75%
No face markings		25%
Female		50%
Male		50%

5. Students should realize that many different combinations of chromosomes could have been selected from each parent. If they have difficulty understanding this, have them pair the chromosomes and select them randomly several times to show them that different combinations of chromosomes occur each time.

EXTEND

1. Work through the Punnett square (Table 8.2.4) with the class. Show them how it can help them figure out the probabilities of genotypes and phenotypes for a specific parental trait.

   The chances are 2 out of 4 (50%) that the puppy will have a straight tail (Tt). There is also a 50% chance that a puppy will have a curly tail (tt).

Table 8.2.4 Punnett Square for Tails

Mother/Father	t	t
T	Tt	Tt
t	tt	tt

2. Students will construct Punnett squares for the two traits of fur color and eye color (Tables 8.2.5 and 8.2.6) to determine the genotype. Then, in the following questions, they will determine the phenotype by referring to the key for decoding the traits.

Table 8.2.5 Punnett Square for Fur Color

	F	f
F	FF	Ff
f	Ff	ff

Table 8.2.6 Punnett Square for Eye Color

	E	e
E	EE	Ee
e	Ee	ee

3. The probability that a puppy will have yellow fur, FF, is 25%. That for red fur, ff, is 25%. Orange fur, Ff, is 50%. This trait is an example of codominance.
4. The probability that a puppy will have brown eyes is 75% because both EE and Ee result in brown eyes. The probability for blue eyes, ee, is 25%.

Table 8.2.7 Punnett Square for Eye Color

	e	e
E	Ee	Ee
E	Ee	Ee

5. The offspring will have a 100% probability for brown eyes.

Teaching Focus

Use a Concept Mapping Program for Creating Pedigrees

You can easily create pedigrees to study family trees by using a concept map computer program such as Inspiration®. The circle (female) and square (male) symbols are available as options. The circles and squares are fully colored if the trait is present in that individual and half filled with color if the individual is a carrier. (A carrier has one dominant and one recessive allele.) This program makes it very simple to link the symbols and arrange the links in "trees."

APPLY

Show the sample pedigree (Figure 8.2.3) to students and explain how they can use it to study the inheritance of a specific trait through several generations. Students are to breed a third-generation dog with their dog. Have them construct a Punnett square to determine the probabilities of dogs having curly or straight tails.

Figure 8.2.3 Three-generation pedigree

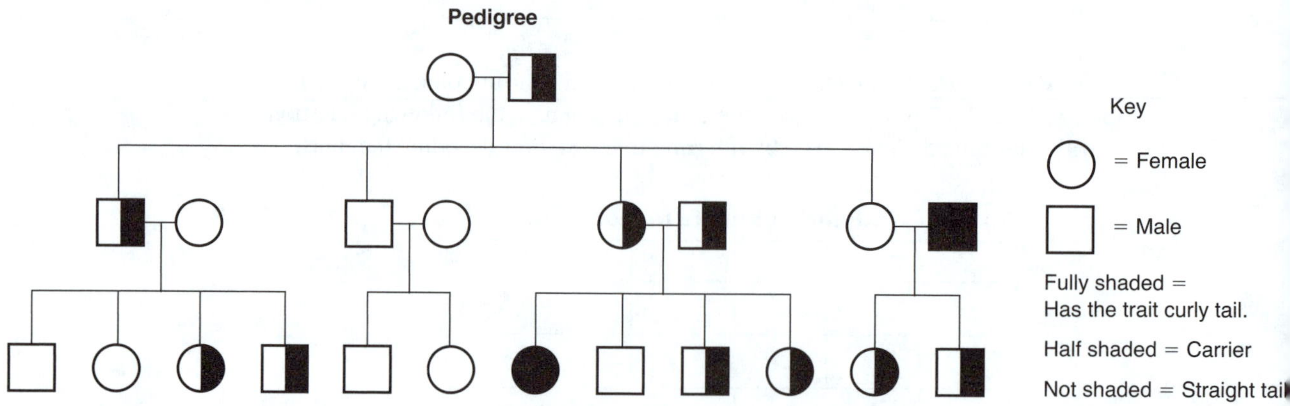

Pedigree

Key

○ = Female

□ = Male

Fully shaded = Has the trait curly tail.

Half shaded = Carrier

Not shaded = Straight tail

Lesson 8.3
Reading Genetic Code*

ENGAGE

Look at the puppy that your teacher is holding. How is it similar to the other puppies? How is it different?

What do you think happened? What information do you think the alleles for tails contained?

In this lesson you will investigate more closely the information contained by the alleles passed on to the offspring by the parents. Sometimes the information on the allele is unreadable. In this lesson you again will simulate producing an offspring from two adult dogs, but this time not all of the genetic information is readable. We will investigate the following question: **What happens to a puppy when the alleles are unreadable?**

EXPLORE

1. Your teacher will provide you with two envelopes that contain the genetic information from the parent dogs. Place all of the strips of paper face down and pair up the mother's chromosomes. Select one chromosome from each pair to pass on to the puppy.

2. Repeat the above process with the father's chromosomes.

3. Read the information on each of the puppy's chromosomes and build the puppy according to the genetic information. Refer to the teacher-supplied key to decode the traits.

*This lesson was adapted from Judy M. Nesmith's *Plantbop Lesson*. Used with permission.

EXPLAIN

1. How are these puppies similar to the ones your class created in the last lesson?

2. How are the puppies different?

3. Compare the readable genes with their unreadable counterparts. What do you think could have happened to the genetic code?

EXTEND

1. What are some human genetic disorders of which you are aware?

2. Research a genetic disorder. Find out the cause of the disorder, how frequently it occurs, and what treatment may be available.

3. Create a presentation to share this information with the class.

APPLY

Read the case study provided by your teacher and use a Punnett square and a pedigree to explain the trait to the family.

Lesson 8.3

Reading Genetic Code

Teaching Focus: Using Educational Technology in Classroom Practice

NSES CONTENT STANDARD, 5–8: REPRODUCTION AND HEREDITY

"Heredity information is contained in genes, located in the chromosomes of each cell. Each gene carries a single unit of information. An inherited trait of an individual can be determined by one or by many genes, and a single gene can influence more than one trait. A human cell contains many thousands of different genes" (National Research Council, 1996, p. 157).

DESCRIPTIVE OBJECTIVE

Students will learn about genetic mutations and genetic disorders in humans.

MATERIALS

For each pair of students, provide a set of parent chromosomes with written instructions (see Figure 8.3.1), a stiff paper copy of the puppy, crayons or markers, scissors, and tape. For the Extend phase, students will need access to resources on genetic disorders.

Figure 8.3.1 Key to puppy traits for reading genetic code

Trait	Mother's Chromosomes	Father's Chromosomes
Tail	MAKEASTRAIGHTTAIL ***makeacurlail***	makeacurlytail ***makeacurlail***
Nose	makearoundnose makearoundnose	MAKEATRIANGLENOSE makearoundnose
Eye color	PRODUCEBROWNEYES produceblueeyes	PRODUCEBROWNEYES produceblueeyes
Fur color	PRODUCEYELLOWFUR ***produceyezxkqllowfur***	Produceredfur ***produceyezxkqllowfur***
White markings on face	TURNONWHITEMARKINGS turnoffwhitemarkings	TURNONWHITEMARKINGS turnoffwhitemarkings
Sex	XX	XY

Note that we have indicated the mutations in boldface italic type.

TEACHER: Grades 5–8

The written genetic codes for the parents' chromosomes are listed in Figure 8.3.1.

1. Straight tail (dominant)= MAKEASTRAIGHTTAIL and makeacurlytail, OR MAKEASTRAIGHTTAIL and makeacurlail
   Curly tail (recessive) = makeacurlytail and makeacurlail
   No tail (mutation)= makeacurlail and makeacurlail
2. Triangle nose (dominant) = MAKEATRIANGLENOSE and makearoundnose
   Round nose (recessive)= makearoundnose and makearoundnose
3. Brown eyes (dominant)= PRODUCEBROWNEYES and produceblueeyes, OR PRODUCEBROWNEYES and PRODUCEBROWNEYES
   Blue eyes (recessive)= produceblueeyes and produceblueeyes
4. Yellow fur (dominant)= PRODUCEYELLOWFUR and produceyezxkqllowfur
   Orange fur (codominant)= PRODUCEYELLOWFUR and produceredfur
   Red fur (recessive)= produceredfur and produceyezxkqllowfur
   White fur (mutation)= produceyezxkqllowfur and produceyezxkqllowfur
5. White markings on face (dominant)= TURNONWHITEMARKINGS and turnoffwhitemarkings OR TURNONWHITEMARKINGS and TURNONWHITEMARKINGS
   No markings on face (recessive)= turnoffwhitemarkings and turnoffwhitemarkings
6. Female puppy = XX Male puppy = XY

As you can see, all the traits are the same as those in the previous lesson except for two. The tail has a deletion mutation in the code for the curly tail. If the puppy has both alleles with this unreadable message (makeacurlail), then the puppy will not have a tail. The fur has an insertion mutation in the code (produceyezxkqllowfur). If the puppy receives this mutation in both alleles, then no color is produced and the puppy will have white fur.

SCIENCE BACKGROUND

Mutations are changes in genes or chromosomes that cause variation in the offspring. Mutations are usually, but not always harmful. They can even be beneficial to organisms such as bacteria that develop resistance to antibiotics. A mutation that prevents bacteria from being destroyed by an antibiotic is beneficial to the bacteria. Some mutations, however, are neither beneficial nor harmful to an organism.

In humans, mutations in genes or chromosomes that are harmful are referred to as *genetic disorders*. Some common genetic disorders are Down syndrome, hemophilia, sickle-cell disease, and cystic fibrosis.

Note: Be aware that some of your students or their families may have genetic disorders. Consider carefully what disorders to study in the Extend phase of the lesson.

Teaching Tip

Using Cooperative Learning Groups

The Explore phase of the Learning Cycle provides a natural opportunity for using small groups. Students, especially English language learners, find cooperative learning groups very helpful because of the interactions between students within the group and between the teacher and individual groups. In cooperative groups, students work together as they learn, but can also be held accountable for individual learning. Students show individual accountability by recording work in individual science journals, through individual assessment in the Apply phase, or by receiving some other assessment by the teacher (Crowther, Vilá, & Fathman, 2006).

CLASSROOM SAFETY

This lesson involves no special safety concerns.

ENGAGE

Show the students a puppy with no tail and begin a discussion about how it could be the offspring of the original parent dogs. Review the previous lesson, reminding students that the alleles represent genetic information from the parents. In rare instances, this information may be unreadable as the result of a mutation. Don't introduce the idea of a mutation at this point unless the students bring it up. Accept their ideas and focus on the following question for the Explore phase: **What happens to a puppy when the alleles are unreadable?**

EXPLORE

1. Provide each pair of students with two envelopes that contain the genetic information from the parent dogs. Tell students to place all of the strips of paper face down so that they randomly select one from each pair of the mother's chromosomes.
2. Repeat the above process with the father's chromosomes.
3. Students will read the information on each of the chromosomes and build the puppy according to the genetic information. Have them refer to the key to decode the traits. Help students understand that when alleles have unreadable messages, the cells cannot carry out the instructions and, therefore, the traits (tail and fur) will experience mutations.

EXPLAIN

1. Students will notice that many of the traits of these puppies are still very similar to those of the previous puppies.
2. The puppies that are homozygous for the mutation will express changes in their phenotypes, such as white fur or no tail. The puppies will also differ as a result of different combinations of chromosomes.
3. When comparing the readable genes with their unreadable counterparts, students will notice that in one case (tail), letters are missing from the code. This is known as a *deletion* mutation. In the other case, the fur, additional letters are present that do not make sense. This is an *insertion* mutation.

EXTEND

1. Students will list some human genetic disorders of which they are aware. These may include Down syndrome, hemophilia, sickle-cell disease, and cystic fibrosis.
2. Students will research one genetic disorder to find out the cause of the disorder, how frequently it occurs, and what treatment is available. Students may work in pairs or in groups for this investigation as they locate resources and information about the disorder.
3. Students will create a presentation to share with the class. If technology is available, students should use it to make their presentations.

TEACHING FOCUS

Using the Internet for Research

Many students enjoy using the Internet at every possible opportunity. Searching for references, however, can be extremely time consuming. If you allow students to search, you should teach them how to search quickly and efficiently. If your school does not allow students to access the Internet, you can take advantage of the resources yourself. These include many great photographs, diagrams, simulations, short videos, and so on. One favorite site of many students is Brainpop.com, which contains many short "movies" that are great for including in the Explain phase of the learning cycle lessons.

TEACHING FOCUS

Equal Access

Some students are more hesitant than others to actively seek out and use technology for completing assignments. Be aware that some of your students will be very adept with many forms of technology while others may not have much experience or access to technology outside the school setting.

TEACHING FOCUS

Using Technology for Presentations

You may wish students to support their presentations by using educational technology such as Microsoft PowerPoint® or other multimedia authoring tools. Students could also share these presentations by posting them on a class Web site.

APPLY

Below is a sample case study that you may have students consider.

Case Study

Mr. and Mrs. Doe are visiting their physician to seek information. They have two children. Their son, John, has cystic fibrosis while their daughter, Jane, does not. They are expecting another baby and are worried that the new baby might also have cystic fibrosis. The doctor wants to know the family's history to track the passing of this genetic disorder from one generation to another. After interviewing Mr. and Mrs. Doe she learns that Mrs. Doe is an only child and does not have family members with the disorder. Mr. Doe has one sister with cystic fibrosis.

Draw a pedigree showing the relationships among the family members and the trait of cystic fibrosis. List the genotypes of each family member. Some members may have more than one possible genotype. Students should draw the pedigree and fill in the information given in the case study. Then, they will have to make inferences about the genotypes of Mr. and Mrs. Doe. Because Mr. Doe has a sister and a son with the trait, he clearly is heterozygous. Students will need to infer that John could have the trait only if both his parents carried the recessive allele. This would also explain why John's sister, Jane, does not have the trait. She could, however, be a carrier.

Make a Punnett square (Table 8.3.1) that shows the probability of each possible genotype for Mr. and Mrs. Doe's baby.

The probabilities for each genotype are:

CC – 25%

Cc – 50%

cc – 25%

Therefore, the probability that the baby will have cystic fibrosis (which is a recessive trait) is 25%.

Figure 8.3.2 Doe family pedigree

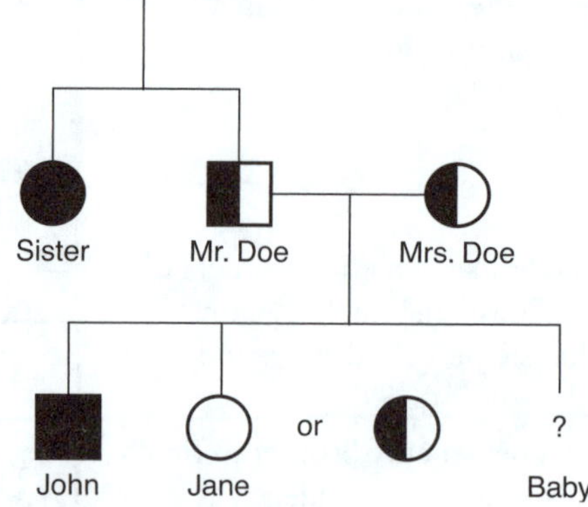

Table 8.3.1 Punnett Square for the Doe Baby

Mother/Father	C	c
C	CC	Cc
c	Cc	cc

Teaching Focus Summary: Using Educational Technology in Classroom Practice

- Have students work with a graphing program to practice making graphs when needed.
- Use a digital camera to record and document student work, publishing it in a variety of ways.
- Have students learn how to use a concept-mapping program to create a map that connects numerous ideas together in a network.
- If you allow students to search for information on the Internet, help them learn efficient searching methods.
- Be aware that some students may not have much experience or access to technology outside the school setting. These students will need additional help or encouragement to effectively use educational technology.
- Encourage students' use of multimedia tools to communicate with others through presentations or class Web sites.

References

Crowther, D., Vilá, J., & Fathman, A. (2006). Learners, programs, and teaching practices. In A. Fathman and D. Crowther (Eds.), *Science for English language learners* (pp. 9–21). Arlington, VA: NSTA Press.

Einstein, A. (1950). *Out of my later years*. New York: Philosophical Library.

International Society for Technology in Education. (2005). *National educational technology standards*. Retrieved from http://cnets.iste.org

National Research Council. (1996). *National Science Education Standards*. Washington, DC: National Academy Press.

UNIT III

Earth/Space Science

INVESTIGATION 9 Soil (K–4)

Teaching Focus: Developing Inquiry Abilities

Lesson 9.1 What Makes Up Soil?
Lesson 9.2 Investigating Soil and Water
Lesson 9.3 Soil Soaking Rates

INVESTIGATION 10 Motions of the Moon (5–8)

Teaching Focus: Identifying Misconceptions

Lesson 10.1 Moon Patterns and Motions
Lesson 10.2 Moon Phases
Lesson 10.3 Eclipses

INVESTIGATION 11 Interpreting Weather Maps (5–8)

Teaching Focus: Integrating Writing and Communication

Lesson 11.1 Comparing Inside Temperatures
Lesson 11.2 Comparing Outside Temperatures
Lesson 11.3 Comparing National Temperatures and Weather

INVESTIGATION 12 The Water Cycle (5–8)

Teaching Focus: Integrating Inquiry in Textbook Instruction

Lesson 12.1 Evaporation
Lesson 12.2 Condensation
Lesson 12.3 The Water Cycle

INVESTIGATION

SOIL

(K–4)

Teaching Focus: Developing Inquiry Abilities

Lesson 9.1

What Makes Up Soil?

ENGAGE

In the summer it is fun to have a garden of flowers or vegetables. Have you ever planted a garden? What is the soil like in a garden? How is it different from the soil in a sandbox? What is soil anyway? What is it made of? How do you think you could find out what soil is?

We will investigate: **What makes up soil?**

EXPLORE

1. Closely observe a sample of soil. Use a hand lens and your pencil point to separate the pieces.

2. Are all of the pieces the same size? The same color?

3. Group the different kinds of materials that make up the soil. Describe the common properties of the materials in each different pile. *Except for taste*, remember to use all of your senses to describe the soil materials.

4. How many different materials make up your soil? How do you know? Wash your hands when you have finished examining the soil.

EXPLAIN

1. Compare your observations and explanations with those of other students.

2. What different kinds of materials make up the soil in your sample?

3. Where might these different materials have come from?

EXTEND

1. Your teacher will give you a different kind of soil. Repeat your investigation with this sample. Describe what makes this soil different.

2. What happens when your soil gets wet? Make a prediction.

3. Make a small pile of each soil. Add several drops of water to each pile. Describe what happens to the water. Observe the wet soils and describe how they react when you gently squeeze them with your fingers.

4. Are you able to roll each of them into a ball? Wash your hands again before you continue.

APPLY

Get several samples of soil from the schoolyard or your neighborhood. Study the soils as you did above. How are they similar to the two soils you studied above? Different?

Which of the soils might be better for growing a bean plant? What are the properties that make it better? How can you find out? Design an investigation to answer this question. Show it to your teacher, then do the investigation and report your results.

Lesson 9.1

What Makes Up Soil?

Teaching Focus: Developing Inquiry Abilities

From the earliest grades, students should experience science in a form that engages them in the active construction of ideas and explanations and enhances their opportunities to develop the abilities of doing science.

National Research Council (1996, p. 121)

NSES CONTENT STANDARD, K–4: PROPERTIES OF EARTH MATERIALS

"Soils have properties of color and texture, capacity to retain water, and ability to support the growth of many kinds of plants, including those in our food supply" (National Research Council, 1996, p. 134).

"As a result of activities in grades K–4, all students should develop: Abilities necessary to do scientific inquiry" (National Research Council, 1996, pp.122–123).

Time Management

If you choose to allow the students to investigate which soil type is better for growing plants, allow 20 minutes for prep time and then several short reporting periods during the bean plant growth period. This part of the investigation should be conducted over a period of 3–4 weeks. Allow 20 minutes at the end for discussion and conclusions.

DESCRIPTIVE OBJECTIVE

To improve inquiry abilities, students observe, group, and describe the components of soil. Using observations, students describe what makes up soil and compare the properties of different types of soil.

MATERIALS

For each group of students, provide two different types of soil (one rich topsoil and one sandy soil), hand lenses, droppers, water, and sheets of plain paper (for sorting soil components). For the Apply phase, provide pinto bean seeds and plastic cups for water and for growing the beans. Obtain several different types of soil from areas around your community. Sources might include friends living in different neighborhoods or local nurseries and plant stores. Soak a cup full of bean seeds overnight before using them in the Apply phase of this investigation.

SCIENCE BACKGROUND

Soil begins as solid rock. Physical and chemical weathering break down the rock into chunks. Further weathering continues to break down the rock and chemically alters minerals. Decaying organic material adds to the mixture. Over time these physical and chemical processes produce a thick profile of soil above the original parent rock. A typical soil profile contains a thin upper zone of topsoil, a thicker zone called *subsoil*, and a zone of broken and weathered parent rock. Topsoil is a mixture of tiny rock bits, weathered minerals, organic matter, air, and water. Particularly rich topsoil is called *loam*. Loam is dark in color, rich in organic material, and allows water to percolate through while retaining enough moisture for plant growth. Subsoil is generally lighter in color, finer in texture, and contains minerals leached out of the topsoil by percolating rainwater.

Soil types vary depending upon the parent rock material and the climate. Thicker soils develop in grassland and forest areas where the climate is warm and moist. In deserts and high mountain regions, however, soil develops very slowly.

Scientists use different field tests to determine the components of soil. One such test detects the presence of clay in a soil sample. Clay becomes somewhat sticky when wet, and forms a ball when rolled. Sandy soils, in contrast, will not roll into a ball.

MISCONCEPTION INFORMATION

Research on student misconceptions for the broad topic of soil and earth materials is limited. Some incorrect ideas that you might find are:

- Soil is the same thing as dirt.
- All soils are the same.
- Pebbles grow from sand in a river.

For related information on misconceptions about rocks, you may refer to the following:

Kusnick, J. (2002). Growing pebbles and conceptual prisms—Understanding the source of student misconceptions about rock formation. *Journal of GeoScience Education, 50*(1), 31–39.

CLASSROOM SAFETY

Students should wash their hands after handling the soils. Soils are not sterile. Because the students are working with sand it is advisable for them to wear goggles.

Teaching Focus

Inquiry and the National Science Education Standards

For more information about inquiry abilities, refer to the *Inquiry and the National Science Education Standards* published by the National Research Council (2000).

ENGAGE

Briefly exchange experiences with planting flowers, vegetable gardens, or trees. Focus the discussion on the nature of soil. What is soil? What is it made of? Ask the children how they could find out the composition of soil by observing and comparing.

Teaching Focus

Focusing Students on an Inquiry Question

Write the question to be explored in large letters and post it for all to see as the investigation continues. As you move from group to group during the investigation, ask the children what question they are trying to answer. Continue to focus on the scientific question being explored.

Teaching Focus

The Nature of Inquiry Questions

Take time to talk about the nature of the question to be explored. Observing, comparing, and experimenting can answer some questions. Other questions can be answered by using reliable resources. To this end the *National Science Education Standards* note that scientific questions are ones that students can answer by "seeking information from reliable sources of scientific information and from their own observations and investigations" (National Research Council, 1996, p. 122).

EXPLORE

1. Distribute samples of rich topsoil (one tablespoon in size) to each group. Show the students how to use a pencil point to spread apart and sort soil particles. Demonstrate the proper use of a hand lens.
2. Help focus student observations on physical properties of the soil such as color, size, and type of material (pieces of rock, sand, insect parts, bits of dry leaves, etc.).
3. After several minutes of exploration, bring the groups back together and ask how many different kinds of materials they have separated from their sample (i.e., how many different piles they have).
4. Briefly compare notes to help focus the different groups on similar properties, then resume observation. Discuss how to record observations in journals. Record observations under headings such as color, size, shape, and type of material.

Teaching Focus

Using the Senses

Remind students to use touch and smell for their soil observations. Taste is not to be part of their observations! Have students wash their hands when they are finished.

EXPLAIN

1. After sufficient time for observation, have students use their journal record to compare the number and types of different materials separated by the different groups.
2. Typically, soils are composed of small bits of rock or sand grains and darker colored, fine-grained organic material.
3. The bits of rock or sand grains come from weathered, broken-down rock material. Organic material comes from decayed plants and animals and may even contain identifiable insect parts and bits of leaves or stems.

Teaching Focus

Using Tools to Extend the Senses

Discuss the role of the hand lens and pencil point in observing. In scientific investigations, tools are used to improve one's senses. The hand lens enables students to see detail that would not be obvious with the unaided eye. The pencil point makes it easier to separate the small pieces of soil. Point out that scientists also use tools and instruments to extend their senses.

EXTEND

1. Provide students with a different type of soil such as sand or a very sandy soil. Have students observe and classify this sample as well. Sand probably will have much less organic matter than will rich topsoil.
2. Encourage students to consider their prior experiences with wet soil as they make their predictions.
3. Review the proper use of an eyedropper, if necessary. Remind students to place just one or two drops of water on their soil sample.
4. Moist soil, depending on its type, will stick together in a clump when you squeeze it with your fingers. Sandy soil is less likely to clump together and roll into a ball when wet.

TEACHING FOCUS

Basing Conclusions on Evidence

Explain to students that their observations serve as evidence that they will use to answer their original question: "What makes up soil?" Answers to scientific questions (explanations) must be supported by evidence. Students can now check their explanations of what makes up soil by reading scientific explanations of the nature of soil in science reference materials.

APPLY

Either provide a broader range of soils or have students collect them from the schoolyard or their neighborhood. Have students analyze these samples as they did with the sand and topsoil earlier. Students should find variations in the amount of clay, sand, and organic matter in each sample.

Ask the students to explain how they will conduct this investigation. What is the question to be investigated? What materials will the students need? What procedures will they carry out? What observations and measurements are important? How can the students ensure that this test will be fair?

TEACHING FOCUS

Conducting a Fair Test

Take this opportunity to discuss a very important aspect of scientific inquiry—the concept of "fair test." When designing an investigation to see which soil best supports plant growth, the students should change only one variable and keep all others the same. In this comparison type of soil is the variable that is different. The amount and frequency of watering should be the same for each plant. The location of the pot—in the sun or the shade—must also be the same. Measurement techniques also must be identical.

Lesson 9.2

Investigating Soil and Water

ENGAGE

The students in a class were getting ready to plant flowers in pots. They decided to plant some of the flowers in sand and the others in gravel. Hector raised a question: Which pots will hold more water, the ones with sand or those with gravel? Several students thought that more water would be needed to fill a pot of gravel. Some thought that fine sand would hold more water. Others did not know.

What do you think? Which will hold more water, a pot of sand or a pot of gravel? Talk with others in your group and make a prediction. Explain your thinking.

We will investigate the following question: **How does the particle size of the soil in a pot affect the amount of water the pot can hold?**

EXPLORE

1. Place one measuring cup of fine sand in a large plastic cup. Fill a large measuring cup with water. Record how much water is in the cup. Slowly pour water into the fine sand. Observe the water as it slowly sinks in. Continue pouring until the water just reaches the top of the sand. Record how much water is left in the measuring cup. How much water did you need to fill the sand? How do you know?

2. Repeat the same procedure with the coarse gravel. Record your results.

Soil	Volume of Water
Sand	
Gravel	

EXPLAIN

1. Which held more water, the cup of sand or the cup of gravel? Compare your results with other groups.

2. Use a hand lens to compare samples of sand and gravel. How does the size of spaces between grains of sand and pieces of gravel compare? How does the number of spaces between grains of sand and pieces of gravel compare?

3. How does this comparison affect how much water sand and gravel can hold?

EXTEND

1. Suppose that you have a cup of sand and gravel mixed together. Will a cup of mixed sand and gravel hold more, less, or the same amount of water as pure sand or gravel? Write down your prediction.

2. Plan an investigation to find out.

3. Explain your results.

APPLY

A family had a problem with a downspout from their roof. Each time it rained, the water flowing down the spout would flood the ground next to their house. They dug a deep hole under the spout and filled it with gravel. It worked! Rainwater from the spout soaked into the gravel and the flooding stopped. Several years later, they noticed that the gravel seemed to fill up with water after heavy rains. Sometimes they even had some flooding. What might be causing this problem? How could they fix it?

Lesson 9.2

Investigating Soil and Water

Teaching Focus: Developing Inquiry Abilities

NSES CONTENT STANDARD, K–4: PROPERTIES OF EARTH MATERIALS

"Soils have properties of color and texture, capacity to retain water, and ability to support the growth of many kinds of plants, including those in our food supply" (National Research Council, 1996, p. 134).

"As a result of activities in grades K–4, all students should develop abilities necessary to do scientific inquiry" (National Research Council, 1996, pp. 121–123).

DESCRIPTIVE OBJECTIVE

To improve inquiry abilities students will design and conduct an investigation to determine the relationship between the size of pore spaces in soil and its capacity to hold water in a closed container.

MATERIALS

For each group of students, provide measuring cups or 100 mL graduated cylinders, 9 oz plastic cups, plastic spoons, hand lenses, clean fine sand, and clean coarse gravel. Building supply stores are a good source for fine sand and gravel.

SCIENCE BACKGROUND

As water seeps into the ground it fills pore spaces in the soil. Gravel has large empty pore spaces between grains. This allows gravel to hold large amounts of water. Pore spaces between sand grains are small. Although sand has excellent holding capacity, it does not hold as much water as an equal volume of gravel. Uniformity of particle size and shape also affects how much water soil can hold. Generally, sand grains are quite uniform in size and space. Thus, they pack together efficiently, reducing the amount of space between them. Gravel, on the other hand, is not uniform in size and shape, so it does not pack efficiently. This leaves large open spaces, allowing gravel to hold large volumes of water.

CLASSROOM SAFETY

Students should wash their hands after handling the soils. Soils are not sterile. Because the students are working with sand it is advisable for them to wear goggles.

Teaching Focus

Scientific Questions

Reinforce the importance of evidence in drawing conclusions. It is evidence that distinguishes between ordinary questions and scientific questions. Answers to scientific questions are based on evidence obtained through investigation. Ask what observations and measurements would be important to obtain scientific evidence in the investigation.

ENGAGE

Find out who has taken care of potted plants or a vegetable garden. Discuss Hector's question about which will hold more water—sand or gravel. Pose the following question: *Which will hold more water, a pot of fine sand or a pot of coarse gravel?* Ask students to defend their prediction and explain their thinking. The sizes of particles and the spaces between them will enter into the discussion.

Rephrase the question to be investigated as follows: **How does the particle size of the soil in a pot affect the amount of water the pot can hold?** Clarify the question and ensure that all the students understand what they will be investigating. Post the question for all to see during the investigation.

EXPLORE

1. Spread newspapers on each group's work area to aid in clean-up. Discuss how to determine the amount of water needed to fill the cup of sand. Help students realize that they need to subtract the amount of water left in the measuring cup from the initial amount to determine the amount of water in the cup of sand. The sample data in Table 9.2.1 was obtained with 9 oz cups of sand and gravel.

Table 9.2.1 Sample Student Data

Soil	Volume of Water
Sand	124 mL
Gravel	141 mL

2. Use separate cups for the gravel and repeat the previous step. Have the students wash their hands after handling the sand and gravel.

TEACHER: Grades K–4

EXPLAIN

1. Make a master chart to record volumes for each group. Expect the groups to report different volumes. Average the reported volumes of water needed to fill the sand and the gravel. As noted in the sample data in Table 9.2.1, the cup of gravel holds more water than does the cup of fine sand.
2. The spaces between grains of sand are smaller than those for gravel. A cup of sand has more spaces between grains than does a cup of gravel.
3. Results indicate that in equal volumes of sand and gravel, the larger spaces between pieces of gravel allow it to hold more water than can sand. The smaller spaces between the grains of sand reduce the total volume of water it can hold.

EXTEND

1. Have students defend their predictions and explain their thinking.
2. Have students develop a plan for their investigation. One method could be as follows: First, place a cup of gravel in the container. Then slowly add sand and shake the container until the spaces in the gravel are full. Pour in water until the sand and gravel mixture is full. Determine the amount of water needed.
3. The sand–gravel mixture will require less water to fill the spaces. Sand grains now occupy some of the space between the grains of gravel. Thus, less water is needed to fill the mixture.

APPLY

Discuss the problem and record solutions proposed by the students. Ask students to explain the thinking that led to their answer. One explanation might be that over time, fine material (like soil or sand) has washed into the gravel, filling up some of the pore spaces. The family may need to remove the old gravel and replace it with clean gravel.

TEACHING FOCUS

Employing Equipment and Tools

Review some of the skills involved in measuring liquid volume using a measuring cup or graduated cylinder. Emphasize consistency in technique. Skills for measuring the volume of sand and gravel are similar to those needed for measuring liquids. Make sure that students know what the marks on the graduated cylinder or measuring cup represent.

TEACHING FOCUS

Importance of Repeatability

Point out to the students that having multiple groups perform the investigation is like one group repeating the investigation many times. This allows the students to average the volume measurements and treat them as acceptable evidence.

TEACHING FOCUS

Understanding Inquiry

"Students do not come to understand inquiry simply by learning words such as 'hypothesis' and 'inference' or by memorizing procedures such as the 'steps of the scientific method.' They must experience inquiry directly to gain a deep understanding of its characteristics" (National Research Council, 2000, p. 14).

Lesson 9.3
Soil Soaking Rates

ENGAGE

All of the pots for Mrs. Green's geraniums had drain holes in the bottom and sat in saucers. While watering the plants, Marissa noticed water in some of the saucers shortly after she had watered the geraniums. The water took longer to drain through the other pots. Marissa told Mrs. Green about her observation. Mrs. Green brought this to the attention of the other students: "Why does the water drain through the soil in some pots faster than in others?" She asked the students to talk about it in their groups and come up with a hypothesis. The students observed that some of the geraniums were planted in sandy soil, some in rich topsoil, and a few others in gravel. They wondered if this was important.

Why do you think some pots drained faster than others? Using what you learned from your earlier investigations with sand, soil, and gravel, come up with a hypothesis. Present your hypothesis to the class and be prepared to explain your thinking.

We will investigate the following question: **Does water flow faster through sand, topsoil, or gravel?**

EXPLORE

1. Design an investigation to answer your question.
   - What equipment and materials will you use?
   - What observations and measurements will you make?
   - How will you organize and record the evidence?
   - Present your plan to the teacher before you begin.

2. Conduct your investigation and record your observations.

EXPLAIN

1. In which material did the water flow the fastest? The slowest?

2. Does the evidence support your hypothesis? Explain.

3. Present your results to the class.

EXTEND

1. When you poured water into sand, topsoil, and gravel, did all of it drain through? How could you find out?

2. Conduct an investigation to find out.

3. Is there a difference among the three samples?

4. If you found that not all of the water passed through the samples, where did it go?

APPLY

Marissa also noticed that some of Mrs. Green's geraniums dried out sooner than the others. Use what you have learned in these soil investigations to hypothesize which pots dry out sooner and explain why. How could you test your hypothesis?

Lesson 9.3
Soil Soaking Rates
Teaching Focus: Developing Inquiry Abilities

NSES CONTENT STANDARD K–4: PROPERTIES OF EARTH MATERIALS

"Soils have properties of color and texture, capacity to retain water, and ability to support the growth of many kinds of plants, including those in our food supply" (National Research Council, 1996, p. 134).

"As a result of activities in grades K–4, all students should develop abilities necessary to do scientific inquiry" (National Research Council, 1996, pp. 121–123).

DESCRIPTIVE OBJECTIVE

To improve inquiry abilities, students will design and conduct an investigation to determine the relationship between the size of a soil's pore spaces and its permeability, or the rate at which water flows through it.

MATERIALS

For each group of students provide a measuring cup or 100 mL graduated cylinder, clean fine sand, clean coarse gravel, topsoil, three 12 oz plastic cups, three clay pots with drain holes, small pieces of window screen material or coffee filters, and a stop watch or a wrist watch with a sweep second hand. (Younger students may have difficulty using stopwatches. They can time the flow rates of the soils directly by pouring the water into them at the same time.)

SCIENCE BACKGROUND

Porosity is the amount of space between grains of soil that allows it to hold water. Unless the pore spaces are connected, water cannot flow through soil. The ability of soil to allow water to flow through is called *permeability*. Water flows more easily through soil with large, connected pore spaces. The smaller the connected pore spaces, the slower water flows through. Even after water has flowed through soil, some of it adheres to grains or is absorbed by organic material and is retained as soil water. After a period of time without recharging, soil water evaporates.

CLASSROOM SAFETY

Students should wash their hands after handling the soils. Soils are not sterile. Because the students are working with sand it is advisable for them to wear goggles.

What Is a Hypothesis?

People use the word *hypothesis* in a variety of ways ranging from a guess, to an informed prediction, to a well-thought-out explanation. At this level, students will most likely predict *what* happens and not necessarily explain *why* something happens.

ENGAGE

Reprise the story of Mrs. Green's class and the potted geraniums. Use the context of Marissa's question to stimulate student thinking about why water drains through some soils faster than others. Pose the following question: **Does water flow faster through sand, topsoil, or gravel?** This question will drive the investigation that the students are asked to design and conduct.

EXPLORE

1. Use the questions in this section to help your students design their investigation. Check the investigation plan for each group. Obtain clay pots with a capacity of at least one cup. Place a round section of window screen or filter paper on the bottom of each pot to prevent sand or gravel from falling out. You can use the sand and gravel from the earlier investigations, but first make sure it is dry.

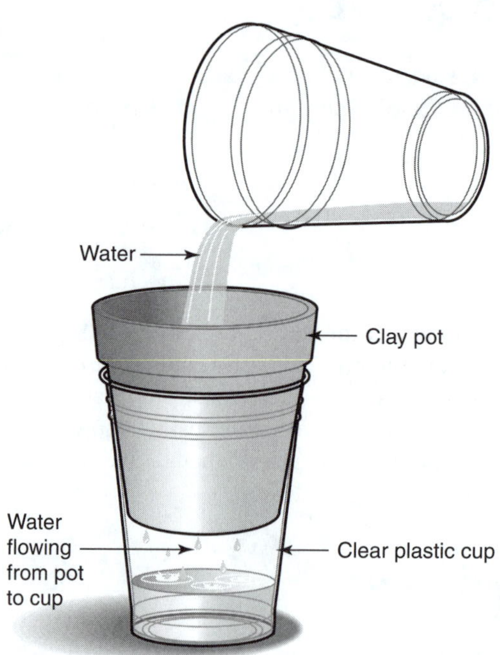

Establishing Procedures and Practicing Techniques

You may want to demonstrate the procedure and agree on what "when the water stops flowing through" means. Does "stops" mean "when the stream stops," "one drop after the stream stops," and so on? This process results in what is called an *operational definition*. Allow student groups to practice a trial to become comfortable with the technique.

2. Place a cup of sand, gravel, or topsoil in each of the three pots. Place the pot with sand in the plastic cup. Quickly pour in one cup of water. Time from the beginning of the pour to when the water stops running through.

EXPLAIN

1. Water flows fastest through the gravel and slowest through the soil.
2. Data should indicate that the smaller the material's particle size, the longer water takes to flow through it. In other words, water flows faster through gravel than it does through sand or soil. In this case it flows the slowest through the soil that contains more organic matter. (If we were using clay, little or no water would flow.)
3. Have students present their results to the class. Individual times will likely vary, but overall conclusions should be similar.

TEACHING FOCUS

Essentials of Inquiry Abilities: Designing Data Tables

Ask students to design a data chart for recording the type of material and the time required for water to flow through. Example:

Material	Time in Seconds for One Cup of Water to Flow Through
Sand	
Gravel	
Topsoil	

EXTEND

1. When measuring the amount of water that flows through the sand and gravel, students should find that some water remains in the sand and in the gravel. Have them plan an investigation to compare the amount of water poured in to the amount that flows out.
2. Students can determine the amount of water left sticking to the grains by subtracting the amount recovered from the beginning volume.
3. More water remains trapped in the soil than in the sand, and more in the sand than in the gravel.
4. The smaller, more tightly packed particles trap and retain more water.

TEACHING FOCUS

Scientific Explanations Are Based on Evidence

Discuss the role of data in determining an explanation. Does the data support the answer to the students' question?

APPLY

Discuss Marissa's observation. Have the students use what they have already learned to hypothesize which pots dry out faster. Arrange for them to present and defend their ideas. Upon conducting the investigation, they should find that the pot that holds the most water will dry out the slowest. Thus, the pot with soil will dry out last, and the pot with gravel will dry out first.

TEACHING FOCUS

Communicate Investigations and Explanations

Point out that, like the students reporting their results, scientists present and defend the results of their experiments to their peers.

Teaching Focus Summary: Developing Inquiry Abilities

- Help students focus on the explorable question by posting it and asking students to explain what they are doing while they are conducting the investigation.
- Encourage students to use their senses, as well as tools that extend their senses, while exploring.

- Students should use their observations as evidence to develop explanations to answer scientific questions.
- Use the term "fair test" with young children when they are conducting an experiment. This helps them understand that they must keep all variables constant except for the one independent variable.
- Students should communicate their results to others and realize that scientists do this as well.

References

National Research Council. (1996). *National Science Education Standards*. Washington, DC: National Academy Press.

National Research Council. (2000). *Inquiry and the National Science Education Standards.* Washington, DC: National Academy Press.

INVESTIGATION 10

MOTIONS OF THE MOON

(5–8)

Teaching Focus: Identifying Misconceptions

Lesson 10.1
Moon Patterns and Motions

ENGAGE

When did you last see the moon? What did it look like? Draw a picture of its shape. Compare your moon picture to those drawn by your classmates. Does the moon always have the same shape? Is the moon visible only at night? Suppose you observed the moon each day for one month. How does the moon change? Draw a picture that shows how you think the moon's shape changes throughout a month's time.

We will investigate the following question: **What happens to the moon's shape during one month?**

EXPLORE

1. Your teacher will help you begin your month-long moon watch. You will begin observing at school and then continue at home. Draw the shape of the moon and record how many "fists" high the moon is above the horizon. In what direction did you look to see the moon? Make a "Moon Watch Data Sheet" like the one below to record your observations and measurements.

Date	Time of Day	Shape	Direction	Number of Fists High

Here are several helpful suggestions for when you continue the moon watch from home. Choose a place in your yard or a nearby location where you can see the southern sky. Your observing place should not be directly under a street light. Draw the moon's shape and note some object on the horizon that is directly beneath it. Be sure to record the time of your observation and indicate whether it was A.M. or P.M.

2. At least twice during your moon watch, make two observations one hour apart. Make both observations from the same spot. For each observation, note an object (a tree, house, fence, etc.) on the horizon directly below the moon and its direction. How has the moon's position changed?

3. Sometime during this investigation, make your observation at the same time and from the same spot for 3 days in a row. Note an object on the horizon directly under the moon each time. How has the moon's position changed?

EXPLAIN

1. Describe how the shape of the moon changed during your month-long watch.

2. Is the moon visible only at night? Cite evidence to support your answer.

3. Was the moon always visible sometime during each 24-hour period? Explain.

4. During your observations, in what direction was the moon when it was the highest above the horizon?

5. In what direction does the moon appear to move each day? Explain.

EXTEND

1. Use your observations and references to name the moon phases.

2. What time of day would be best to view each of the major moon phases?

3. Do you think the moon rises and sets at about the same time each day? Cite evidence to support your answer.

4. At approximately what time of day does the full moon rise? Use your data sheet for evidence.

5. The moon is above the horizon for about 12 hours each day. At approximately what time does the full moon set?

6. Suppose that it was cloudy for a period of 3 or 4 days during your moon watch. Infer what the moon's shape would have been during that time. Explain.

APPLY

Suppose you see the moon high in the sky on your way to school in the morning. Draw a picture showing the shape you think the moon would have. Explain your thinking.

Lesson 10.1
Moon Patterns and Motions
Teaching Focus: Identifying Misconceptions

It's not what you don't know that hurts you. It's what you do know that ain't so!

Will Rogers

NSES CONTENT STANDARD, 5–8: EARTH IN THE SOLAR SYSTEM

"Most objects in the solar system are in regular and predictable motion. Those motions explain such phenomena as the day, the year, phases of the moon, and eclipses" (National Research Council, 1996, p. 160).

DESCRIPTIVE OBJECTIVE

Students will investigate the moon's regular pattern of shapes and motions during a month-long observation.

TIME ALLOTMENT

Allow a period of at least 4 weeks to conduct this investigation. The daily time required is quite short. (**Special note:** In order to begin this activity during the school day, you need to start 2 or 3 days prior to the first quarter moon. Check the daily newspaper for moon phase dates.) The introduction and practice stage may require just two or three 30-minute lessons over several days. During the month-long observations, you may need only a couple of minutes for reminders and problem solving each week. Thus, you can conduct other lessons in your curriculum during most of the month. Set aside several 30-minute time periods at the end of the investigation for discussions and summarizing.

MATERIALS

For each group of students provide a Moon Watch Data Sheet, calendar, and magnetic compass.

SCIENCE BACKGROUND

The moon revolves in a counterclockwise orbit around the Earth. This produces a regular cycle of moon phases. The phases appear as changes in the amount of the moon's lighted surface that we can see. One complete cycle of moon phases takes about 29.5 days. If we begin the cycle with the new moon phase, approximately 2 days later a thin crescent moon becomes visible low in the

Figure 10.1.1 Phases of the moon

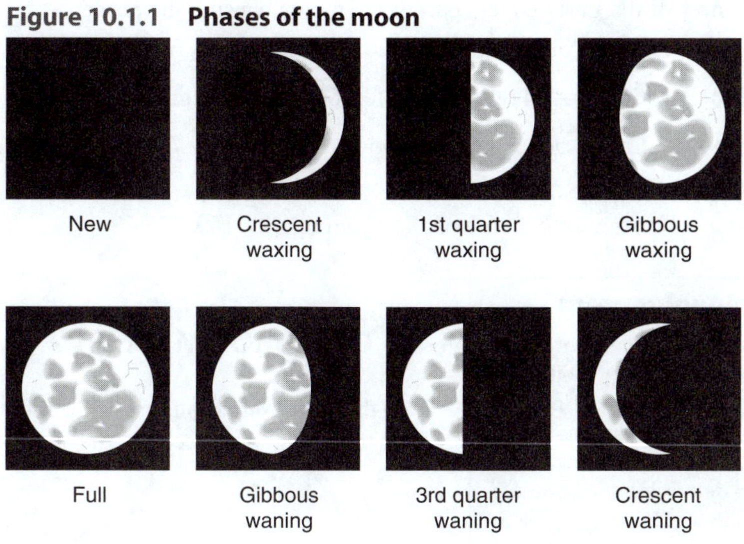

western sky just after sunset. During the next week, the lighted portion of the moon that we see increases (waxes) to one half (lighted on the right-hand side). This half-moon is called the *first quarter* moon. In the following week, the visible portion waxes, entering what is referred to as the *waxing gibbous* phase, until all of the side of the moon facing Earth is lighted. This is the *full* moon phase. The full moon rises in the east about the same time as the sun is setting in the west. During the week following full moon, the lighted portion begins to decrease (wane), progressing through the *waning gibbous* phase, until one half (the left-hand side) is lighted. This phase is called the *third quarter* moon. (Sometimes this phase is referred to as the *last quarter* moon. Most astronomers, however, refer to this phase as the third quarter moon.) Just as the first quarter moon occurs at the end of the first week (one quarter of the full cycle), the third quarter moon occurs at the end of the third week of the full cycle. In the final (fourth) week of the cycle, the lighted portion of the moon continues to decrease or wane until only a thin crescent phase appears on the left, just 2 days before the next new moon. The waning crescent is visible in the eastern sky just before sunrise.

The lunar phases are caused by the moon's orbit around the Earth, and the sunlight reflected from its surface. Half of the moon is always illuminated by the sun. On Earth, we see different amounts of the moon's lighted side as it moves in its orbit. During the new moon, the moon is located between Earth and the sun. As a result, the new moon rises as the sun rises, and then sets as the sun sets. During the full moon the moon has moved around to the opposite side of Earth, away from the sun. This results in the full moon rising as the sun sets. First and third quarter moons occur halfway between the new moon and full moon. Consequently, the first quarter moon rises in our eastern sky at noon and sets below the western horizon at midnight. The third quarter moon rises at midnight and sets at noon. The moon rises and sets on average approximately 50 minutes later each day during its month-long orbit around Earth. Thus, if you view the moon from the same location at the same time for several consecutive days, it will appear a little farther to the left (east) in the sky each day.

MISCONCEPTION INFORMATION

Much research has been conducted on student misconceptions about the topic of lunar phases. This topic can be difficult for many students as it requires them to visualize the positions of the Earth, sun, and moon as they would appear in space and then combine that image with their perspective from on Earth. Some of the more common misconceptions include:

- Clouds cover part of the moon in such a way that part of the moon can't be seen, thus causing the phases.

- The shadow of the Earth covers part of the moon, causing the phases.
- People in different locations on Earth see different phases of the moon.

For additional information, you may wish to refer to the following:

Philips, W. C. (1991). Earth science misconceptions. *The Science Teacher, 58*, 21–23.

Stahly, L., Krockover, G., & Shepardson, D. (1999). Third grade students' ideas about the lunar phases. *Journal of Research in Science Teaching, 36*(2), 159–177.

Teaching Tip

Parental Involvement

Notify parents that this investigation requires some night viewing by their child. Encourage the parents to participate in the daily moon watch. Help the child choose an appropriate viewing site and become a regular viewing partner. Also help the child determine the compass directions from his or her viewing site to different places on the horizon—especially in the southern half of the horizon.

Teaching Tip

KWL Charts

KWL stands for What do I **K**now, What do I **W**ant to know, and What did I **L**earn. It was first introduced as a technique to assist students in increasing their reading comprehension. Students now widely use it as an organizer to conceptualize and reflect on their thinking about the study of some new topic (Ogle, 1986).

Teaching Tip

Staying Focused on Your Objectives

It is not important at this time to discuss why the moon has phases. Should that question come up, record it in the KWL chart, but do not emphasize cause and effect at this time. Observing changes in shape and motion is the objective of this lesson.

Teaching Focus

Assessing Students' Prior Understanding

It is very important to solicit what students know about the changing moon phases. "Students come to the classroom with preconceptions about how the world works. If their initial understanding is not engaged they may fail to grasp the new concepts and information that are taught, or they may learn them for purposes of a test but revert to their preconceptions outside the classroom" (National Research Council, 2000, pp. 14–15).

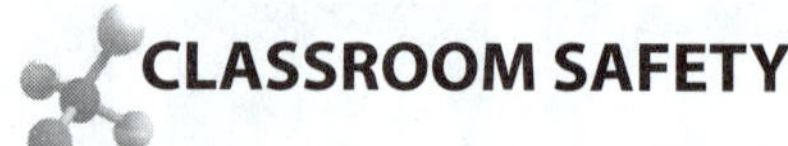

CLASSROOM SAFETY

Even though observations are of the moon, remind students to never look directly at the sun.

ENGAGE

Ask the students when they last saw the moon. Have students draw a picture of the moon they observed. Compare the drawings and discuss why they think the shapes are different. Ask them what they know about moon phases. Make a chart showing what the students know, and what they would like to find out. Keep the chart for discussion at the end of the investigation.

It is important to focus discussion on the following question: How does the moon change? Have the children share their drawings of how they think the moon's shape will change during the month. Save the drawings to compare with their observations at the end of the investigation. Establish the question to be investigated: What happens to the moon's shape during one month?

EXPLORE

1. Begin the moon watch at the first quarter phase. Conduct the first week of the watch at school. Students can work in small group teams during this part of the investigation. The first quarter moon rises at about noon. This will make it visible in the eastern to southeastern sky during the afternoon. Choose a location on the school grounds where this part of the sky is relatively unobstructed. Help the students learn to record their data on the Moon Watch Data Sheet. Allow the students to practice using a compass to determine the direction to the horizon directly below the moon. Draw an east–west line on the ground and a north–south line crossing it at a right angle.

Label the line points and orient the students to directions on the school grounds.

Show the students how to measure the elevation of the moon above the horizon. Do this by extending an arm straight out to the horizon directly below the moon. Make a fist that just sits on the horizon. Then extend the other arm straight out so that the second fist sits just on top of the first one. Continue placing one fist on top of the other until you reach the moon. Each fist is approximately 10 degrees. Nine fists, one on top of the other, should end up directly overhead—90 degrees from the horizon. Students can practice this technique on the playground by measuring the heights, in fists, of the flag pole, a tree, or a nearby building. Introduce the students to the Moon Watch Data Sheet. Students may need several days to become comfortable with the procedures of observing and recording. Remind them that they will use the same data sheet throughout the month-long investigation.

> **Classroom Management** *Teaching Tip*
>
> It is often unnecessary to have the entire class perform each step of an activity, especially a long-term one. In this case a group of students can share the daily responsibility of observation on a weekly basis (see below).

2. During the second week you may want to assign home observations to members of two or more teams. Each day these students can report back to the rest of the class. They are to report the time, moon shape, direction, and elevation (in fists) above the horizon. Individual members of other groups can make observations this week if they wish, but the primary responsibility tests on the assigned team. All students can then update the observation data for the previous day. Assign different teams for the third week, and the remaining teams for the fourth week. Each day they are to report their observations. This way, each student is responsible for actual observations for just one week. All students should be encouraged to be responsible because the entire class is depending on their data. If you think it is more valuable, have each student conduct individual observations each day. In this case you may not need daily reports. A better course of action, however, may be to hold a brief session once a week to discuss problems, answer questions, share unusual observations, and provide encouragement.
3. Students can conduct this task during their assigned week of observation and report the observed movement along with the time, shape, direction, and elevation. They should conduct both observations from the same spot. The moon will have moved to the right (toward the west) because of the Earth's rotation from west to east.
4. Students should make these three observations from the same spot, and identify and record an object on the horizon directly below the moon for each observation. The moon, when observed from the same location at the same time two days in a row, appears to the left from where it was on the first day. Put another way, the moon is farther to the east on the second day from where it was on the first day. In other words, the moon is actually moving from west to east in its orbit. During any one day the "apparent" motion is east to west. Viewed over several days, however, the moon actually moves west to east in its orbit around the Earth.

EXPLAIN

1. The lighted part of the moon steadily grew from half (lighted on the right side) to full during the first week of observation. During the second week the lighted part steadily went from full to half (lighted on the left side). During the third week the lighted part shrunk from half to a thin crescent (lighted on the left) and then was not visible. During the fourth week the moon was not visible for several days, then reappeared as a crescent (lighted on the right) and grew to a half (lighted on the right).
2. The moon is visible during the day as well as at night. Remind the students of their discussion of this question at the opening of the investigation, and discuss the evidence that supports this conclusion.

Teaching Focus

Addressing Prior Understanding

Students often think that the moon appears only in the night sky and is not "out" during the day. Further probing may reveal that some have actually seen the moon during the day but have not yet confronted their prior understanding with this discrepant evidence. Scientific explanations are always evidence-based.

3. The moon was not visible for several days at the end of the third week (during the new moon phase), and for several days at the beginning of the fourth week. Sometimes the sky is cloud covered and the moon is obscured. Students may be able to see some light in the clouds in the area where they expect the moon.
4. The moon is generally at its highest in the south. It rises in the east and sets in the west. The moon reaches the highest part of its path across the sky approximately halfway between its rising and setting points.
5. The moon appears to move across the sky from east to west (left to right) each day. The moon's path is similar to that of the sun in that it rises each day in the east and sets in the west.

EXTEND

1. The watch began with the first quarter phase (right half lighted). Each day more of the moon was lighted (waxing gibbous) until full moon. After the full phase, the lighted portion steadily decreased (waning gibbous) until its left half was lighted (third quarter). During the next week, the lighted portion continued to decrease, becoming a waning crescent (lighted on the left). In the final week of observation, the moon disappeared as it entered and left the new moon phase. Several days after the new moon, a thin waxing crescent appears in the southwest just after sundown. The waxing crescent grows larger in size each day until it again reaches the first quarter moon phase. The term *waxing* means that the lighted side is getting larger, and *waning* means it is getting smaller.
2. The first quarter moon is visible in the afternoon until about midnight. Full moon is visible just after sunset until about sunrise. The third quarter moon rises at midnight, so it is best seen in the morning sky.
3. If the moon were to rise and set at the same time each day, then it would always be in the same place at any given time each day. The moon rises and sets about 50 minutes later each day. Data from the students' observations at the same time for 3 days in a row should show that the moon is located farther to the left (east) on the second day than on the first day at the same time. It is farther to the left on the third day than it was on the second.
4. Observation data should show that the full moon rises at about the same time as the sun sets. This may not be obvious if the horizon is cluttered with trees, houses, tall buildings, and so on. Visibility may also vary depending on the time that students choose to observe the moon. The moon could be visible only several hours after moonrise, and so the relationship between sunset and moonrise might not be obvious. Discuss the idea that an observer in a large open agricultural area often can see the sun go down in the west and then the full moon rise immediately afterward in the east. It is a beautiful sight!
5. The full moon rises at about sunset and moves across the sky until it sets about 12 hours later (around sunrise).
6. Yes, you could predict the moon's shape during those days. The month-long watch reveals the predictable pattern of phases from one new moon to the next. By noting the shapes that lead up to the cloudy period and occur for a few days afterward, one can infer what the shapes would have been.

A moon seen in the morning sky would vary between the shapes of the third quarter moon phase (left half lighted) and a waning crescent (lighted on the left).

Return to the KWL chart you started at the beginning of this lesson and list some of the things that the students now think they know. The next lesson deals with a model of how moon phases are formed, so you may want to list some questions students may have about what causes the phases.

Lesson 10.2
Moon Phases

ENGAGE

During your moon watch, you observed the changing shapes of the moon over a period of one month. Now let's make some classroom observations using a model. Study the pictures showing the moon phases. Use what you learned in the moon watch investigation to place the pictures in the proper order for each month. Compare your sequence with those of other groups. What do you think causes this sequence of moon phases? Write an explanation. You may include pictures to help explain. Compare your explanation with those of other groups.

How do you think the relative positions of the sun, the Earth, and the moon affect the different moon phases? In this investigation you will make a model of the sun, Earth, and moon to determine their positions during the different moon phases.

We will investigate the following: **How do the positions of the sun, Earth, and moon cause the monthly pattern of moon phases?**

EXPLORE

1. Develop a model of the sun, Earth, and moon system. Your teacher will set up a strong light to act as the sun. A white ball will be the moon. You are the observer on the Earth (imagine that your head is the Earth).

2. Stick the model moon on the tip of a pencil or pen. Hold the "moon" at arm's length between you and the sun. Move the moon in an orbit around "Earth" (your head) so that you see each of the different moon phases in order. Note the relative positions of sun, Earth, and moon that produce each phase. (**Important reminder:** As you move the "moon" in its orbit around "Earth," always keep it in the light from the "sun.")

3. Draw a diagram that shows the positions of the sun, moon, and Earth for each of the moon phases in the pictures. Your teacher will give you tips on constructing the diagram.

EXPLAIN

1. Set up your model to produce a first quarter moon. Compare it to your drawing of the sun, Earth, and moon for the first quarter moon.

2. Discuss your original ideas with some of your classmates. Look at one of the explanations that the evidence does not seem to support. Manipulate your model to try and produce the sequence of moon phases using these other explanations. What are some of the problems you encounter? Explain.

3. Write an explanation for what causes the repeating pattern of moon phases each month.

EXTEND

1. In your model, which direction did you move the moon around Earth to produce the moon phases in order—clockwise or counterclockwise? What happens if you move the moon in the opposite direction?

2. So far, we have been viewing the moon phases as they appear to an observer on the Earth. To fully understand moon phases you should also consider what the moon looks like from the perspective of an observer in space. Repeat the above investigation and record how much of the "moon" is lighted as seen by an observer looking down on the model—that is, from a "bird's-eye" view. Record this observation for each phase of the moon.

3. Compare the top view of the moon with the view from the Earth. Describe.

4. Study several pictures of different moon phases. Describe where the sun would be for each picture.

Figure 10.2.1 The Earth as viewed from the moon

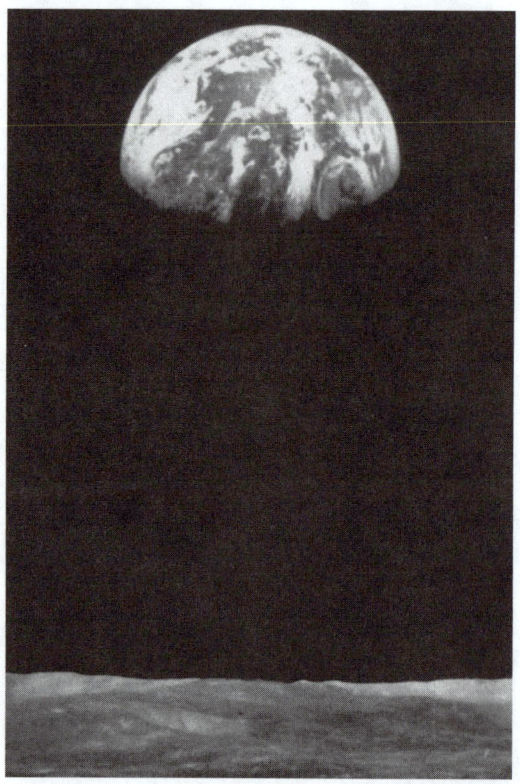

Guy Worthey, University of Michigan/NASA

APPLY

Refer back to your Moon Watch Data Sheet. Look at your data for the observations you made at the same time on 2 consecutive days. In which direction did the moon move from the first day to the second day? In what direction does the moon move around the Earth? Is this consistent with your model? Explain.

Suppose you were an observer on the moon. What would Earth look like? Look at Figure 10.2.1 and then arrange your model to show how the sun, the Earth, and the moon would have to be positioned. Use your model to simulate what Earth looks like from the moon during one month. (**Hint:** This time you will be the moon. The white ball is Earth.)

Lesson 10.2

Moon Phases

Teaching Focus: Identifying Misconceptions

NSES CONTENT STANDARD, 5–8: EARTH IN THE SOLAR SYSTEM

"Most objects in the solar system are in regular and predictable motion. Those motions explain such phenomena as the day, the year, phases of the moon, and eclipses" (National Research Council, 1996, p. 160).

DESCRIPTIVE OBJECTIVE

Students will manipulate a model of the sun, Earth, and moon to develop an explanation for the cause of moon phases.

MATERIALS

For each group of students provide a Moon Watch Data Sheet, unordered pictures of moon phases, smooth white foam ball for each student (about 3 inches in diameter), and a lamp (without shade) with a 150-watt clear bulb.

SCIENCE BACKGROUND

As the moon revolves around Earth in a counterclockwise orbit, we see different amounts of the moon's lighted surface. This results in a regular pattern of changing moon phases. This pattern of change repeats itself every 29.5 days. For more information see the Science Background section of the previous lesson.

> **TEACHING FOCUS**
>
> **Noting Common Misconceptions**
>
> Many children and adults alike hold alternative explanations for the cause of moon phases. They associate moon phases with the moon moving into the Earth's shadow. In their reasoning, they see a crescent or quarter moon because the shadow of the Earth covers up part of the moon's surface. One important part of this investigation is to provide experiences and evidence that challenge this explanation of moon phases.

CLASSROOM SAFETY

Caution students about the very hot light bulb. Be sure to let the bulb cool down after turning it off and before unscrewing it.

> **Using Models** — *Teaching Tip*
>
> Many students in grades five through eight have difficulty imagining what objects look like from different locations or frames of reference. Physical models provide concrete experiences that allow learners to manipulate objects.

ENGAGE

Arrange a series of unordered pictures of moon phases on a wall in your room before the lesson begins. Students will refer to them in the engagement activity. Using observational data from their moon watch, students should be able to place the phases in order as follows: new, waxing crescent, first quarter, waxing gibbous, full, waning gibbous, third quarter, and waning crescent. This now prompts the question to be investigated: **How do the positions of the sun, Earth, and moon cause the monthly pattern of moon phases?**

Have the students gather in small groups to discuss what they think causes moon phases. Pull the groups back together and summarize the different explanations. Accept all explanations without bias at this point.

> Teaching Tip
>
> **Advanced Preparation**
>
> Use an extension cord to place a lamp with a bare 150-watt clear light bulb in the center of the room. Close all window shades to make the room as dark as possible. Stand 5 or 6 feet away from the bulb and hold a model moon ball at arm's length directly in front of the light. Move the ball to the left until you see a lighted crescent shape appear on the right side of the ball. Continue moving the ball around your head in a circle to observe the lighted portion as it changes in size and shape, duplicating the phases of the moon. Now you are ready for the students.

EXPLORE

1. Place a bare 150-watt clear light bulb in the center of the room. Arrange your students in a circle around the light bulb. Close all window shades to make the room as dark as possible.
2. Standing in the circle, demonstrate how to hold the model moon ball at arm's length in front of the light bulb. Suggest to students that they should note the relationship of the sun, Earth, and moon in their model as they observe each moon phase. Students should refer to the pictures of moon phases in order for reference.
3. These sketches will be from the point of view of an observer in space. At this stage of the lesson your students may have difficulty visualizing the relationship of the two views—that is, the one looking at the moon from the Earth with the one looking at the moon from a point in space.

   During their manipulation of the model, some student groups may ask about lunar and solar eclipses. They may notice that the moon moves into the Earth's shadow at the full moon phase. This should cause a lunar eclipse. They may also know, however, that we do not have a lunar eclipse each month. They may have a similar problem with new moons and potential solar eclipses. Acknowledge their concern and ask them to determine which orientation of the moon's orbit would produce the full moon phase without causing a lunar eclipse. Focus on lunar phases and assure students that they will have a chance to address eclipses in the next investigation.

> **TEACHING FOCUS**
>
> ### Diversity—Accessing Misconceptions with English Language Learners
>
> English language learners may find it especially difficult to replace their misconceptions with scientifically accurate ideas because of cultural perspectives and prior knowledge in another language. "As a result, the learner 1) may not be able to wrestle with the underlying concepts and their fit or lack of fit with existing ideas or assumptions, and 2) may misinterpret new information because of inaccurate prior knowledge, language differences, and cultural differences" (Katz and Olson, 2006, pp. 62–63).

EXPLAIN

1. Help students who have difficulty going from the three dimensions of the model to the two dimensions of the drawing and vice versa. Be sure they have a correct model of the sun, Earth, and moon that depicts the first quarter moon (see Figure 10.2.2).
2. If students have a misconception that the Earth's shadow causes the moon phases, focus their attention on the direction in which the Earth's shadow actually points. Show also where the moon's shadow points. Do the same for the third quarter moon. Draw these shadows on your

Figure 10.2.2 Positions of the sun, Earth, and moon during the first quarter moon

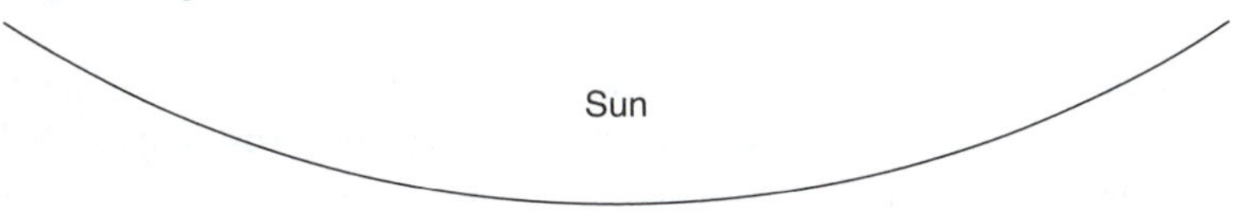

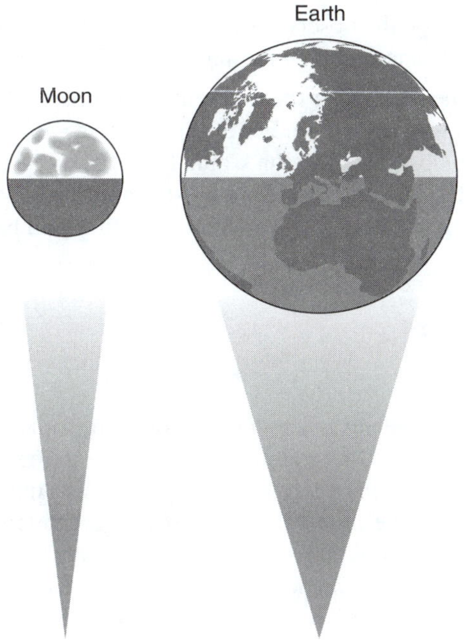

diagram. Refer to your explanations for moon phases. Choose either the first or the third quarter moon phase. Demonstrate a bird's-eye view of the sun, Earth, and moon in the positions needed to produce that phase. At all times during the month, Earth's shadow extends in the opposite direction of the sun. During the first and third quarters, the moon is at right angles to the line connecting the sun and Earth. Therefore, the Earth's shadow cannot possibly fall on the moon.

To produce traditional phases using the shadow explanation requires very creative, but impossible motions of the moon. Each phase would have to occur in the vicinity of the Earth's shadow. To accomplish this, the moon's path could not orbit the Earth but instead would have to follow a "jumpy" and illogical path in a small area on the opposite side of the Earth from the sun.

3. We see different amounts of the lighted half of the moon as the moon travels in orbit around the Earth. This results in a repeating pattern of moon phases.

TEACHING FOCUS

Using Evidence to Address Misconceptions

Earth's shadow position during first and third quarter moons is critical in analyzing evidence to construct explanations of moon phases. This evidence challenges those who think that Earth's shadow covers up part of the moon, causing the first quarter moon. Faced with evidence to the contrary, these learners are forced to rethink their naïve explanations.

EXTEND

1. In this model, the moon phases appear in the correct sequence when the moon is moved around the Earth in a counterclockwise direction (west to east). When you move the moon in the opposite direction—clockwise—the sequence of phases is reversed.
2. Using this model, students will observe that no matter where the moon is positioned (regardless of phase), half of it is *always* lighted. This may surprise some students, therefore each student should have the opportunity to view this model.
3. Although half of the moon is always lighted, the amount that an observer sees illuminated depends on the observer's position. An observer on the Earth will see the same phases the students observed during their moon watch.
4. Refer students to the pictures of the different moon phases. Have them determine the location of the sun for each phase. For example, during a full moon, the sun would be directly behind the observer. The sun would be to the right (west) when viewing a first quarter moon, and to the left (east) for a third quarter moon. Students should be able to observe any moon phase and point to where the sun would be to produce that shape.

APPLY

Refer here to the observations students made of the moon at the same time on 2 consecutive days. The students should have observed that the moon was a little to the left on the second day. Although the moon appears to move from left to right (east to west) during one day (due to the rotation of the Earth on its axis), the moon actually moves right to left (west to east) in its orbit around the Earth. This is consistent with the direction of travel in the model.

As observed from the moon, Earth goes through the same cycle of phases as the moon. The "new Earth" phase occurs in the position of a full moon. Beginning in this position an observer on the moon would then see a waxing crescent Earth, a first quarter Earth, and so on through the cycle. Students use their light bulb model to observe these Earth phases.

For further information on moon phases consult the following:

Great Explorations in Math and Science (GEMS). (1986). *Earth, moon, and stars.* Berkeley: University of California.

Educational Development Center. (1968). *Elementary science study: Where is the moon?* New York: McGraw-Hill.

Lesson 10.3
Eclipses

ENGAGE

You have observed and explored the monthly cycle of moon phases. You know that moon phases are related to the motions and positions of the sun, Earth, and moon. Maybe you have seen a total eclipse of the moon. By comparison, few people ever get to see a total eclipse of the sun. Draw a picture of what you think an eclipse of the moon looks like. Draw a picture of a solar eclipse. Compare your pictures with those of other students. How are eclipses different from moon phases? What causes them? Record your ideas below.

We will investigate the following: **How do you construct models of eclipses of the moon and the sun?**

EXPLORE

1. Use the same model you used to simulate moon phases. Turn on the "sun" and move the "moon" around "Earth" until you see an eclipse of the moon. Draw a picture showing the positions of the sun, Earth, and moon that produce a lunar eclipse.

2. Manipulate your model to produce an eclipse of the sun. Draw a picture to show the positions of the sun, Earth, and moon that produce a solar eclipse.

EXPLAIN

1. What causes a lunar eclipse? Write your explanation.

2. What causes a solar eclipse? Write your explanation.

3. Describe the relationship between moon phases and eclipses.

EXTEND

1. Assemble the eclipse simulator provided by your teacher. Position the moon in this model in a way that results in lunar and solar eclipses.

2. Do we see one lunar and one solar eclipse each month? Explain.

3. How many times a year might a solar eclipse be possible? Explain why.

4. A lunar eclipse follows a solar eclipse exactly 2 weeks later. Explain why this happens.

APPLY

Some lunar or solar eclipses are partial and not total at any location on Earth. Explain what would make this happen.

Lesson 10.3
Eclipses
Teaching Focus: Identifying Misconceptions

NSES CONTENT STANDARD, 5–8: EARTH IN THE SOLAR SYSTEM

"Most objects in the solar system are in regular and predictable motion. Those motions explain such phenomena as the day, the year, phases of the moon, and eclipses" (National Research Council, 1996, p. 160).

DESCRIPTIVE OBJECTIVE

Students will investigate the relative positions and motions of the sun, Earth, and moon that result in lunar and solar eclipses.

MATERIALS

For each group of students provide a foam ball (one for each student), a strong light, and reference photos of lunar and solar eclipses (a good source can be found at http://www.mreclipse.com/). The eclipse simulator is required for the Extend phase of this lesson. It is best to reproduce the eclipse simulator on heavy paper to card stock.

SCIENCE BACKGROUND

Although moon phases and eclipses are different, there is a direct relationship between them. Lunar eclipses occur only during the full moon phase. Solar eclipses occur only at new moon. During a lunar eclipse (see Figure 10.3.1), the moon moves from west to east through the Earth's shadow. If it passes near the mid-line of the shadow, a total lunar eclipse occurs. Observers will see the Earth's shadow first appear on the left side (east limb) of the moon. Then the shadow gradually creeps across until the moon is fully in the center and darkest part of the shadow (the umbra). The moon then slowly moves out of the shadow to the left. From start to finish, a lunar eclipse can last over 3 hours. When the moon passes above or below the central umbra, through the lighter part of the shadow (the penumbra), a partial lunar eclipse occurs. Lunar eclipses are visible over a very large area of the Earth up to an entire hemisphere.

During a total solar eclipse (see Figure 10.3.2), the moon moves directly in between Earth and the sun. The moon's shadow is cast back onto Earth's surface. Observers in the central part of the shadow (umbra) witness a total solar eclipse. The sun is totally blocked from view. Observers nearer the outside of the shadow see a partial solar eclipse in which only part of the sun is blocked from view.

During much of the moon's orbit around Earth, the apparent diameters of sun and moon are nearly equal. The orbit of the moon, however, is not a perfect circle. The diameter of the moon, at its closest approach (perigee), is slightly larger than that of the sun. At the farthest point of the moon's orbit (apogee), its apparent diameter is slightly smaller than the apparent diameter of the sun. If the solar eclipse alignment occurs during or near apogee, an annular solar eclipse occurs. The moon blocks out all of the sun except for a thin ring on the outer perimeter. Solar eclipses of any type are visible only when the observer is located in the shadow that the moon

Figure 10.3.1 Lunar eclipse

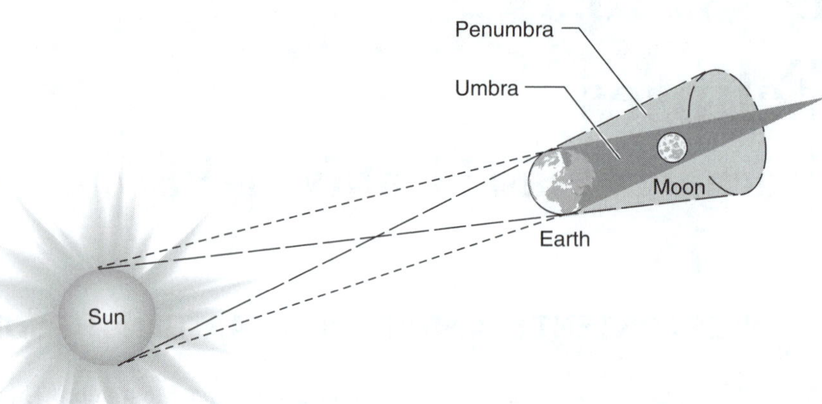

Figure 10.3.2 Total solar eclipse

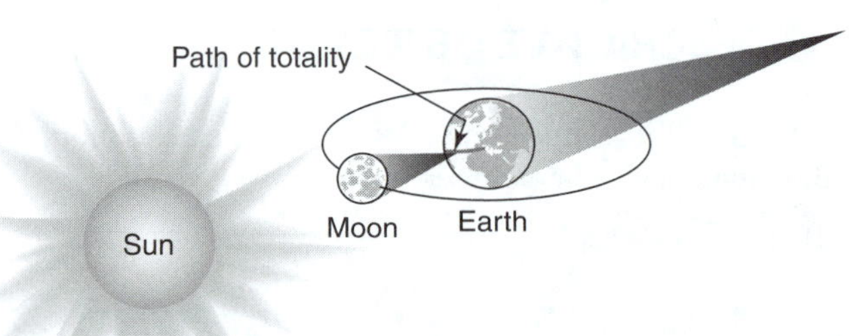

casts back onto Earth. This shadow moves from west to east as Earth turns on its axis. During most years the orientation of sun, Earth, and moon are in a straight line just two times. Because the cycle of moon phases takes just 29.5 days, one year (365.25 days) is enough time for approximately 12.4 moon phase cycles. This means the proper orientation occurs more than twice in some years.

CLASSROOM SAFETY

Emphasize that it is never safe to look directly at the sun without special filters. Radiation from the sun is very intense and can burn the retina of the eye in an instant, causing severe damage and possibly blindness. Special viewing filters that are suitable for viewing solar eclipses are available commercially from some astronomical observatories or supply houses. The sun can also safely be observed indirectly by projecting it through a pinhole onto the ground or a piece of paper.

Teaching Tip

Recalling Earlier Questions or Concerns

This is a good time to bring up questions that students may have asked during the moon phase investigation. Some students may have recognized the relationship between eclipses of the moon and the full moon phase. Observations may include, "It looks like there should be an eclipse of the moon every month!" Assure them that they will pursue that idea in more detail in this lesson.

ENGAGE

Begin by finding out how many students have seen an eclipse of the moon. Ask them to describe what it looked like and estimate how long it took. Have them draw and label a picture of a lunar eclipse. If possible, show your students a picture of a lunar eclipse and compare it to their drawings.

Do the same with solar eclipses. Has anyone ever seen a solar eclipse? What did it look like and how long did it last? Show them pictures of a total and a partial solar eclipse. Point out that many people get to see an eclipse of the moon, but very few ever see a total solar eclipse. Discuss students' ideas about why this happens. At this point you are assessing prior understanding and not teaching specifics.

Focus attention on the question to be investigated: **How do you construct models of eclipses of the moon and sun?** Have student groups discuss the question and develop an explanation that is based on their prior knowledge before beginning the Explore phase of the lesson. Compare explanations that vary in concept and record them for later reference.

EXPLORE

1. Quickly review how to set up the light ("sun") and manipulate the model "moon" around their head ("Earth"), this time to simulate eclipses. During an eclipse of the moon, the sun, Earth, and moon (in that order) are in a *straight* line.
2. To produce a solar eclipse, the moon should be directly between the sun and the Earth. The order is sun, moon, and Earth—in a *straight* line.

EXPLAIN

1. Lunar eclipses occur at full moon when the moon moves into Earth's shadow.
2. Solar eclipses occur at new moon when the moon moves directly between the Earth and sun. When the moon is in this position, its shadow falls on the surface of the Earth and blocks all or part of the sun from view.
3. Eclipses of the moon occur only during full moon. Solar eclipses occur only at new moon. They are not associated with any of the other moon phases (because the sun, Earth, and moon cannot be in a straight line during any other phase).

Using Demonstrations to Explain

Teaching Tip

Allow students to explore the sun, Earth, and moon model for themselves. Then use a flashlight, a small "moon" ball, and a globe to demonstrate the shadows involved in eclipses. Shine the light on the globe and move the moon ball directly into the shadow behind the globe to demonstrate a lunar eclipse.

To demonstrate a solar eclipse place the moon ball between the light and the globe so that the ball casts a shadow on the surface of the globe. Point out that the observer would have to be near the center of the shadow on the globe to see the eclipse. You can slowly rotate the globe, demonstrating how the shadow moves from west to east during a total eclipse.

EXTEND

1. Cut out each of the four squares containing the Earth and moon (see Figure 10.3.3). On the eclipse simulator, make a slit at each of the four straight lines on the orbit of the Earth. Insert one square into each slit so that the Earth is positioned on the orbit of the simulator and the square is (very) slightly tilted. All four squares should be tilted in the same plane. Place a piece of tape on the underside of the simulator to hold each square in place. The sun, Earth, and moon are in a straight line (in the same plane) in only two positions along Earth's orbit around the sun.

Figure 10.3.3 Eclipse simulator

Sun

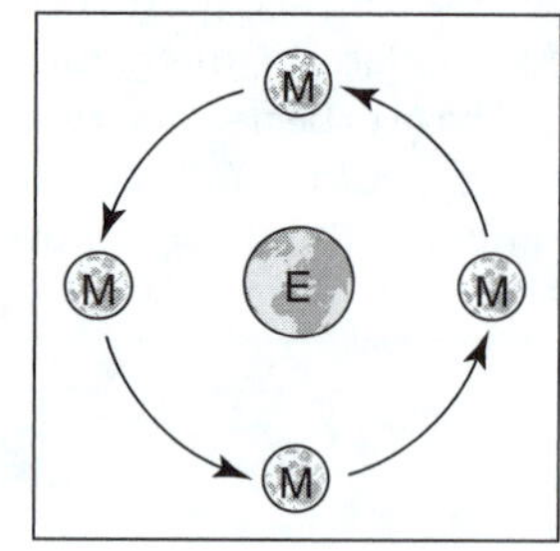

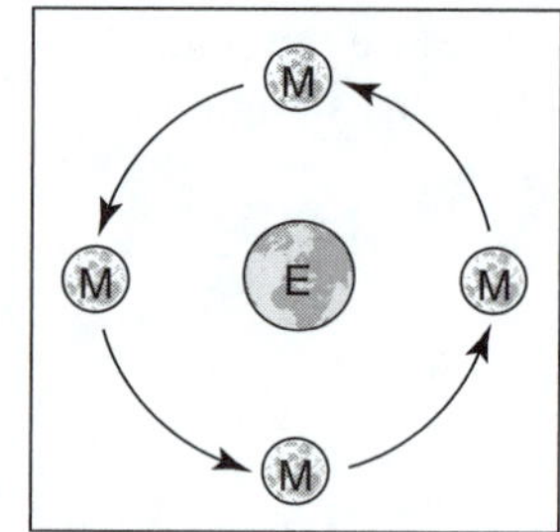

Figure 10.3.4 Sample areas of total and partial solar eclipse

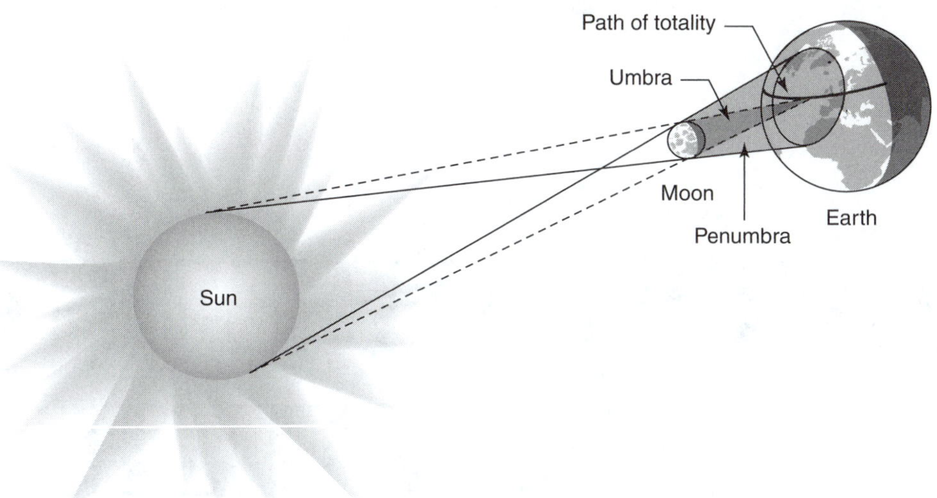

2. The orbit of the moon is tilted to Earth's orbit around the sun. Most of the time, Earth's shadow at full moon passes either below or above the moon. Thus, an eclipse does not occur. Likewise, most of the time, the moon's shadow at new moon passes above or below the Earth. Thus, an eclipse of the sun does not occur.
3. Solar eclipses are possible twice a year. Each occurs at a spot in Earth's orbit where the moon aligns directly with Earth and the sun.
4. Two weeks after the solar eclipse, the moon is in its full phase and is still oriented such that it aligns with Earth and the sun.

APPLY

To produce a total lunar eclipse, the moon must pass inside the dark area (umbra) of the Earth's shadow. If the moon moves along a line that puts part of it in the umbra and part in the lighter penumbra of the Earth's shadow, we see a partial eclipse. See Figure 10.3.4 above to note areas on the Earth where one would observe a total or a partial solar eclipse. The locales on Earth where partial and total eclipses can be viewed will vary from one eclipse to another.

Teaching Focus Summary: Identifying Misconceptions

- Pre-assess students' prior knowledge and possible misconceptions to guide teaching.
- Have students collect and analyze evidence to challenge a misconception.
- When faced with evidence that is contrary to their thinking, students are forced to rethink their ideas.

References

Katz, A., & Olson, J. (2006). Strategies for assessing science and language learning. In A. Fathman and D. Crowther (Eds.), *Science for English language learners* (pp. 61–77). Arlington, VA: NSTA Press.

National Research Council. (1996). *National Science Education Standards*. Washington, DC: National Academy Press.

National Research Council. (2000). *Inquiry and the National Science Education Standards*. Washington, DC: National Academy Press.

Ogle, D. M. (1986, February). K-W-L: A teaching model that develops active reading of expository text. *The Reading Teacher, 39*(6), 564–570.

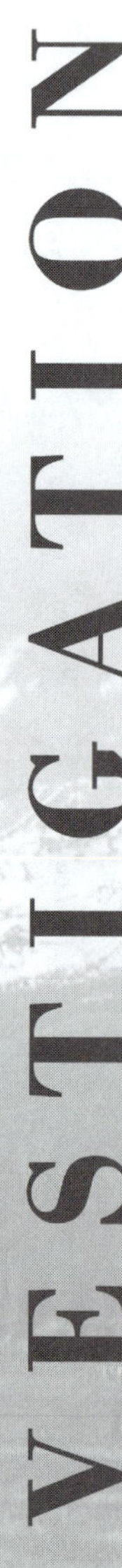

INTERPRETING WEATHER MAPS

(5–8)

Teaching Focus: Integrating Writing and Communication

Lesson 11.1

Comparing Inside Temperatures

ENGAGE

1. When the thermostat says that the room temperature is 72 degrees, is that the temperature everywhere in the room? Have you ever noticed warmer or cooler areas in your classroom? Where?

2. How many degrees different do you think the warmest and coolest locations could be? Write your prediction.

3. Does the time of day make a difference?

4. What might cause temperature differences?

We will investigate the following: **What factors affect the temperature in different parts of our classroom?**

EXPLORE

1. Select ten stations evenly distributed on the classroom floor. Use tape to mark the location of each station and its number.

2. Record location notes for each station. Is the station near a door opening or window, in the center of the room, and so on? What air temperature differences do you expect to find at each location?

3. At each location, take three readings: one at the floor, one at the desktop, and one at the ceiling. How do you think these temperatures might vary?

4. Use a thermometer to find out. Record the temperatures in the chart below.

Comparing Air Temperatures Around the Classroom

Station	Floor	Desktop	Ceiling	Location Notes
1.				
2.				
3.				
4.				
5.				
6.				
7.				
8.				
9.				
10.				

EXPLAIN

1. Describe the pattern of temperatures across the floor.

2. What might explain some of the temperature differences? What effect do doors, windows, and heating and cooling ducts have on floor temperature? What evidence supports your explanation?

3. How do temperatures around the room at desktop height compare to floor temperatures? Explain your results.

4. How do temperatures near the ceiling compare to those at the desktop and floor? Does the evidence support your prediction? Explain.

5. How many degrees difference did you observe between the warmest and coolest areas? How accurate was your prediction? Propose an explanation for the difference.

EXTEND

1. What location in your classroom do you think represents the average temperature?

2. Calculate the average of all your temperature readings.

3. Find the areas in the classroom that are closest to the average that you calculated.

4. Do you think the temperature in other classrooms will be about the same as the average temperature? How could you find out?

5. With your teacher's permission, find the temperature of other classrooms in the school. Based on what you found, agree on the one location that is easiest to measure in the other classrooms.

6. How do the average temperatures in each of the classrooms compare? Explain.

APPLY

Write a report to the principal that explains the temperature variation in your school. Include the locations, time of day, and possible reasons for these differences. Suggest ways to help keep the school more uniform in temperature.

Lesson 11.1
Comparing Inside Temperatures
Teaching Focus: Integrating Writing and Communication

Scientific literacy implies that a person can identify scientific issues underlying national and local decisions and express positions that are scientifically and technologically informed.

National Research Council (1996, p. 23)

NSES CONTENT STANDARD, 5–8: EARTH AND SPACE SCIENCE

"Weather changes from day to day and over the seasons. Weather can be described by measurable quantities, such as temperature, wind direction and speed, and precipitation" (National Research Council, 1996, p. 134).

DESCRIPTIVE OBJECTIVE

Students conduct an investigation to identify and analyze factors affecting temperature differences in their classroom and school.

MATERIALS

For each group of students provide tape, thermometers, and a meter stick (students will tape the thermometer to the meter stick to measure ceiling temperatures—so any long stick will work). Before you hand out the thermometers spread them out on a table. Allow them to sit for several minutes, then check their readings. Select the number of thermometers you will need from those that show the same temperature reading. A calculator will be useful for the Extend phase of the lesson.

SCIENCE BACKGROUND

For most of us, room temperature is the temperature shown on the wall thermostat. The temperature displayed on the thermostat actually is just the temperature at that location. Temperatures vary in different parts of the room. The presence of windows (particularly those on a south wall or north wall) is a significant factor. Windows with southern exposure admit direct sunlight that is absorbed by walls, floors, and furniture and is converted to thermal energy. In winter, windows on the north allow thermal energy to radiate out of the room. On cool nights, all windows radiate heat out of the room. The air temperature near these windows is often cooler than in other parts of the room (or warmer for southern windows on sunny days). The location of outside doors as well as of heating and air conditioning ducts is also a factor.

In general, a room will be warmer near the ceiling and cooler near the floor. A major reason for this is *convection*. Convection is the process by which thermal energy is transferred in fluids—liquids and gases. As air is heated, the molecules have greater energy and thus move more rapidly. When these faster moving particles collide they bounce off one another with greater energy. As a result, the molecules have more space between them, resulting in lower density. Gravity pulls the colder, denser air to the floor, thus displacing the warmer air to the ceiling.

MISCONCEPTION INFORMATION

Students encounter weather on a daily basis and have developed ideas about how the world works. While much research has been conducted on physical science misconceptions, less has been done to understand children's ideas in the earth sciences. Many concepts related to weather have actually been researched based on the physical properties of water. (**Note:** See the misconception information relating to the water cycle in Lesson 12.1.) Some possible misconceptions that you may find with your students include:

- The *H* on a weather map stands for hot temperatures and the *L* stands for low temperatures.
- Heat rises.
- Heat is a substance that moves in or out of objects.

For additional information, you may wish to refer to the following:

Henriques, L. (2002). Children's ideas about weather: A review of the literature. *School Science and Mathematics, 102*(5), 202–215.

Stepans, J. (1996). *Targeting students' science misconceptions*. Riverview, FL: Idea Factory, Inc.

CLASSROOM SAFETY

Be sure not to use mercury thermometers for this (or any) investigation. Ceiling temperatures should be taken by taping a thermometer to a stick rather than by climbing a ladder or standing on furniture. Students should also handle the glass thermometers with care.

ENGAGE

Ask about experiences your students have had with warm or cool spots at home or in school. Question them about their classroom. Does it have warm or cool spots? Where are they located? Ask them to predict the number of degrees difference between the warmest and the coolest spot in the room. Ask them to explain their reasoning. Record their predictions.

TEACHING FOCUS

Standards for English Language Arts

Standards for writing and communication are included in the International Reading Association (IRA) and the National Council of Teachers of English (NCTE). This chapter focuses on Standard 5, "Students employ a wide range of strategies as they write and use different writing process elements appropriately to communicate with different audiences for a variety of a purposes" (National Council of Teachers of English, 1996).

TEACHING FOCUS

Communicating Predictions Visually

Have students construct a (two-dimensional) map of the classroom and then mark it where they predict the warmest and coolest temperatures will be found. Have students communicate their predictions by sharing maps with several classmates. You may wish ultimately to combine all of the predictions on one map for discussion.

Focus the students on the question to be explored: **What factors affect the temperature in different parts of our classroom?** Post the question for all to see.

> Teaching Tip
>
> **Thermometer Reading Skills**
>
> Demonstrate proper handling of thermometers. Remind students to keep their fingers off the thermometer bulb. Place the thermometer on the floor. Allow the thermometer time to adjust after it is placed in a new location. It should adjust to any change in temperature within 2 minutes. Read the thermometer with the top of the red column at eye level.

> Teaching Tip
>
> **Classroom Management Strategies**
>
> Each student group may be responsible for taking temperatures at several stations. Post a master chart of stations and have one person from each group record readings in the appropriate spaces on the chart.

EXPLORE

1. Assist the students in selecting floor temperature sites. At least one site should be close to a door opening, one near a heat or air conditioning vent, and several along a row of windows. You may want to create a general floor map on which the students can mark the temperature sites for reference. Prepare a master chart identical to the student data chart. All data should be displayed on the master chart as well as on the individual student charts.
2. Have students indicate factors they think might affect air temperature at each location.
3. Have students make their predictions prior to taking the actual temperatures.

Figure 11.1.1 Student measuring temperature near ceiling

4. To measure the temperature near the ceiling, have students tape a thermometer to one end of a meter stick (see Figure 11.1.1). Hold the other end and raise the stick above your head. Wait 2 minutes, and then lower the meter stick and read the temperature.

EXPLAIN

1. Depending on the time of day, the location of your room in the building, its number and size of windows, and the quality of insulation, you can expect up to 5 or 6 degrees difference in floor temperatures. Look for patterns or areas with similar temperatures.
2. In the morning the floor temperatures near windows may be several degrees cooler than those in the center or opposite side of the room. If the windows are on the south side of the room, the floor temperatures may be warmer in the afternoon. The floor area in front of doors may be cooler than in the center of the room. If both the door and windows are open you may be able to track the flow of cool air across the floor between them. Floor areas near heat vents may be warmer, and those around air conditioning vents may be cooler. Measured and recorded floor temperatures provide scientific evidence.
3. Discuss the question as a group. Place thermometers on the desktop, wait for 2 minutes, and then read the temperature. Typically, desktop temperatures are a degree or two warmer than those on the floor (unless, of course, the classroom has a floor heating system). The pattern of differences may vary from that of the floor.
4. Typically, temperatures at the ceiling will be several degrees higher than those at the tabletop. Temperatures will vary from location to location, not necessarily in the same pattern as seen on the floor and desktop.
5. Discuss the maximum temperature difference. Compare the locations of the highest reading and the lowest. This may help explain the difference.

> Teaching Tip
>
> **Comparing Predictions and Hypotheses**
>
> Predictions are based on prior experience and understanding. Hypotheses go one step further. They contain an explanation for the prediction.

EXTEND

1. Answers will vary depending on the factors noted above.
2. Have students use a calculator to average the 30 readings they collected.
3. The location of the average temperature depends on the location of heat registers, windows, and doors. Several locations probably will be at the average temperature. As implied in the Science Background section, it is unlikely that all 30 readings will be the same.
4. Initiate a discussion with the students about the factors they have been studying and how these might apply to other rooms in the school.
5. Students should agree on a standard procedure to use when measuring the temperatures of the various classrooms.

> **TEACHING FOCUS**
>
> **Using E-mail**
>
> Encourage students to compose a formal e-mail to selected teachers in your school to request permission to take the temperature in their classrooms. Many students do not use e-mail for anything other than casual messaging.

TEACHING FOCUS

Diversity—Use Graphic Organizers for Pre-Writing

Academic writing can be difficult for students, so provide opportunities for them to organize their learning graphically prior to writing. Some very popular graphic organizers include concept webs or maps, charts, and Venn diagrams. In constructing an organizer, students have to consider what they know, practice using the needed vocabulary, and arrange the information in meaningful ways. This cognitive work can be demanding on students. English language learners may need assistance in preparing a graphic organizer, so you may wish to construct the organizer as a whole class or in small groups. A graphic organizer constructed ahead of time allows students to focus more on the writing required (Maatta, Dobb, & Ostlund, 2006).

TEACHING FOCUS

Writing in Science

Teaching inquiry science provides many opportunities to meet your school's language arts standards. The writing of a business letter is a typical language arts requirement.

Integrating writing and inquiry science is beneficial as noted by Miller and Calfee: "Writing, in conjunction with other activities such as reading and hands-on experiences, contributes to greater critical thinking, thoughtful consideration of ideas, and better concept learning" (2004, p. 20).

6. The temperatures are likely to be different in the various classrooms due to the direction the room faces, what floor it is on, the number of windows, heating and cooling equipment, size, ceiling height, and so on.

APPLY

Discuss students' ideas on how to minimize temperature differences in the school. You could discuss how adding ceiling fans might affect the air temperature distribution in classrooms. Students might also consider the location of thermostats in each of the classrooms. The students' letters should summarize their findings as well as provide suggestions on how to maintain a more uniform temperature throughout the school building.

Lesson 11.2

Comparing Outside Temperatures

ENGAGE

1. Look out the windows of your classroom. What is the weather like today?

2. Is the outside air temperature the same everywhere on the school grounds?

3. Study a diagram of your school grounds. List the factors you think affect the temperature around the school building and explain why.

We will investigate the following question: **How do certain factors affect the outside air temperature around our school building?**

EXPLORE

1. Study a diagram showing the outline of your school building, recreation areas, and parking lots. Select sites around the building to measure air temperatures, and number them on your diagram. Predict where you think it will be warmest and coolest. Propose reasons why.

2. Estimate how many degrees difference there will be between the warmest and the coldest locations.

3. At each site measure and record the surface type, surface temperature, and air temperature at eye level in the table below.

Comparing Outside Air Temperatures

Site	Surface Type	Surface Temperature	Eye Level Temperature	Location Notes
1.				
2.				
3.				
4.				
5.				
6.				
7.				
8.				
9.				
10.				

EXPLAIN

1. Which location was the warmest? Explain your thinking.

2. What areas were coolest? Why do you think so?

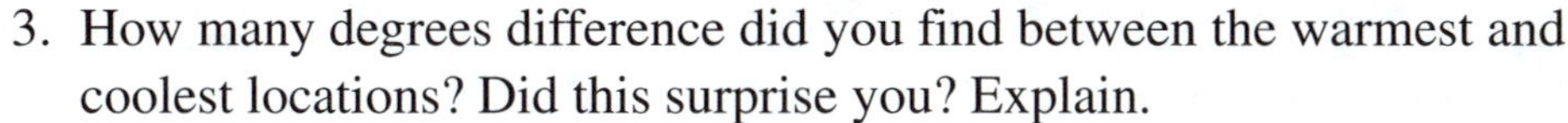

3. How many degrees difference did you find between the warmest and coolest locations? Did this surprise you? Explain.

4. How do surface and eye level temperatures compare?

EXTEND

1. How do you think the type of surface affects the air temperature above it?

2. Design an investigation to test your hypothesis. If you were to carry out this investigation, what variables would you control?

APPLY

Which classrooms in your building may be warmer than others in the afternoon? Why? Which rooms may be cooler year-round? Why? What could you do to maintain a more even temperature in all of the rooms? Write a letter to the PTA asking for their support of your ideas.

Lesson 11.2

Comparing Outside Temperatures

Teaching Focus: Integrating Writing and Communication

NSES STANDARDS, 5–8: EARTH AND SPACE SCIENCE

"Weather changes from day to day and over the seasons. Weather can be described by measurable quantities, such as temperature, wind direction and speed, and precipitation" (National Research Council, 1996, p. 134).

DESCRIPTIVE OBJECTIVE

Students conduct an investigation to analyze the factors affecting temperature variation around the outside of their school building.

MATERIALS

For each group of students provide a diagram map showing an outline of the school building and grounds, and thermometers. Recheck your thermometers and select those that read the same temperature for this activity.

SCIENCE BACKGROUND

Air temperatures can vary widely at different locations around school buildings and grounds. Factors affecting these temperatures include: direct sunshine, shade, type of surface (grass, concrete, asphalt, dirt), evaporation from recently watered lawns, and building walls heated by the sun. Air temperatures above asphalt and concrete in direct sunlight are much warmer than temperatures over grass because different materials absorb thermal energy at different rates. In addition, darker surfaces absorb (and radiate) thermal energy to a greater extent than do lighter ones. Wind may mix air, reducing temperature difference between locations.

CLASSROOM SAFETY

Be sure not to use mercury thermometers for this (or any) investigation. Students should handle the glass thermometers with care.

ENGAGE

Discuss outside temperature variation. Have the students predict where it will be warmer and cooler and tell why. Brainstorm a list of factors that affect the air temperature around the building. Have students predict the effect of each factor and explain why. Save the predictions and explanations and compare them with the measured temperatures.

Focus student attention on the question to be investigated: **How do these factors affect the outside air temperature around our school building?**

EXPLORE

1. Help students select a variety of sites where they are likely to notice temperature variations. Suggest that they consider the results of the previous investigation to inform their predictions. Sites for temperature measurement can be distributed evenly around the building or individually selected for testing certain factors (sun, shade, type of surface) (see Figure 11.2.1).

> *Teaching Tip*
>
> **Management Strategies**
>
> You could have each group read and record temperatures at all ten sites, or assign one or two teams to a specific site and then have them record their data on a master chart.

Figure 11.2.1 Possible sites for data collection

2. Again, students might consider the previous investigation.
3. Students will tabulate their data in the table provided. Have students wait for about 2 minutes at each location for the temperature to stabilize.

> *Teaching Tip*
>
> **Temperature Measuring Skills**
>
> Set common standards for measuring techniques. For example: Measure air temperatures at some standard measure above the surface. To measure surface temperatures, place the thermometer on the surface, wait at least 2 minutes, and then quickly pick up the thermometer and read it at eye level.

Teaching Focus

Organizing Data

Remind students to record their predictions and explanations. Discuss the importance of organization and accuracy. Well-organized and accurate data improve the ability to communicate results both orally and in written form.

EXPLAIN

1. The warmest locations will normally be those in direct sunlight—especially those that have been in the sun for an hour or more. Temperatures should also be warmest in sunny areas over asphalt surfaces (usually on the south side of the building).
2. The coolest areas will be those in the shade, especially places that have been in the shade for several hours (usually on the north side of the school building).
3. On warm still days temperature differences of at least 10 degrees Fahrenheit are possible between the warmest and coolest locations.
4. Surfaces (especially dark surfaces) that have been exposed to the sun for some time will be warmer.

EXTEND

1. Asphalt, concrete, and bare dirt areas absorb thermal energy from incoming sunlight and heat up. Asphalt in direct sunlight for several hours can become too hot to touch. Heat radiating from such a surface warms the air above it.
2. Surface temperatures should be measured with the thermometer in contact with the asphalt, concrete, dirt, or grass. Air temperatures can then be measured at waist level above each different surface. Measurement techniques should be consistent. The type of surface is the independent variable. Controlled variables would include time of day, the amount of time the thermometer is exposed to the surface, and other measurement techniques.

APPLY

Classrooms with south-facing windows are generally the warmest rooms in the building as they receive direct sunlight for several hours each sunny day. Temperatures are even higher in these rooms near the beginning and end of the school year, when the afternoon sun is higher in the sky. Classrooms with north-facing windows are generally cooler than other rooms in the school as they receive little if any direct sunlight.

Encourage students to think of practical ways to address temperature variation, such as the addition of curtains, blinds, awnings, trees, and so on.

Teaching Focus

Persuasive Writing

Students will use evidence to support their stand on an issue—in this case their recommendations. You may wish to have them determine the cost of each of their suggested solutions.

Lesson 11.3

Comparing National Temperatures and Weather

ENGAGE

Everyone wants to know about the weather. How warm will it get? Is it going to rain? The answer to questions like these can be found in your local newspaper. Each day newspapers publish weather maps for the United States. Have you ever looked at one of these weather maps? How do you read a weather map?

We will investigate the following: **How do you interpret information on a weather map?**

EXPLORE

1. Observe the weather map provided. Study the map legend to learn the kinds of information provided on the map.

2. Find areas where the temperatures will be warm. Locate areas that will be cold.

3. Find cloudy areas and where precipitation is expected.

4. What are the weather conditions in your area?

EXPLAIN

1. What is the general trend in air temperature as you move from north to south?

2. What area can expect cloudy skies? What kind of pressure system is associated with this area? What area will have clear skies? What kind of pressure is associated with this area?

3. Describe the weather expected in Birmingham, Alabama. Include expected high and low temperatures, sky conditions (cloudy or clear), and any precipitation.

EXTEND

1. Locate a cold front on the weather map. Fronts move in the direction of the symbols (triangles for cold fronts and semicircles for warm fronts). How do the air temperatures in the area ahead of the cold front compare with those in the area behind it?

2. Do the same for a warm front.

3. Compare the types of precipitation associated with each front on the map below. This map shows weather conditions for a day in late November. How might this change if it were late May instead?

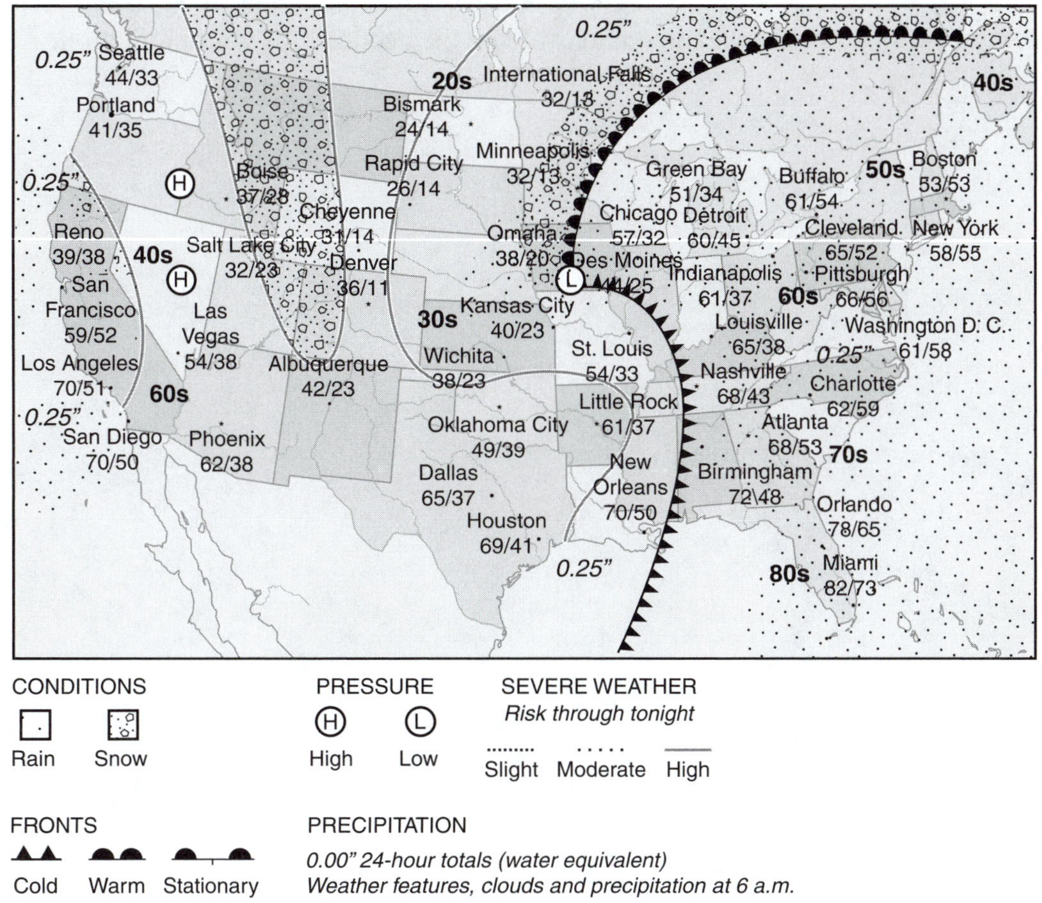

4. Weather systems move from west to east each day. This includes the passage of fronts like the one to the west of Birmingham, Alabama. Predict the weather conditions for Birmingham for the next day after the front has moved to the east. Include expected temperatures, cloud cover, and precipitation.

Use today's weather map from your local daily paper. Analyze information provided on the map for your community. Write and present a TV weather spot describing today's weather and make a prediction for tomorrow. Wait until tomorrow, observe the weather, and evaluate the accuracy of your prediction.

Lesson 11.3

Comparing National Temperatures and Weather

Teaching Focus: Integrating Writing and Communication

NSES CONTENT STANDARD, 5–8: EARTH AND SPACE SCIENCE

"Weather changes from day to day and over the seasons. Weather can be described by measurable quantities, such as temperature, wind direction and speed, and precipitation" (National Research Council, 1996, p. 114).

DESCRIPTIVE OBJECTIVE

Students analyze information provided on a weather map to determine weather conditions at given locations and to predict the next day's weather.

MATERIALS

For each group of students you need the weather map provided, and a newspaper (or Internet) weather map for your area for the Apply phase of the lesson.

SCIENCE BACKGROUND

The data for daily weather maps are compiled from ground level observations and measurements of atmospheric conditions at stations distributed across the world. The data are then transposed to weather maps using symbols and numbers. Instruments aboard weather balloons and on satellites gather high-elevation temperatures, pressures, and wind data that are used to develop upper atmospheric maps. These maps are then distributed electronically to both print and broadcast media.

When large air masses come in contact with each other, the boundary between them forms a front. Cold air advancing into a warmer air mass produces a cold front. The advancing cold air, being greater in density, wedges underneath, lifting the warmer, less dense air to higher elevations. As the warm air is lifted it cools. If it cools enough, condensation may occur causing clouds and possible precipitation. When warm air advances into cooler air it is called a warm front. The advancing warm air (being less dense) slides up and over the frontal boundary. As the warm air rises it cools and may form clouds and precipitation. Fronts are named cold or warm depending upon which is the aggressor. Changing weather conditions are the result of the passing of cold or warm fronts. When a cold front passes through your area you may expect possible clouds, precipitation, and falling temperatures. A warm front passage produces gradually increasing temperatures with possible clouds and precipitation. Frontal systems generally move from west to east across the continental United States. The weather changes you experience today generally move east between 300 and 500 miles in one day.

TEACHING FOCUS

Using Maps to Communicate Information

Point out the value of weather maps in communicating information to others. The use of map symbols allows a large amount of information to be displayed in a small space. This enables users to select specific information efficiently in a short period of time.

ENGAGE

Find out how many of your students are familiar with weather maps and how to interpret them. Show them a weather map from a local or regional newspaper. Point out the different kinds of markings on the map (do not try to teach what all of the markings mean at this point). Ask: How do you read a weather map? Use the discussion to pose the following question: **How do you interpret information on a weather map?**

EXPLORE

1. The weather map used in this activity shows weather conditions across the continental United States on November 28, 2005. Have students explore the information on the map in small groups. Bring them together to discuss where they found areas of low and high temperatures, sunny and cloudy regions, areas of precipitation, and the location of the two major fronts. Review the map legend and its symbols. Point out that temperatures for each city are given in pairs (e.g., 57/32 in Chicago). The first temperature is the expected high and the second the expected low for the day. Arrowhead symbols appear on the leading edge of cold fronts. Rounded bump-shaped symbols appear on the leading edge of warm fronts.
2. The warmest temperatures are in the southwest and south: Los Angeles, 70, Houston, 69, and Miami, 82. The coldest temperatures are in the north central portion of the country: Bismarck, 24, Rapid City, 28, and Cheyenne, 31.
3. The map implies cloudy conditions in the east. Rain or snow is indicated over large portions of the central and eastern United States.
4. Identify your location on the map for this date.

EXPLAIN

1. As one might expect, the temperatures trend higher as you move from the northern states to the southernmost states.
2. The map shows that most of the eastern United States is cloud covered. This area is affected by a large low-pressure system centered in eastern Iowa. Low-pressure systems are usually associated with cloudy conditions and often with precipitation. Most of the southwestern and western areas have clear skies and are affected by several high-pressure systems. High-pressure systems are usually associated with fair weather and clear skies.
3. In Birmingham the expected high is 72 and the low 48, with cloudy skies and rain.

EXTEND

1. A cold front extends from just east of Omaha, Nebraska, and curves down through New Orleans and farther south. Ahead of the front, in cities like Louisville, Nashville, Birmingham, and New Orleans, the temperatures are in the low 70s. The temperatures behind the cold front in St. Louis and Little Rock are cooler (54 and 61, respectively). It is even cooler just to the west of these cities.
2. The temperatures are cold ahead of the warm front, and behind it the temperatures are warmer.
3. It is snowing ahead of the warm front. It is raining ahead of the cold front. Where the air is cold it is snowing, and where it is warm it is raining.
4. The following day, Birmingham might expect the temperatures to drop with a high in the low 60s and a low temperature around 37. The skies should clear later in the day. The prediction is made by looking at the temperature in a city of about the same latitude that is behind the front. In this case one could look at Little Rock to predict temperatures in Birmingham.

TEACHING FOCUS

E-mail Pen Pals

To create an authentic writing experience you can arrange for students to exchange weather information with other children around the country. Services are available online for identifying other interested classrooms. You could also arrange for e-mail pals internationally, which would allow you to compare weather information with classrooms that are experiencing a different season or climate (Bryson, 2004).

APPLY

Make copies of the newspaper weather map for the day and give one to each group. Have students apply what they have learned to predicting tomorrow's weather. Predictions should include expected high and low temperatures, sky conditions (cloudy or sunny), precipitation, and locations of any fronts and pressure systems that might affect local weather.

Have one group volunteer (or select one) to present a short television weather spot predicting the next day's weather. Encourage them to use maps or diagrams as visual aids to enhance their weather forecasts.

If your school has a closed-circuit TV system, request permission for your class to produce and to record a weather forecast spot. The program should be aired each morning for one week.

TEACHING FOCUS

Writing a Script

All students benefit from expressing their knowledge in a variety of ways. Organizing and communicating explanations often enhances understanding and comprehension of science content knowledge.

Teaching Focus Summary: Integrating Writing and Communication

- Provide opportunities for students to use and create maps to communicate ideas visually as well as to gain information.
- Integrate writing opportunities in science to meet both language arts and science standards.
- Science investigations can provide students with evidence to use in persuasive writing.
- Use e-mail to create authentic writing experiences with others both locally and internationally.
- Students can communicate their learning to others by writing and delivering weather forecasts.

References

Bryson, L. (2004). S'cool science. *Science and Children 41*(8), 24–27.

Maatta, D., Dobb, F., & Ostlund, K. (2006). Strategies for teaching science to English language learners. In A. Fathman and D. Crowther (Eds.), *Science for English language learners* (pp. 37–59). Arlington, VA: NSTA Press.

Miller, R. G., & Calfee, R. C. (2004). Making thinking visible. *Science and Children 42*(3), 20–25.

National Council of Teachers of English. (1996). *Standards for the English language arts*. Urbana, IL: Author.

National Research Council. (1996). *National Science Education Standards*. Washington, DC: National Academy Press.

INVESTIGATION 12

THE WATER CYCLE

(5–8)

Teaching Focus: Integrating Inquiry in Textbook Instruction

Lesson 12.1
Evaporation

ENGAGE

One morning after a rain, Jenny noticed puddles of rainwater in the school parking lot. Later that morning, she observed that the puddles were getting smaller, and several were completely gone. She wondered why some of the puddles were gone and others were not. She asked her teacher, who suggested she do an experiment for the science fair to find out. Jenny thought that maybe the ones that dried up first were in the sun. She decided to investigate the following question: **How does the sun affect how fast water evaporates?**

EXPLORE

1. Get two plastic lids and label one "Sun" and the other "Shade." Place one drop of water in the center of each lid.

2. Place one lid in direct sunlight and the other in the shade. Observe each lid every 10 minutes. Record how much time it takes for the water to evaporate from each lid.

EXPLAIN

1. Compare your results to those reported by other groups. How do the times compare?

2. How does exposure to direct sunlight affect how fast the water evaporated?

3. Summarize the evidence that supports your answer.

4. How might you try to explain the results?

EXTEND

1. What other factors do you think might affect how fast water evaporates? Make a list.

2. Choose one factor and write a scientific question to be investigated.

3. Write a hypothesis explaining how this factor affects evaporation.

4. Design a procedure to carry out the investigation to test your hypothesis.

5. Share your results with other groups.

In what parts of the world might you expect the drop of water to evaporate quickly? Slowly? Explain.

Lesson 12.1
Evaporation
Teaching Focus: Integrating Inquiry in Textbook Instruction

Learning science is something students do, not something that is done to them.

National Research Council (1996, p. 2)

NSES CONTENT STANDARD, 5–8: STRUCTURE OF THE EARTH SYSTEM

"Water, which covers the majority of the earth's surface, circulates through the crust, oceans, and atmosphere in what is known as the 'water cycle.' Water evaporates from the earth's surface, rises and cools as it moves to higher elevations, condenses as rain or snow, and falls to the surface where it collects in lakes, oceans, soil, and in rocks underground" (National Research Council, 1996, p. 160).

TEACHING FOCUS

Textbooks and Inquiry

"Although the *Standards* emphasize inquiry, this should not be interpreted as recommending a single approach to science teaching. Teachers should use different strategies to develop the knowledge, understandings, and abilities described in the content standards. Conducting hands-on science activities does not guarantee inquiry, nor is reading about science incompatible with inquiry. Attaining the understandings and abilities described . . . cannot be achieved by any single teaching strategy or learning experience" (National Research Council, 1996, pp. 23–24).

Many teachers follow a curriculum that uses a science textbook as the major source of instructional materials. Some believe that this precludes the use of inquiry in their classroom. "However, a teacher's curriculum is not defined by the materials alone, but more broadly by what students focus their attention on, how they learn, and how and on what they are assessed" (National Research Council, 2000, p. 138). The sequence of investigations in this chapter emphasizes strategies for helping teachers integrate inquiry with science textbook instruction.

DESCRIPTIVE OBJECTIVE

Students will conduct an investigation to determine the effect of sunlight on how fast water evaporates. In the Extend portion of the lesson they will conduct additional investigations to determine the effect of other factors (wind, surface area, and humidity) on evaporation.

Teaching Tip

Time Allotment

Allow a period of approximately 20 minutes for the Engage phase and to set up the investigation. Students can then make observations at 15-minute intervals during the day. Observations may occur over a period of 1–3 hours depending upon the availability of direct sunlight and the relative humidity. Allow a second period of 30 to 45 minutes to complete the Explain phase and to set up investigations for the Extend phase. Observations at 30-minute intervals are also required for the Extend phase. Allow 30 minutes to discuss results and discuss the Apply questions.

TEACHING FOCUS

Identifying Major Concepts

Many textbook chapters on the water cycle include numerous concepts such as evaporation, condensation, precipitation, surface runoff, and underground storage. Evaporation and condensation, however, are the two driving concepts that are key to understanding the water cycle. Students should be given the opportunity to conduct scientific investigations on specific factors affecting these key processes. As a result, this chapter comprises three science investigations: one each on evaporation and condensation, and a unifying investigation on the interacting processes involved in the water cycle.

MATERIALS

For each group of students provide a dropper and plastic margarine tub lids (or petri dishes). For the Extend phase of the lesson students will need a variety of things such as sponges (rectangular type used in the kitchen or bath), an electric fan, two cotton face cloths, paper towels, a 1-quart sealable plastic bag, a double pan balance (optional), and filter paper or cotton balls (optional).

SCIENCE BACKGROUND

Evaporation is the process involved when liquid water changes to water vapor. Evaporation occurs at the surface of a liquid when molecules have enough energy to escape into the air. Water vapor is simply water molecules with greater energy. Thus, the molecules in water vapor are farther apart than they are in the liquid state. Some of the factors that affect evaporation are thermal energy, wind, water temperature, surface area, and relative humidity of the air above the water. Water exposed to direct sunlight warms. This increases the kinetic energy of the water molecules, which increases the number of molecules with sufficient energy to escape into the atmosphere. Warm water evaporates faster than cold water, again due to the higher energy of the water molecules. Air blowing over the surface of water increases the evaporation rate. This happens because in still air the water, as it evaporates, saturates the area above it with water vapor, resulting in a state of equilibrium in which as many water vapor molecules return to the liquid as liquid molecules escape. If the air above the water is moving, however, the saturated air above the water is blown away, leaving drier air above the liquid. This results in an increased rate of evaporation. Because evaporation takes place at the surface, all else being equal, the larger the exposed surface area, the faster the rate of evaporation. Also, as implied above, water evaporates faster into dry air than it does into humid air.

MISCONCEPTION INFORMATION

The phase changes of water can be a difficult topic for students because they cannot directly observe the water molecules. Some of the common misconceptions related to the water cycle include the following:

- Water evaporates only from oceans or lakes.
- The bubbles in boiling water are air, oxygen, or hydrogen.

- Condensation on the outside of a container is water that seeped through the container.
- Clouds are smoke, cotton, or bags of water.
- Rain comes from holes in the clouds.

For additional information, you may wish to refer to the following:

Bar, V. (1989). Children's views about the water cycle. *Science Education, 73*(4), 481–500.

Henriques, L. (2002). Children's ideas about weather: A review of the literature. *School Science and Mathematics, 102*(5), 202–215.

CLASSROOM SAFETY

Have students use caution when manipulating spotlights or electric fans. Be alert for water spills.

TEACHING FOCUS

Modifying the Order of Textbook Instruction

A typical textbook chapter on the water cycle begins by defining terms. Students then read facts that support explanations together with appropriate examples. Hands-on activities generally follow written descriptions and explanations. In many cases these activities are conducted as demonstrations designed to verify what has already been read and discussed.

Rather than assigning readings to initiate learning about the water cycle, you may choose instead to employ strategies more consistent with inquiry and the Learning Cycle. You would begin by engaging the students in an interesting and real-world context. As this unfolds, you could assess students' prior knowledge and develop the context for a specific and relevant question about evaporation. The question becomes the focus for the science investigation. Note the nature of the Engage phase in this student activity.

ENGAGE

Discuss the puddle story while focusing on Jenny's question: "Why are some of the puddles gone and others not?" Ask your students what happens to the water in puddles when they dry up. Where does the water go? If the term *evaporation* comes up, ask students to explain what it means to them. Resist the temptation to correct their misconceptions at this point. This will allow you to assess your students' prior understanding of evaporation.

Ask your students for a hypothesis about how direct sunlight affects evaporation. Make sure everyone understands the question to be investigated: **How does the sun affect how fast water evaporates?**

TEACHING FOCUS

Moving from Verification to Inquiry

In many textbooks, this investigation would be designed to demonstrate (or verify) how energy from the sun increases evaporation. Note that this investigation begins with a question: "How does the sun affect how fast water evaporates?" Students conduct the investigation to answer the question.

EXPLORE

1. Use plastic margarine lids, petri dishes, or other flat dishes.

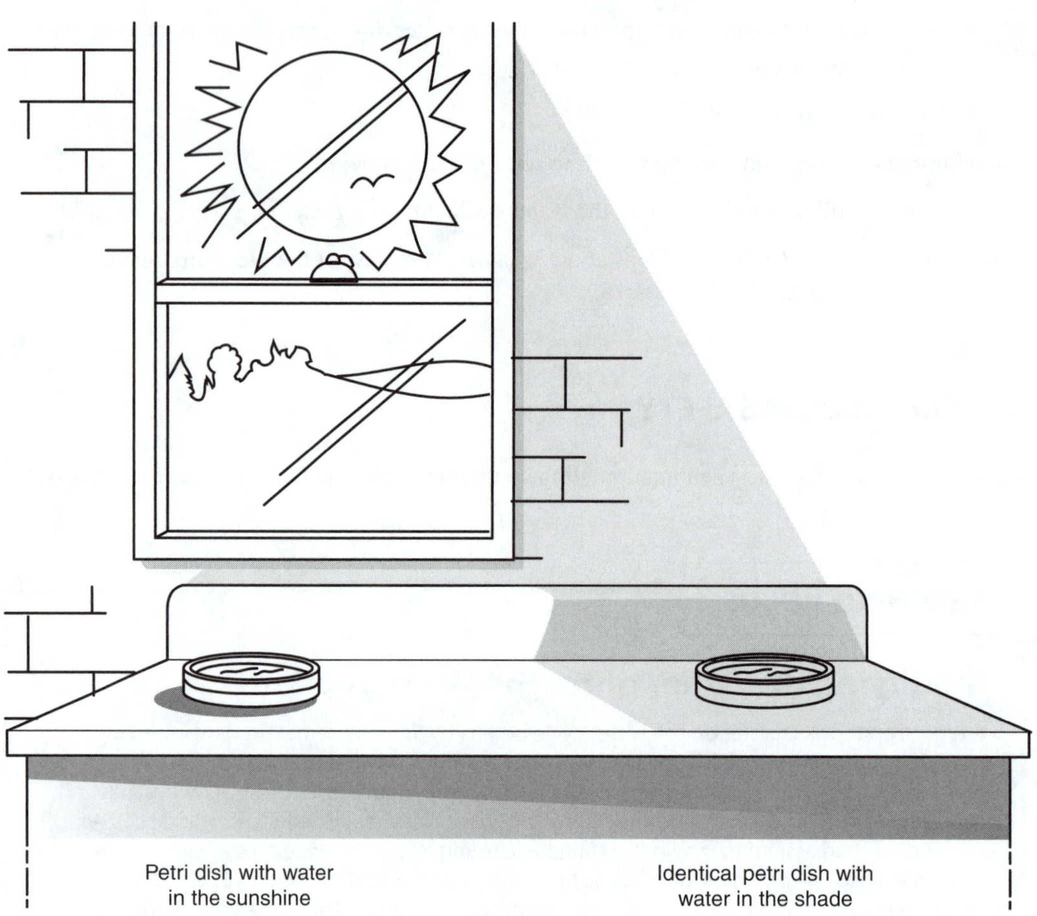

Teaching Tip

Management Suggestion

One member of each team can be assigned to make the 10-minute observations. This will allow you to conduct other lessons in the interim without frequent interruptions.

Teaching Tip

Alternative Investigation

You can modify this investigation to reduce observation time. Place a piece of filter paper (or folded paper towel) on an electronic balance sensitive to 0.1 gram. Note the mass of the filter paper first, then add ten drops to the filter paper (or cotton ball) and record the mass again. Depending on your dropper, ten drops will be approximately 0.3 gram. See how long it takes the filter paper to return to its original mass. Repeat, but this time shine a spotlight on the filter paper and compare how long it takes to return to the original mass.

2. The amount of time needed for the drops of water to evaporate will depend upon the availability of direct sunshine and relative humidity. If you live in an area that is cloudy much of the time, you may want to use spotlights as model suns. Also you should allow more time in climates where the relative humidity is high.

EXPLAIN

1. Water in direct sunlight evaporates faster than water in the shade. Individual group times may vary.
2. The higher temperatures result in greater kinetic energy of the molecules and thus increased evaporation rate.
3. Difference in time to dry serves as evidence.

4. Student explanations will vary. This is an appropriate time for reading as well as discussion. Stress to the students that they keep in mind the evidence they have discovered as they read.

TEACHING FOCUS

Gathering Evidence to Develop Explanations

In this investigation students develop an explanation from observational evidence. In verification activities, the explanation has been provided, so evidence is used to verify what is already known. *Evidence to explanation* is the hallmark of scientific inquiry. The appropriate time for reading text is at this point, after students have obtained evidence of the relationship between temperature and evaporation rate. You would now select relevant passages from the textbook to enhance and strengthen conceptual understanding. (Note the emphasis on reading "relevant" and "selected" passages, rather the entire chapter!) Students, because of their exploration, extended activities, and concept application to the real world, are now better able to read about evaporation with understanding. Students also can use relevant illustrations, photos, charts, and graphs from the text or other instructional materials more effectively at this time.

EXTEND

1. Other common factors affecting evaporation rate include wind, surface area, and humidity.
2. Have each group determine a factor to investigate and a question to answer.
3. Have students construct a hypothesis regarding the effect of their selected factor on evaporation rate.
4. Have each group present a plan for the procedures, observations, and measurements they will employ. Some suggestions for investigation procedures include the following:

   Wind—Use a fan to simulate wind.

   Surface area—Soak two face towels in water. Wring them out, and lay one out unfolded. Fold the other in half and then in half again (one-fourth of the area facing up).

   Humidity—Have one water sample in a closed plastic bag, and the other exposed.
5. Students could share their findings with classmates in a number of ways including whiteboards, PowerPoint presentations, and so on.

TEACHING FOCUS

Extending Conceptual Understanding

Many textbook activities end with verification of the central concept. Inquiry enriches development of understanding by extending thought to further questions and explorations of factors affecting the central concept (in this case, evaporation).

APPLY

The water will evaporate quickly in places that are hot, windy, or dry such as a desert. It will evaporate slowly in humid areas like the Midwest in the summer. It will also evaporate more slowly in cold areas, although winter is quite dry in many locales.

TEACHING FOCUS

Applying Concepts

This would be a good place for you to incorporate real-world examples from your textbook into your lesson. Application of factors that affect evaporation in a real-world context strengthens learners' understanding as well as providing relevance.

Lesson 12.2
Condensation

ENGAGE

On some summer mornings the grass is very wet. Your shoes become soaked with water when you walk across the lawn. Where does the water come from? Sometimes a glass of ice water "sweats," forming a puddle on the table. Where did the puddle come from? Did it come through the glass like sweat from a human body, or did it come from outside the glass? Write your hypothesis.

We will investigate the following: **Where does the puddle around the glass of ice water come from?**

EXPLORE

1. Describe an investigation you might conduct to test your hypothesis. What materials would you need? What evidence would support your explanation? Develop a plan for your investigation and show it to your teacher.

2. Conduct your investigation and record your results.

EXPLAIN

1. Explain what you think produced the water on the outside of the glass and in the puddle.

2. Cite evidence to support your explanation.

EXTEND

1. What other factors do you think might affect how much a pitcher of ice water "sweats"? List possible variables.

2. Design and carry out an investigation to test one of the factors.

3. Share your results with your classmates.

APPLY

Why does dew appear on grass some mornings and not other mornings? Explain.

Lesson 12.2
Condensation
Teaching Focus: Integrating Inquiry in Textbook Instruction

NSES CONTENT STANDARD, 5–8: STRUCTURE OF THE EARTH SYSTEM

"Water, which covers the majority of earth's surface, circulates through the crust, oceans, and atmosphere in what is known as the 'water cycle.' Water evaporates from the earth's surface, rises and cools as it moves to higher elevations, condenses as rain or snow, and falls to the surface where it collects in lakes, oceans, soil, and in rocks underground" (National Research Council, 1996, p. 160).

DESCRIPTIVE OBJECTIVE

Students conduct an investigation to determine the source of condensation forming on a glass of ice water and the factors that affect the process.

MATERIALS

For each group of students provide several 9 oz clear plastic cups, water, ice, food coloring, and paper towels.

SCIENCE BACKGROUND

As air cools, the humidity (the mass of water vapor in a given volume of air) remains constant, but the relative humidity (the percent of water vapor that the air can hold at a given temperature) increases. Put another way, as air cools, its capacity for water vapor already present decreases. Thus, as air cools its relative humidity increases. If it cools enough the relative humidity reaches 100%. The temperature at which air reaches 100% relative humidity is called its *dew point*. At the dew point temperature, water vapor begins to condense on surfaces such as blades of grass, rocks, and automobiles.

Most of us have experienced condensation on a glass or can of cold beverage. The air next to the cold glass or aluminum transfers heat to the cold container. In the process this air becomes cooler than the surrounding air. As this air cools its relative humidity becomes higher. If the air contains enough water vapor, it becomes saturated when it reaches the dew point. Very humid air may have a dew point temperature just a few degrees below the present air temperature. Dry air, with little water vapor to begin with, may have to cool significantly before it reaches saturation—the dew point temperature. This explains why humid locations have dew on specific mornings and why dry areas seldom have dew. Clouds form when the air cools to the dew point temperature and water vapor condenses on tiny dust or smoke particles to form cloud droplets. When this process occurs near the ground, the cloud formed is called *fog*.

> **TEACHING FOCUS**
>
> **Modifying Textbook Activities**
>
> Study any activities in the chapter that deal with condensation. If they are cookbook-type verification activities, convert them to inquiry-oriented investigations that answer an explorable question. Use the 5-E instructional design that is employed in the lessons throughout this book. Investigate condensation, then read to enhance understanding. For more information on adapting textbook activities to the Learning Cycle, see the article "An Evaluation of the Use of a Technique Designed to Assist Prospective Elementary Teachers to use the Learning Cycle with Science Textbooks (Barman, 1992).

ENGAGE

Ask students for their experiences of a "sweating" glass or beverage can (see Figure 12.2.1). Ask them where the water on the container and the puddle come from. Ask them if they think it comes from the air around the container or from inside the container. Ask students to propose a hypothesis. If they do not propose the idea of "sweat" coming from inside the container to the outside, tell them that some might think this is possible. Ask students how they could find out whether the water comes from inside. Ask them to propose an investigation to answer the following question: **Where does the puddle around the glass of ice water come from?** This becomes the question that they will answer by an experiment they design and conduct.

Figure 12.1.1 Sweating glass

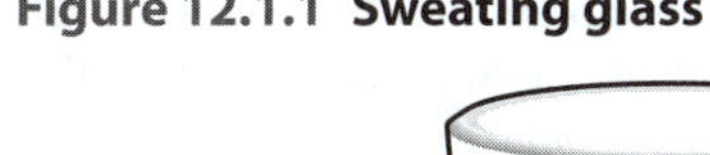

EXPLORE

1. Ask the students for examples of evidence that would show that the liquid comes from inside the container. If they cannot do this, ask them what they might observe if red or blue water were inside the container. How would they then proceed? What materials will they need? What will count as evidence? Ask them what question they are trying to answer. Have them describe their procedures before you give them permission to begin.
2. Help students stay focused as they conduct the investigation by asking them to explain what they are trying to find out.

EXPLAIN

1. Water forming on the outside of the container and in the puddle underneath is clear and free of any food coloring.
2. This is evidence that the water did not come from the inside. Note that while the evidence *suggests* that the water condensed from the air around the container, it does not necessarily constitute *proof*. This evidence indicates only that the water did not come from inside the container. We cannot prove that the water came from the atmosphere, although it would be a valid inference.

TEACHING FOCUS

Content Reading

Select specific reading passages in the chapter that explain the process of condensation. Use photos, diagrams, charts, and graphs from the text to enhance understanding.

EXTEND

1. Some factors students might suggest include humidity, temperature of the water, temperature of the room, the amount of water, and so on.
2. For example, if students suggest that humidity in the air affects the amount of condensation they might conduct the following investigation. Quickly place a glass of ice water in a quart-sized sealable plastic bag and seal. Use the smallest bag that you can seal. Compare the condensation that forms on this glass with another that is not enclosed in a sealed bag. Because the bag contains less air, noticeably less condensation will form on the glass in the bag.
3. Encourage students to question each other's results as a scientist would. That is, each group should be prepared to provide the evidence that supports its conclusions.

APPLY

Several factors are at work here. One (not explored here) is that the grass produces increased water vapor due to transpiration. In addition, cooler air tends to stay near the ground. For these reasons, the air is more likely to become saturated and reach its dew point.

Lesson 12.3
The Water Cycle

ENGAGE

The water we have on Earth today has always been here. The glass of water you drink today may have flowed in a stream where dinosaurs stopped to drink. The rain falling on the rain forest may have been locked in glaciers that melted 10,000 years ago. What processes cycle water from where it is today to other places in the future?

One way to explore the Earth's water cycle is to use a model. For example, we can represent all of the water on Earth by water in a sealed plastic bag.

We will investigate the following question: **What will happen to the water in the sealed bag?**

EXPLORE

1. Put 125 mL of colored water into a sealable plastic bag. Predict what will happen to the water if we tape the bag to a sunny window?
   - Will any evaporate?
   - Will the mass of the bag and water change? Record the beginning mass of the bag plus the water.
   - Will the volume of the water change (you started with 125 mL)?

2. Tape the bag to a sunny window and observe it for several days. Record your observations each day. Do not disturb the bag as you make your observations.

3. After several days, carefully find the bag's mass. Then pour out the water and find the bag's final volume.

EXPLAIN

1. Did you observe any evidence of evaporation? Condensation? Explain.

2. Did the mass of the bag and water system change? Why or why not?

3. Did the volume of water in the bag and water system change? Why or why not?

4. How does the water in the bag model what happens to water on the Earth?

5. Write a summary of your results.

EXTEND

1. Refer to your textbook to find a diagram of Earth's water cycle. Study the different ways water is distributed in the water cycle. Identify as many local examples of these as you can. At each location record whether the water is liquid, solid, or gas.

2. Select two locations where water is in different states. What process or processes changed the water from one state to another (e.g., water from a lake turns into falling snow)?

3. Give an example of a location on the Earth where water might remain in the same state (solid, liquid, gas) for a very long time. Explain why.

4. Where might water remain in the same state for a relatively short period of time? Explain why.

APPLY

Pretend you are a drop of water moving through the water cycle. Write a creative story telling where you have been for the last 100 years. Include whether you were solid, liquid, or gas at each stop and what type of process allowed you to move from place to place.

Lesson 12.3

The Water Cycle

Teaching Focus: Integrating Inquiry in Textbook Instruction

NSES CONTENT STANDARD, 5–8: STRUCTURE OF THE EARTH SYSTEM

"Water, which covers the majority of the earth's surface, circulates through the crust, oceans, and atmosphere in what is known as the 'water cycle'. Water evaporates from the earth's surface, rises and cools as it moves to higher elevations, condenses as rain or snow, and falls to the surface where it collects in lakes, oceans, and soil, and in rocks underground" (National Research Council, 1996, p. 160).

DESCRIPTIVE OBJECTIVE

Students construct and observe a model water cycle to determine what happens to water in a sealed system. Next, they analyze a diagram of Earth's water cycle to determine what processes move water from location to location in the global cycle.

MATERIALS

For each group of students provide a sealed plastic bag, tape, graduated cylinder, water, food coloring, and an electronic balance.

SCIENCE BACKGROUND

Earth's water is probably its most valuable resource. But we must make do with what we have as Earth receives practically no new water. Earth's water circulates through the oceans, atmosphere, and crust driven by the processes of evaporation, condensation, precipitation, percolation, and storage.

Countless liters of water evaporate daily from our oceans. According to Tarbuck and Lutgens (2006), approximately 380,000 cubic kilometers of water evaporate from Earth each year. Ocean water absorbs thermal energy from the sun, which changes it from a liquid to water vapor, a gas. The water vapor cools as the air containing it rises to higher altitudes. The air's relative humidity increases as it cools until it reaches saturation. The water vapor then condenses, forming liquid cloud droplets or tiny crystals of ice that can grow in size and fall as rain or snow. Some precipitation falls directly back into the oceans, lakes, and streams. The rest falls on land where it soaks into the soil or runs off into streams, rivers, and lakes. Some rainwater soaks through soil and percolates into permeable layers of rock underground. Water stored in underground rock slowly moves through rock layers to lakes and oceans. Some snow falls on glaciers and ice caps remaining there remain for centuries before returning to the atmosphere or melting into lakes, rivers, and the oceans. Plants and animals also receive and store water. This water also returns to the atmosphere by transpiration through plant leaves and perspiration through the skin of animals.

The water cycle is commonly described as following a continuous path from the oceans, to the atmosphere (evaporation, condensation, precipitation, infiltration, and runoff) and back to the oceans. The cycle is actually much more complex and is probably more like a web. Water moves in many directions other than in a simple cycle. Sometimes water moves in reverse—cloud droplets evaporate back to water vapor, or ice melts during the day only to refreeze at night. Water can also remain as frozen glacial ice, or as deep ocean water for centuries before melting or moving to the surface of the ocean, respectively.

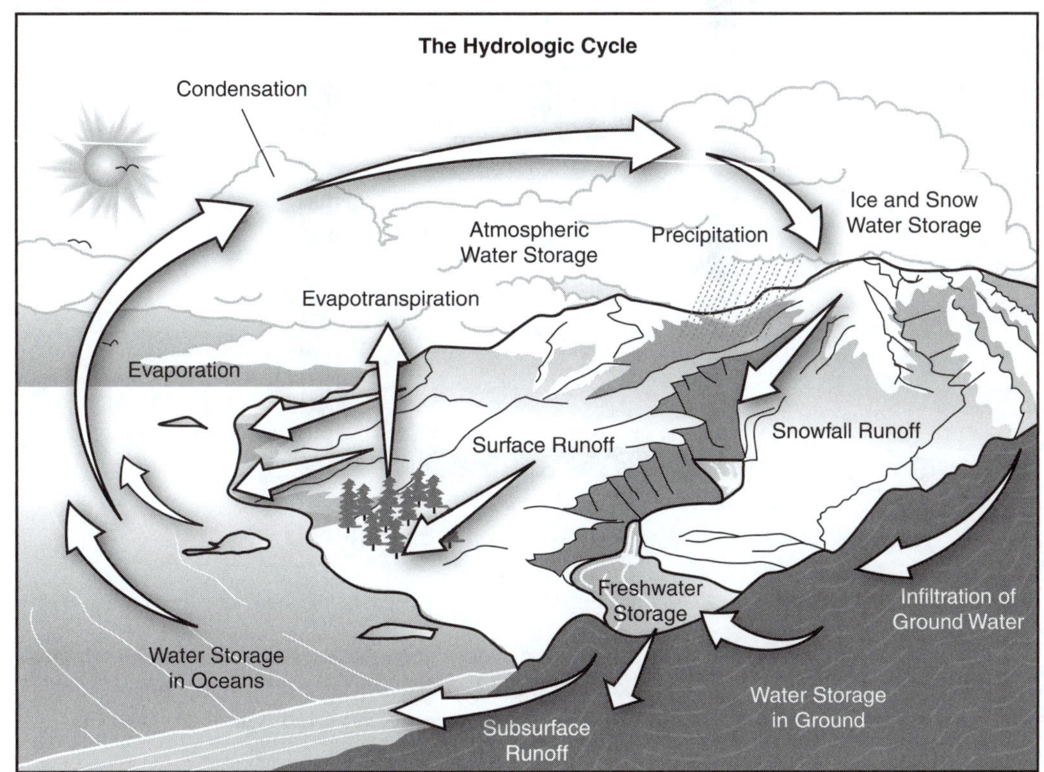

CLASSROOM SAFETY

No special safety concerns are involved here. Remember that food dye can stain clothing.

ENGAGE

Without defining the water cycle, discuss the students' understandings of the movement of water on Earth. Listen to their explanations to assess their prior knowledge. Pose the following question: **What will happen to water in the sealed bag?**

EXPLORE

1. Have the students write their predictions after placing the water into the bags and sealing them. The predictions can be written as testable hypotheses.

TEACHING FOCUS

Sequencing Learning Experiences

Proper sequencing of learning experiences provides coherence and enhances the learners' understanding. Note that the three lessons in this investigation are sequenced, moving from evaporation to condensation and concluding with a model of the water cycle that combines these two concepts.

Figure 12.3.1 Sealed bag of water taped to window

TEACHING FOCUS

Textbook Resources

Review observation and measurement skills, pointing out how using a balance extends the senses. Most text series include an addendum that contains helpful information and guidelines for developing the skills needed to complete inquiry investigations.

2. Where possible, tape the bags on south-facing windows (see Figure 12.3.1). Set aside a 5-minute observation period each morning and afternoon. Have students record all observations.
3. Remind your students to use proper measuring techniques in using the balance and graduated cylinder. Students should remove tape used to mount the bag on the window before measuring it, unless the tape was present when the bag was first massed.

EXPLAIN

1. Although the bag provides little, if any, direct evidence of evaporation of water, tiny drops of condensed water will collect inside the bag. The students can infer evaporation from the evidence of condensation. Notice that the condensate is not colored because the food dye did not evaporate.
2. The bag–water system should not lose mass. Some of the liquid water inside the bag evaporated to water vapor and then condensed back to liquid water, but none escaped outside the bag. Therefore, the amount of matter is the same.
3. The volume of water should remain the same provided the bag was tightly sealed. The bag is a closed system, so nothing is added or taken away from inside it. Demonstrate how to tip and rotate the bag to incorporate the condensed droplets into the total liquid volume before pouring the water into the graduated cylinder.

4. The sealed bag represents the Earth. Water inside the bag represents all of Earth's liquid water (oceans, lakes, rivers, and streams). Just as on Earth, liquid water in the bag evaporates and rises to higher levels, then condenses to form droplets and raindrops that fall back to the surface. Water cycles from place to place but, just as on Earth, it does not escape.
5. The summary should include the question being investigated, a description of the model, observations and measurements, an analysis of findings, and an answer to the inquiry question.

Teaching Tip

Developing Conservation Thinking Abilities

Conservation of mass or volume is a difficult concept for many students. Some will not yet have developed the ability to think in these terms. Wadsworth notes that conservation of volume is typically one of the last conservation concepts that students grasp, usually around the age of 11 to 12 (Wadsworth, 2004).

EXTEND

1. Describe the processes (evaporation, condensation, precipitation, runoff, infiltration into soil and rock, and freezing into glaciers and ice caps). Identify local examples where some of these changes take place (e.g., evaporation from local lakes or rivers, last rainfall or snow, runoff into gutters and storm sewers, ice on the surface of a lake, etc.).
2. Besides the major locations shown on the textbook diagram, have students select additional parts of the water cycle (e.g., liquid water freezing to ice, ice or snow melting to liquid water, water absorbed by plants and then transpired into the atmosphere as water vapor, etc.).
3. Water can remain frozen in the center of a glacier, where the thermal energy necessary to melt it is absent; or it can stay at the bottom of an ocean far from the surface, where evaporation takes place.
4. Water evaporating from an ocean may remain a gas for just minutes before rising, cooling, and condensing in a large thunderstorm or hurricane. Water vapor can change to an ice crystal in a cloud, then fall toward the ground and melt as it moves through warmer air at lower elevations, and so on.

TEACHING FOCUS

Using Diagrams

Assign reading of the chapter section that explains the water cycle. Your text will have a large diagram of the water cycle describing the processes involved. Discuss the strengths and weaknesses of the diagram in light of the investigation modeling the path of a drop of water over time.

APPLY

Students who can create a story that contains the proper elements of the water cycle, have at least synthesis level understanding of the concept.

TEACHING FOCUS

Developing Deeper Understanding

Role playing a drop of water moving through the water cycle involves students in thought processes that enhance understanding. It also stimulates more complex thinking. Seeing so many different possible paths inside the model shows students the complexity so often unseen when learning is confined to reading and talking about the water cycle. It also challenges the typical image (misconception) that all water follows the same path from evaporation to condensation, to precipitation, to runoff, to oceans again for evaporation, and so on.

Teaching Focus Summary: Integrating Inquiry in Textbook Instruction

- Identify the major concepts for the inquiry investigations to focus on within a science topic.
- Modify the order of the information and activities in the textbook, if necessary, to follow the learning cycle.
- If the textbook activities are verification activities, modify them into explorations that students will conduct to answer questions.
- Have students read the appropriate passages from the textbook after they conduct the investigations.
- Use the applications, examples, diagrams, photographs, and so on from the text to enhance students' understanding after they finish the investigations.

References

Barman, C. R. (1992). An evaluation of the use of a technique designed to assist prospective elementary teachers to use the learning cycle with science textbooks. *School Science and Mathematics, 92*(2), 59–63.

National Research Council. (1996). *National Science Education Standards*. Washington, DC: National Academy Press.

National Research Council. (2000). *Inquiry and the National Science Educational Standards.* Washington, DC: National Academy Press.

Tarbuck, E. J., & Lutgens, F. K. (2006). *Earth science*, 11th ed. Upper Saddle River, NJ: Pearson Prentice Hall.

Wadsworth, B. J. (2004). *Piaget's theory of cognitive and affective development*, 5th ed. Boston: Pearson.

In Conclusion

Developing Learning Cycle Lessons

DEVELOPING LEARNING CYCLE LESSON PLANS

As a teacher, you can adapt lessons you find in textbooks, resource books, activity guides, and Web sites into an inquiry-based learning cycle pedagogical plan. Recall, however, that most of the activities you will encounter while searching for ideas are of the verification/demonstration type. In fact, most are designed for use after a concept has been taught for purposes of verification of that concept. This pedagogy is quite different from the inquiry learning cycle that you have experienced in this book. Nonetheless, you can profitably adapt most of the lessons or activity ideas you find into inquiry learning cycle explorations. You can do this by following the steps below.

Begin with an Explorable Question

First, think about the most important aspect of a learning cycle lesson: The activity must answer some explorable question for the learner. An explorable question is one that a learner can answer through firsthand experiences with materials. The first thing you should do when revising an activity is to determine whether it answers an explorable question. If it does not, then you must decide whether you can alter it so that it does answer an explorable question.

For example, a typical activity found in many resource books involves making a cloud in a glass jar. This is commonly done by putting a small amount of hot water in a jar, dropping a lighted match in the jar, covering it, and then placing a bag of ice on top of the jar. This results in a visible cloud in the jar. Note that this activity doesn't really answer any question, although many students erroneously assume that it answers the question "How is a cloud formed?" Students *see* that this combination of components forms a cloud, but the activity doesn't help students understand *how* the components interact. To answer the question of how requires further exploration and explanation. Thus, the cloud activity above is not an exploration (it answers no question); rather, it is a demonstration (or verification) of a model of cloud formation.

How can we turn the above demonstration into an inquiry activity? As noted, we must alter the activity so that it answers an explorable question. One way to do this is to select one variable in the demonstration that students can manipulate in order to investigate the effects of that factor. For instance, students could manipulate the water temperature to determine its effect on cloud formation. This activity now becomes a true investigation because it answers the following explorable question: What effect does water temperature have on cloud formation? Another way to alter the activity might be to broaden the investigation so that students explore several factors. In that case the explorable question could become the following: What factors affect cloud formation? Students then could manipulate the water temperature, the volume of water, the amount of ice, the location of the ice or water, the amount of smoke, and so on. Note that we did not ask a question such as "Why are clouds formed?" Students would find it difficult to answer such a question using an exploration. As a general rule, "how" and "why" questions do not make good explorable questions at this level. A better strategy is to provide questions that answer "what" or "when."

Write the Engage Portion of the Lesson

After you have decided on the Explore activity and explorable question, you can write the Engage phase of the inquiry activity. Recall that the most important function of the Engage phase is to set up the explorable question. That means that the students must know exactly what they are trying to find out. It is helpful if the Engage phase provides some real-world context for the questions we are asking about this concept. In the case of the clouds, for example, a discussion regarding the conditions that exist when we have clouds and when we do not would be appropriate. Because learners construct new knowledge based on what they already know, beginning with what is known is the best way to do this.

Students also need to understand how the specific procedure(s) they are going to perform will help them find the answer(s). If students do not know why they are following a procedure, then they are merely following a procedure—cookbook style. If students focus on the explorable question, however, then they should be able, at any step in the investigation, to answer the question, "Why are you doing this?" Students who cannot explain why they are doing any given procedure (beyond saying that it is step 3) have not been engaged appropriately.

You can use a demonstration in the Engage phase of a learning cycle lesson to set up the explorable question for the students. In the example of the cloud in a jar, the students view the demonstration in the Engage phase to generate the variables to test in the exploration (water temperature, amount of ice, etc). Without this experience they really could not get started. Furthermore, conducting a demonstration in the Engage phase can pique curiosity, motivation, and cognitive dissonance. In other words, it can cause students to ask, "What's going on here?"

Let's review the process so far. First, you want to consider what concept you are trying to teach. Then you either think of an activity or, more likely, locate an appropriate activity in a book or an online source. Then you must determine whether that activity answers some explorable question. An activity that does not answer any question is not an inquiry activity but more likely a demonstration. If the activity is a demonstration you must alter it so that it leads to some explorable question. Having settled these issues, you are ready to write the Engage phase of your lesson, followed by the exploration.

Present the Explanation

The Explain phase of your lesson should begin with the results of the exploration and, through teacher-guided discussion, help students construct an appropriate explanation. This phase is also an appropriate time for the students to read textual material. Recall that in the activities of this text, the exploration sets up students for the explanation, either through reading, lecture, and/or discussion. The Explain phase is what most people regard as the act of teaching. Here, however, the explanation builds on the results that the students have gathered—it is itself set up by the exploration. In our cloud lesson, the Explain phase should begin with students sharing the findings of their various investigations. That is, students share what they find and the teacher guides them to understand why. For example, students might report that they developed better clouds with hot water. The teacher would use this finding as a starting point to discuss the increased evaporation of the water, which results in more water vapor to form clouds.

Extension: Apply the Activity to the Real World

You can now write the Extend and Apply phases of your lesson. Often, you can return to the real-world context of the Engage phase for an Extend and Apply idea. In the cloud example we have been using, you could return to a discussion of the factors that must be present for a cloud to form. Another extension would be to consider what conditions of warm and cold temperatures are necessary to produce fog. You could also ask students to consider the variables that affect the formation of "clouds" in their bathrooms as they shower. You do not want to introduce new concepts in this part of the lesson, however. The purpose is to reinforce the concept of the lesson by showing its application.

Evaluate the Lesson

Evaluation should be an ongoing process throughout your lesson. But one way to assess students' understanding is to determine how well they can apply their new understanding in the Extend and Apply phases. You should also ensure that your assessment measures the objectives you (or your school district) have established. In the lesson discussed here, for example, the teacher can assess student understanding by evaluating their responses to the question about fog in a bathroom during a hot shower.

For further help in using the Learning Cycle to develop your own lesson plans, see Table C.1. It summarizes the procedures you can use to develop your own learning cycle lessons.

Table C.1 Developing Learning Cycle Lessons

Procedures	Planning Focus	What to Do. . .	What Not to Do. . .
Preliminary planning	Be sure the activity answers an explorable question for the students. If it does not, alter it so that it does.	• Identify a specific science focus for the lesson. • Consider all safety issues including clean-up.	• Do not try to teach everything about a concept in one lesson. • Do not list vague, general suggestions for materials.
Determine an appropriate investigation	Find an explorable question for students. Alter the investigation you choose if it does not have one.	• Base your activities on your school's curriculum. • Refocus demonstrations so they answer an explorable question.	• Do not use a demonstration activity in the Explore phase without modifying its purpose. • Do not use activities that are unsafe for your students.
Engage	Students should share prior knowledge in order to develop the explorable question. Ensure during this stage that students understand how the procedure in the Explore phase answers their question. Try to begin the Engage discussion with a real-world context.	• Ask students for their ideas and experiences. • Encourage students to brainstorm ideas. • Use open-ended questions when possible.	• Do not include new terminology in the Engage phase of the lesson. • Do not teach new concepts. • Do not ask students to read the textbook before the exploration. • Do not "lecture" about the concept before students engage and explore the concept in the activity.
Explore	Students actively investigate the answer to the explorable question by collecting evidence and manipulating data.	• Encourage students to try out their own ideas. • Encourage students to think critically. • Encourage students to record evidence. • Ensure students understand how the procedure may answer their question.	• Do not ask students to simply follow directions to complete the activity. • Do not use activities that fail to meet the lesson objective.

Explain	Determine how students will share and explain their findings, and learn additional information to understand and ground the concept.	• Encourage students to learn from each other and other groups. • Include appropriate, applicable terminology. • Require students to write explanations in their own words. • Have students read science content after exploring a science concept.	• Do not copy explanations from a resource. • Do not include unnecessary terminology just for the purpose of loading students up with new science vocabulary.
Extend and Apply	Plan for students to use the knowledge gained from the Explore and Explain phases by conducting deeper investigations, applying the knowledge to everyday life, or making connections to related concepts or other subject areas.	• Ask students to apply what they have learned in some interactive way. • Encourage students to use prior knowledge or experiences to make connections. • Ask students to relate what they have learned to real-world contexts whenever possible. • When appropriate, return to the real-world context noted in the Engage phase.	• Do not simply tell students what the science connections are to real-world applications. • Do not teach a new concept in this stage of the lesson.
Evaluation	Review students' explanations and extensions to assess their ongoing understanding. Determine how students will show what they know and whether they can go beyond simply repeating words or phrases from the lesson by applying the concept to a new situation.	• Assess students for their understanding. • Require students "to do" something with the new concept.	• Do not ask only for recall of knowledge. • Do not assess only new vocabulary words.

Appendix I

K–4 National Science Education Standards*

PHYSICAL SCIENCE

Fundamental concepts and principles that underlie this standard include:

Properties of Objects and Materials

- Objects have many observable properties, including size, weight, shape, color, temperature, and the ability to react with other substances. Those properties can be measured using tools, such as rulers, balances, and thermometers.
- Objects are made of one or more materials, such as paper, wood, and metal. Objects can be described by the properties of the materials from which they are made, and those properties can be used to separate or sort a group of objects or materials.
- Materials can exist in different states—solid, liquid, and gas. Some common materials, such as water, can be changed from one state to another by heating or cooling.

Position and Motion of Objects

- The position of an object can be described by locating it relative to another object or the background.
- An object's motion can be described by tracing and measuring its position over time.
- The position and motion of objects can be changed by pushing or pulling. The size of the change is related to the strength of the push or pull.
- Sound is produced by vibrating objects. The pitch of the sound can be varied by changing the rate of vibration.

Light, Heat, Electricity, and Magnetism

- Light travels in a straight line until it strikes an object. Light can be reflected by a mirror, refracted by a lens, or absorbed by the object.
- Heat can be produced in many ways, such as burning, rubbing, or mixing one substance with another. Heat can move from one object to another by conduction.
- Electricity in circuits can produce light, heat, sound, and magnetic effects. Electrical circuits require a complete loop through which an electrical current can pass.
- Magnets attract and repel each other and certain kinds of other materials.

* Reprinted with permission from National Science Education Standards © 1996 by the National Academy of Science, courtesy of the National Academies Press, Washington, DC.

LIFE SCIENCE

Fundamental concepts and principles that underlie this standard include:

The Characteristics of Organisms

- Organisms have basic needs. For example, animals need air, water, and food; plants require air, water, nutrients, and light. Organisms can survive only in environments in which their needs can be met. The world has many different environments, and distinct environments support the life of different types of organisms.
- Each plant or animal has different structures that serve different functions in growth, survival, and reproduction. For example, humans have distinct body structures for walking, holding, seeing, and talking.
- The behavior of individual organisms is influenced by internal cues (such as hunger) and by external cues (such as a change in the environment). Humans and other organisms have senses that help them detect internal and external cues.

Life Cycles of Organisms

- Plants and animals have life cycles that include being born, developing into adults, reproducing, and eventually dying. The details of this life cycle are different for different organisms.
- Plants and animals closely resemble their parents.
- Many characteristics of an organism are inherited from the parents of the organism, but other characteristics result from an individual's interactions with the environment. Inherited characteristics include the color of flowers and the number of limbs of an animal. Other features, such as the ability to ride a bicycle, are learned through interactions with the environment and cannot be passed on to the next generation.

Organisms and Their Environments

- All animals depend on plants. Some animals eat plants for food. Other animals eat animals that eat the plants.
- An organism's patterns of behavior are related to the nature of that organism's environment, including the kinds and numbers of other organisms present, the availability of food and resources, and the physical characteristics of the environment. When the environment changes, some plants and animals survive and reproduce, and others die or move to new locations. [See Content Standard F (grades K–4)]
- All organisms cause changes in the environment where they live. Some of these changes are detrimental to the organism or other organisms, whereas others are beneficial.
- Humans depend on their natural and constructed environments. Humans change environments in ways that can be either beneficial or detrimental for themselves and other organisms.

EARTH SCIENCE

Fundamental concepts and principles that underlie this standard include:

Properties of Earth Materials

- Earth materials are solid rocks and soils, water, and the gases of the atmosphere. The varied materials have different physical and chemical properties, which make them useful in different ways, for example, as building materials, as sources of fuel, or for growing the plants we use as food. Earth materials provide many of the resources that humans use.
- Soils have properties of color and texture, capacity to retain water, and ability to support the growth of many kinds of plants, including those in our food supply.
- Fossils provide evidence about the plants and animals that lived long ago and the nature of the environment at that time.

Objects in the Sky

- The sun, moon, stars, clouds, birds, and airplanes all have properties, locations, and movements that can be observed and described.

- The sun provides the light and heat necessary to maintain the temperature of the earth.

Changes in the Earth and Sky

- The surface of the earth changes. Some changes are due to slow processes, such as erosion and weathering, and some changes are due to rapid processes, such as landslides, volcanic eruptions, and earthquakes.
- Weather changes from day to day and over the seasons. Weather can be described by measurable quantities, such as temperature, wind direction and speed, and precipitation.
- Objects in the sky have patterns of movement. The sun, for example, appears to move across the sky in the same way every day, but its path changes slowly over the seasons. The moon moves across the sky on a daily basis much like the sun. The observable shape of the moon changes from day to day in a cycle that lasts about a month.

INQUIRY ABILITIES AND UNDERSTANDINGS

Fundamental abilities and concepts that underlie this standard include:

Abilities Necessary to Do Scientific Inquiry

Ask a Question About Objects, Organisms, and Events in the Environment. This aspect of the standard emphasizes students asking questions that they can answer with scientific knowledge, combined with their own observations. Students should answer their questions by seeking information from reliable sources of scientific information and from their own observations and investigations.

Plan and Conduct a Simple Investigation. In the earliest years, investigations are largely based on systematic observations. As students develop, they may design and conduct simple experiments to answer questions. The idea of a fair test is possible for many students to consider by fourth grade.

Employ Simple Equipment and Tools to Gather Data and Extend the Senses. In early years, students develop simple skills, such as how to observe, measure, cut, connect, switch, turn on and off, pour, hold, tie, and hook. Beginning with simple instruments, students can use rulers to measure the length, height, and depth of objects and materials; thermometers to measure temperature; watches to measure time; beam balances and spring scales to measure weight and force; magnifiers to observe objects and organisms; and microscopes to observe the finer details of plants, animals, rocks, and other materials. Children also develop skills in the use of computers and calculators for conducting investigations.

Use Data to Construct a Reasonable Explanation. This aspect of the standard emphasizes the students' thinking as they use data to formulate explanations. Even at the earliest grade levels, students should learn what constitutes evidence and judge the merits or strength of the data and information that will be used to make explanations. After students propose an explanation, they will appeal to the knowledge and evidence they obtained to support their explanations. Students should check their explanations against scientific knowledge, experiences, and observations of others.

Communicate Investigations and Explanations. Students should begin developing the abilities to communicate, critique, and analyze their work and the work of other students. This communication might be spoken or drawn as well as written. [See Teaching Standard B]

Understandings About Scientific Inquiry

- Scientific investigations involve asking and answering a question and comparing the answer with what scientists already know about the world. [See Content Standard G (grades K–4)]
- Scientists use different kinds of investigations depending on the questions they are trying to answer. Types of investigations include

describing objects, events, and organisms; classifying them; and doing a fair test (experimenting).

- Simple instruments, such as magnifiers, thermometers, and rulers, provide more information than scientists obtain using only their senses. [See Program Standard C]
- Scientists develop explanations using observations (evidence) and what they already know about the world (scientific knowledge). Good explanations are based on evidence from investigations.
- Scientists make the results of their investigations public; they describe the investigations in ways that enable others to repeat the investigations.
- Scientists review and ask questions about the results of other scientists' work.

Appendix II

5–8 National Science Education Standards*

PHYSICAL SCIENCE

Fundamental concepts and principles that underlie this standard include:

Properties and Changes of Properties in Matter

- A substance has characteristic properties, such as density, a boiling point, and solubility, all of which are independent of the amount of the sample. A mixture of substances often can be separated into the original substances using one or more of the characteristic properties.
- Substances react chemically in characteristic ways with other substances to form new substances (compounds) with different characteristic properties. In chemical reactions, the total mass is conserved. Substances often are placed in categories or groups if they react in similar ways; metals is an example of such a group.
- Chemical elements do not break down during normal laboratory reactions involving such treatments as heating, exposure to electric current, or reaction with acids. There are more than 100 known elements that combine in a multitude of ways to produce compounds, which account for the living and nonliving substances that we encounter.

Motions and Forces

- The motion of an object can be described by its position, direction of motion, and speed. That motion can be measured and represented on a graph. [See Content Standard D (grades 5–8)]
- An object that is not being subjected to a force will continue to move at a constant speed and in a straight line.
- If more than one force acts on an object along a straight line, then the forces will reinforce or cancel one another, depending on their direction and magnitude. Unbalanced forces will cause changes in the speed or direction of an object's motion.

Transfer of Energy

- Energy is a property of many substances and is associated with heat, light, electricity, mechanical motion, sound, nuclei, and the nature of a chemical. Energy is transferred in many ways.
- Heat moves in predictable ways, flowing from warmer objects to cooler ones, until both reach the same temperature.
- Light interacts with matter by transmission (including refraction), absorption, or scattering (including reflection). To see an object, light from that object—emitted by or scattered from it—must enter the eye.

- Electrical circuits provide a means of transferring electrical energy when heat, light, sound, and chemical changes are produced.
- In most chemical and nuclear reactions, energy is transferred into or out of a system. Heat, light, mechanical motion, or electricity might all be involved in such transfers. [See Unifying Concepts and Processes]
- The sun is a major source of energy for changes on the earth's surface. The sun loses energy by emitting light. A tiny fraction of that light reaches the earth, transferring energy from the sun to the earth. The sun's energy arrives as light with a range of wavelengths, consisting of visible light, infrared, and ultraviolet radiation.

LIFE SCIENCE

Fundamental concepts and principles that underlie this standard include:

Structure and Function in Living Systems

- Living systems at all levels of organization demonstrate the complementary nature of structure and function. Important levels of organization for structure and function include cells, organs, tissues, organ systems, whole organisms, and ecosystems. [See Unifying Concepts and Processes]
- All organisms are composed of cells—the fundamental unit of life. Most organisms are single cells; other organisms, including humans, are multicellular.
- Cells carry on the many functions needed to sustain life. They grow and divide, thereby producing more cells. This requires that they take in nutrients, which they use to provide energy for the work that cells do and to make the materials that a cell or an organism needs.
- Specialized cells perform specialized functions in multicellular organisms. Groups of specialized cells cooperate to form a tissue, such as a muscle. Different tissues are in turn grouped together to form larger functional units, called organs. Each type of cell, tissue, and organ has a distinct structure and set of functions that serve the organism as a whole.
- The human organism has systems for digestion, respiration, reproduction, circulation, excretion, movement, control, and coordination, and for protection from disease. These systems interact with one another.
- Disease is a breakdown in structures or functions of an organism. Some diseases are the result of intrinsic failures of the system. Others are the result of damage by infection by other organisms.

Reproduction and Heredity

- Reproduction is a characteristic of all living systems; because no individual organism lives forever, reproduction is essential to the continuation of every species. Some organisms reproduce asexually. Other organisms reproduce sexually.
- In many species, including humans, females produce eggs and males produce sperm. Plants also reproduce sexually—the egg and sperm are produced in the flowers of flowering plants. An egg and sperm unite to begin development of a new individual. That new individual receives genetic information from its mother (via the egg) and its father (via the sperm). Sexually produced offspring never are identical to either of their parents.
- Every organism requires a set of instructions for specifying its traits. Heredity is the passage of these instructions from one generation to another.
- Hereditary information is contained in genes, located in the chromosomes of each cell. Each gene carries a single unit of information. An inherited trait of an individual can be determined by one or by many genes, and a single gene can influence more than one trait. A human cell contains many thousands of different genes.
- The characteristics of an organism can be described in terms of a combination of traits. Some traits are inherited and others result from interactions with the environment.

Regulation and Behavior

- All organisms must be able to obtain and use resources, grow, reproduce, and maintain stable internal conditions while living in a constantly changing external environment.

- Regulation of an organism's internal environment involves sensing the internal environment and changing physiological activities to keep conditions within the range required to survive.
- Behavior is one kind of response an organism can make to an internal or environmental stimulus. A behavioral response requires coordination and communication at many levels, including cells, organ systems, and whole organisms. Behavioral response is a set of actions determined in part by heredity and in part from experience.
- An organism's behavior evolves through adaptation to its environment. How a species moves, obtains food, reproduces, and responds to danger are based in the species' evolutionary history.

Populations and Ecosystems

- A population consists of all individuals of a species that occur together at a given place and time. All populations living together and the physical factors with which they interact compose an ecosystem.
- Populations of organisms can be categorized by the function they serve in an ecosystem. Plants and some micro-organisms are producers—they make their own food. All animals, including humans, are consumers, which obtain food by eating other organisms. Decomposers, primarily bacteria and fungi, are consumers that use waste materials and dead organisms for food. Food webs identify the relationships among producers, consumers, and decomposers in an ecosystem.
- For ecosystems, the major source of energy is sunlight. Energy entering ecosystems as sunlight is transferred by producers into chemical energy through photosynthesis. That energy then passes from organism to organism in food webs.
- The number of organisms an ecosystem can support depends on the resources available and abiotic factors, such as quantity of light and water, range of temperatures, and soil composition. Given adequate biotic and abiotic resources and no disease or predators, populations (including humans) increase at rapid rates. Lack of resources and other factors, such as predation and climate, limit the growth of populations in specific niches in the ecosystem.

Diversity and Adaptations of Organisms

- Millions of species of animals, plants, and microorganisms are alive today. Although different species might look dissimilar, the unity among organisms becomes apparent from an analysis of internal structures, the similarity of their chemical processes, and the evidence of common ancestry.
- Biological evolution accounts for the diversity of species. developed through gradual processes over many generations. Species acquire many of their unique characteristics through biological adaptation, which involves the selection of naturally occurring variations in populations. Biological adaptations include changes in structures, behaviors, or physiology that enhance survival and reproductive success in a particular environment.
- Extinction of a species occurs when the environment changes and the adaptive characteristics of a species are insufficient to allow its survival. Fossils indicate that many organisms that lived long ago are extinct. Extinction of species is common; most of the species that have lived on the earth no longer exist.

EARTH SCIENCE

Fundamental concepts and principles that underlie this standard include:

Structure of the Earth System

- The solid earth is layered with a lithosphere; hot, convecting mantle; and dense, metallic core.
- Lithospheric plates on the scales of continents and oceans constantly move at rates of centimeters per year in response to movements in the mantle. Major geological events, such as earthquakes, volcanic eruptions, and mountain building, result from these plate motions. [See Content Standard F (grades 5–8)]

- Land forms are the result of a combination of constructive and destructive forces. Constructive forces include crustal deformation, volcanic eruption, and deposition of sediment, while destructive forces include weathering and erosion.
- Some changes in the solid earth can be described as the "rock cycle." Old rocks at the earth's surface weather, forming sediments that are buried, then compacted, heated, and often recrystallized into new rock. Eventually, those new rocks may be brought to the surface by the forces that drive plate motions, and the rock cycle continues.
- Soil consists of weathered rocks and decomposed organic material from dead plants, animals, and bacteria. Soils are often found in layers, with each having a different chemical composition and texture.
- Water, which covers the majority of the earth's surface, circulates through the crust, oceans, and atmosphere in what is known as the "water cycle." Water evaporates from the earth's surface, rises and cools as it moves to higher elevations, condenses as rain or snow, and falls to the surface where it collects in lakes, oceans, soil, and in rocks underground.
- Water is a solvent. As it passes through the water cycle it dissolves minerals and gases and carries them to the oceans.
- The atmosphere is a mixture of nitrogen, oxygen, and trace gases that include water vapor. The atmosphere has different properties at different elevations.
- Clouds, formed by the condensation of water vapor, affect weather and climate.
- Global patterns of atmospheric movement influence local weather. Oceans have a major effect on climate, because water in the oceans holds a large amount of heat.
- Living organisms have played many roles in the earth system, including affecting the composition of the atmosphere, producing some types of rocks, and contributing to the weathering of rocks.

Earth's History

- The earth processes we see today, including erosion, movement of lithospheric plates, and changes in atmospheric composition, are similar to those that occurred in the past. earth history is also influenced by occasional catastrophes, such as the impact of an asteroid or comet.
- Fossils provide important evidence of how life and environmental conditions have changed. [See Content Standard C (grades 5–8)]

Earth in the Solar System

- The earth is the third planet from the sun in a system that includes the moon, the sun, eight other planets and their moons, and smaller objects, such as asteroids and comets. The sun, an average star, is the central and largest body in the solar system. [See Unifying Concepts and Processes]
- Most objects in the solar system are in regular and predictable motion. Those motions explain such phenomena as the day, the year, phases of the moon, and eclipses.
- Gravity is the force that keeps planets in orbit around the sun and governs the rest of the motion in the solar system. Gravity alone holds us to the earth's surface and explains the phenomena of the tides.
- The sun is the major source of energy for phenomena on the earth's surface, such as growth of plants, winds, ocean currents, and the water cycle. Seasons result from variations in the amount of the sun's energy hitting the surface, due to the tilt of the earth's rotation on its axis and the length of the day.

INQUIRY ABILITIES AND UNDERSTANDINGS

Fundamental abilities and concepts that underlie this standard include:

Abilities Necessary to Do Scientific Inquiry

Identify Questions That Can Be Answered Through Scientific Investigations. Students should develop the ability to refine and refocus broad and ill-defined questions. An important aspect of this ability consists of students' ability to clarify questions and inquiries and direct them toward objects and phenomena that can be described, explained, or predicted by scientific investigations. Students should develop the ability to identify their questions with scientific ideas, concepts, and quantitative relationships that guide investigation.

Design and Conduct a Scientific Investigation. Students should develop general abilities, such as systematic observation, making accurate measurements, and identifying and controlling variables. They should also develop the ability to clarify their ideas that are influencing and guiding the inquiry, and to understand how those ideas compare with current scientific knowledge. Students can learn to formulate questions, design investigations, execute investigations, interpret data, use evidence to generate explanations, propose alternative explanations, and critique explanations and procedures.

Use Appropriate Tools and Techniques to Gather, Analyze, and Interpret Data. The use of tools and techniques, including mathematics, will be guided by the question asked and the investigations students design. The use of computers for the collection, summary, and display of evidence is part of this standard. Students should be able to access, gather, store, retrieve, and organize data, using hardware and software designed for these purposes.

Develop Descriptions, Explanation, Predictions, and Models Using Evidence. Students should base their explanation on what they observed, and as they develop cognitive skills, they should be able to differentiate explanation from description—providing causes for effects and establishing relationships based on evidence and logical argument. This standard requires a subject matter knowledge base so the students can effectively conduct investigations, because developing explanations establishes connections between the content of science and the contexts within which students develop new knowledge.

Think Critically and Logically to Make the Relationships between Evidence and Explanations. Thinking critically about evidence includes deciding what evidence should be used and accounting for anomalous data. Specifically, students should be able to review data from a simple experiment, summarize the data, and form a logical argument about the cause-and-effect relationships in the experiment. Students should begin to state some explanations in terms of the relationship between two or more variables.

See the example entitled "Pendulums."

Recognize and Analyze Alternative Explanations and Predictions. Students should develop the ability to listen to and respect the explanations proposed by other students. They should remain open to and acknowledge different ideas and explanations, be able to accept the skepticism of others, and consider alternative explanations.

Communicate Scientific Procedures and Explanations. With practice, students should become competent at communicating experimental methods, following instructions, describing observations, summarizing the results of other groups, and telling other students about investigations and explanations. [See Teaching Standard B]

Use Mathematics in All Aspects of Scientific Inquiry. Mathematics is essential to asking and answering questions about the natural world. Mathematics can be used to ask questions; to gather, organize, and present data; and to structure convincing explanations. [See Program Standard C]

Understandings About Scientific Inquiry

- Different kinds of questions suggest different kinds of scientific investigations. Some investigations involve observing and describing objects, organisms, or events; some involve collecting specimens; some involve experiments; some involve seeking more information; some involve discovery of new objects and phenomena; and some involve making models.
- Current scientific knowledge and understanding guide scientific investigations. Different scientific domains employ different methods, core theories, and standards to advance scientific knowledge and understanding.
- Mathematics is important in all aspects of scientific inquiry.
- Technology used to gather data enhances accuracy and allows scientists to analyze and quantify results of investigations.
- Scientific explanations emphasize evidence, have logically consistent arguments, and use scientific principles, models, and theories. The scientific community accepts and uses such explanations until displaced by better scientific ones. When such displacement occurs, science advances.
- Science advances through legitimate skepticism. Asking questions and querying other scientists' explanations is part of

scientific inquiry. Scientists evaluate the explanations proposed by other scientists by examining evidence, comparing evidence, identifying faulty reasoning, pointing out statements that go beyond the evidence, and suggesting alternative explanations for the same observations.

- Scientific investigations sometimes result in new ideas and phenomena for study, generate new methods or procedures for an investigation, or develop new technologies to improve the collection of data. All of these results can lead to new investigations.

Appendix III

NSTA Position Statement: Safety and School Science Instruction*

PREAMBLE

Inherent in many instructional settings including science is the potential for injury and possible litigation. These issues can be avoided or reduced by the proper application of a safety plan.

RATIONALE

High quality science instruction includes laboratory investigations, interactive or demonstration activities and field trips.

DECLARATIONS

The National Science Teachers Association recommends that school districts and teachers adhere to the following guidelines:

- School districts must adopt written safety standards, hazardous material management and disposal procedures for chemical and biological wastes. These procedures must meet or exceed the standards adopted by EPA, OSHA and/or appropriate state and local agencies.
- School authorities and teachers share the responsibility of establishing and maintaining safety standards.
- School authorities are responsible for providing safety equipment (i.e., fire extinguishers), personal protective equipment (i.e., eye wash stations, goggles), Material Safety Data Sheets and training appropriate for each science teaching situation.
- School authorities will inform teachers of the nature and limits of liability and tort insurance held by the school district.
- All science teachers must be involved in an established and on-going safety training program relative to the established safety procedures which is updated on an annual basis.
- Teachers shall be notified of individual student health concerns.
- The maximum number of occupants in a laboratory teaching space shall be based on the following:
  1. the building and fire safety codes;
  2. occupancy load limits;
  3. design of the laboratory teaching facility;
  4. appropriate supervision and the special needs of students.
- Materials intended for human consumption shall not be permitted in any space used for hazardous chemicals and or materials.
- Students and parents will receive written notice of appropriate safety regulations to be followed in science instructional settings.

References

Section 1008.0 Occupant Load—BOAC National Building Code/1996

Section 10-1.7.0 Occupant Load—NFPA Life Safety Code 101-97

40 CFR 260-70 Resource Conservation and Recovery Act (RCRA)

29 CFR 1910.1200 Hazard Communication Standard (Right to Know Law)

29 CFR 1910.1450 Laboratory Standard, Part Q The Laboratory Standard (Chemical Hygiene Law)

National Research Council (1995). Prudent Practices in the Laboratory, National Academy Press.

Furr, K. Ed. (1995). Handbook of Laboratory Safety, 4th Ed. CRC Press.

Fleming, et al Eds. (1995). Laboratory Safety, 2nd Ed. ASM Press.

National Science Education Leadership Position Paper. (1997). Class size in laboratory rooms. The Navigator. 33(2). Authors

George R. Hague, Jr., Chair Science Safety Advisory Board, St. Mark's School of Texas, Dallas, TX 75230

Douglas Mandt, Immediate Past-Chair Science Safety Advisory Board, Science Education Consultant, Edgewood, WA 98372

Dennis D. Bromley, Safety Instructor, Independent Contractor, Anchorage, AK 99502

Donna M. Brown, Radnor Township School District, Wayne, PA 19087

Frances S. Hess, Cooperstown H.S., Cooperstown, NY 13326

Lorraine Jones, Kirby H.S., Nashville, TN

William F. McComas, Director NSTA District XVI, University of Southern California, Los Angeles, CA 90089

Kenneth Roy, Glastonbury Public Schools, Glastonbury, CT 06033

Linda D. Sinclair, South Carolina Department of Education, Columbia, SC 29201

Colette Skinner, Henderson, NV 89015

Olivia C. Swinton, Patricia-Roberts Harris Education Center, Washington, D.C.

Nina Visconti-Phillips, Assistance & Resources Integrating Science Education (ARISE) Dayton, NJ 08810

—Adopted by the NSTA Board of Directors, July 2000

Index